Bologna

Fiesole
FLORENCE

Arezzo

Cortona

Perugia

Chiusi

Todi

iano
Sovana
Orvieto

Viterbo
Castel d'Asso

Norchia

Corneto Tarquinia
Falerii

Bieda

Sutri

Cerveteri
Veii
Fidenae
Pyrgi
ROME

DENNIS OF
ETRURIA

BY THE SAME AUTHOR

The Writings of Edward Hutton: A Bibliography

*India, Pakistan, Ceylon, Burma and Thailand
(The Spread of Printing)*

La Stampa a Viterbo

John Argentine, Provost of King's

La vita e le opere di Castore Durante

Yanoama. By Ettore Biocca. (Translator)

In an Eighteenth Century Kitchen (Editor)

Essays in Honour of Victor Scholderer (Editor)

George Dennis, about 1888

DENNIS OF ETRURIA

THE LIFE OF GEORGE DENNIS

BY DENNIS E. RHODES

LONDON
CECIL & AMELIA WOOLF

For
DON WILKS
*of Santa Fe Springs, California
whom I first met
in Etruscan lands*

CONTENTS

ILLUSTRATIONS

Frontispiece: George Dennis, from a photograph taken probably in 1888, when he received the C.M.G. Courtesy of Mr S. L. Dennis

12 Edward Cooke, RA: drawing from *The Illustrated London News*, 1864. Courtesy of the Trustees of the National Portrait Gallery

13 Edward Falkener: photo taken about 1890 or 1895. Courtesy of Cambridge University Library

14 George Dennis: photo taken about 1875. Courtesy of Mr. S. L. Dennis

15 Henry Layard: pencil drawing by G. F. Watts, undated. Courtesy of the Trustees of the National Portrait Gallery

16 Aphrodite, from Centorbi, Sicily. Acquired by the British Museum from George Dennis in 1863. Courtesy of the Trustees of the British Museum

17 Aphrodite carrying Eros (second century BC) from Centorbi, Sicily. Acquired by the British Museum from George Dennis in 1863. Courtesy of the Trustees of the British Museum

18 Plaque: Eros (second century BC) from Centorbi, Sicily. Acquired by the British Museum from George Dennis in 1863. Courtesy of the Trustees of the British Museum

19 Greek statuette of Aphrodite (third century BC) from Cyrenaica. Acquired by the British Museum from George Dennis in 1868. Courtesy of the Trustees of the British Museum

CHRONOLOGICAL TABLE

GEORGE DENNIS 1814-1898

21 July 1814	Born in London, son of John Dennis of the Excise Office
1828	Enters Charterhouse
1829	Made to work in his father's office
c. 1832	Visits Wales
June 1834	Tours Scotland
May 1836	Spends three months in Portugal and Southern Spain
1839	Publishes his anonymous first book, *A Summer in Andalucia*
July 1839	Visits Switzerland and Northern Italy, and first meets Henry Layard in Venice
July 1840	Travels via Paris to Northern Spain and Madrid
1841	Publishes a series of anonymous articles on the Cid
April 1842	Leaves London via France for Italy
May 1842	In Florence
June-July 1842	First Etruscan tour with Samuel Ainsley, the artist: Tarquinia, Viterbo, Orvieto
Oct.-Nov. 1842	Second Etruscan tour with Ainsley: Veii, Castel d'Asso, Sutri
Winter 1842-43	Rome
April-July 1843	Third Etruscan tour with Ainsley: Cerveteri, Todi, Perugia, Volterra, Vetulonia, Sovana, Cortona, Florence
Summer 1843	Contracts with John Murray to write *The Cities and Cemeteries of Etruria*
February 1844	Leaves London for Etruria: works in Rome
1845	Publishes first article on Etruria and his book, *The Cid*
February 1846	Leaves London for Rome where he meets Edward Cooke, the artist. Continues writing his book on Etruria
June 1846	Visits Florence and meets Professor Migliarini. Returns to London about Christmas. Meets Edward Falkener
1847	First visit to Sicily

1848	Publishes *The Cities and Cemeteries of Etruria*; terminates his post at the Excise Office and joins the Colonial Office
January 1849-63	Sails for British Guiana to become Private Secretary to the Governor. Visits Sicily in 1852 and 1856-57. Works for John Murray on a Handbook of Sicily. Writes a book on Neapolitan misrule in Sicily which is never published. Made Inspector of Schools in June 1851
c. 1860	George Dennis marries
March 1863	The Dennises leave South America for Sicily. Excavations at Terranova and Girgenti
May 1863	Returns to London
Feb. 1864-April 1868	Vice-Consul at Benghazi. On extended leave in England in 1867. Excavations at Cyrene, Teucheira and Ptolemais
June 1868	Goes to live in Smyrna. Preliminary excavations at Sardis
July 1869	Promoted Consul for Crete
1870	Appointed Consul for Sicily at Palermo. Resident there from May 1870 to summer of 1879, with several trips on leave to England and Etruria
1878	Second edition, revised, of *Cities and Cemeteries of Etruria*, dedicated to Layard
June 1879	Appointed Consul at Smyrna. Resident there from September 1879 to 1888. Resumes work at Sardis and makes further tours of Southern Turkey
1885	Honorary doctorate at Oxford
April 1888	Death of Mrs Dennis
1 May 1888	George Dennis retires
1888-98	Further travels in Italy, Spain, Tangier and France. Gives several lectures to the British and American Archaeological Society in Rome
15 November 1898	Death in London aged eighty-four.

FOREWORD

GEORGE DENNIS'S *Cities and Cemeteries of Etruria* is probably less well-known in Britain at the present time than it was at the beginning of the century when it achieved the crowning distinction of being reprinted in Everyman's Library (1907). In France, Germany and Italy, however, where interest in Etruscan civilisation is still vigorous, it has never ceased to be regarded as a classic. *'Encore aujourd'hui,'* wrote an eminent Etruscologist recently, *'il n'est pas de meilleure introduction à l'étude de l'ancienne Etrurie que la lecture de ce petit chef d'oeuvre; un siècle d'existence ne lui a rien ôté de son charme ni de sa valeur'.*

The continuing archaeological value of Dennis's work lies in its comprehensiveness and accuracy. His knowledge of ancient Etruria was both extensive and intimate, and he describes its sites with a graphic objectivity which is all the more precious now that a great deal of what he recorded has perished. But it is above all Dennis's ability to delight as well as to instruct which sets *Cities and Cemeteries* apart from the ordinary guidebook or archaeological handbook and gives it a more humane quality and a more universal appeal. How refreshing it is, for example, in these days when archaeology seems on the point of capitulating to the computer, to interrupt a tour of the ruins of Veii with a visit to a nearby *capanna* to watch the shepherds drawing their daily ration of *ricotta*. Genre scenes such as this, together with the many vivid landscape vignettes, make Dennis a perpetual joy to read.

A man who could write as well as this must surely be worth writing about; and here we come upon the strange fact, noted by Dr Rhodes in his preface, that even the *Dictionary of National Biography* passes him over in silence. Can it really be, one wonders irreverently, that James Blatch Piggot Dennis's paper 'On the Mode of Flight of the Sterodactyles of the Coprolite bed near Cambridge' is more deserving of national commemoration than *Cities and Cemeteries*? Be that as it may, we must be thankful that George Dennis has at last found a worthy biographer, one who has sought out the evidence — much of it difficult to come by — with conscientious diligence and set it out with a directness and unpretentiousness of which Dennis himself would certainly have approved. Here, for once, is a book which truly does fill a gap.

Denys Haynes

12

PREFACE

ONE DAY in late summer, three or four years ago, I had just returned to Viterbo from a visit to the enchanting ruins of the Etrusco-Roman city of Ferento, about five miles away in the heart of that delightful countryside. The previous day I had visited the eerie and utterly remote site of Castel d'Asso with its Etruscan necropolis where Italian workmen were still excavating in banks still gay with wild cyclamen and yellow mullein and blue chicory.

I was sitting in Schenardi's, that famous old bar so familiar to anyone who knows Viterbo, drinking with a group of local friends who included a librarian, a schoolmaster, a museum curator and a municipal secretary. The conversation lighted upon the Etruscans, and one of my Italian friends (the librarian) happened to mention that he and a group of his companions were busily engaged in translating into Italian that immensely long book, the *Cities and Cemeteries of Etruria* by George Dennis, even though they had little hope of finding a publisher for the whole work. But, they complained, they knew next to nothing about the author, and could not find his name mentioned even in the English *Dictionary of National Biography* which they had consulted in vain in Rome. Who was he? How had he come to write such an amazing book one hundred and twenty years ago?

This set me thinking. I had once revised George Dennis's heading in the British Museum's General Catalogue of Printed Books, and I had read Edward Hutton's lavish words of praise of him in his recent book *Assisi and Umbria Revisited*. But that was all I knew about George Dennis, until I returned to England and was lucky enough to find, in a tiny bookshop in Sussex, a good copy of the first edition of 1848, which I bought and read from cover to cover. Thus was the idea for this biography born.

It has indeed been difficult to find the necessary facts, and even now I doubt whether I have found them all; yet I venture to hope that what I have managed to collect and put together may give a true picture of a man whom I consider to have been in every way extraordinary and admirable: a thoroughly honest Victorian gentleman, whose energy for work and adventure was boundless; an antiquary who knew frequent disappointments but who never knew fatigue or defeat; a Christian citizen whose only aim was to penetrate the secrets of past civilizations, above all of the Etruscans, and communicate his results to the world of scholarship with little or no thought for personal gain or for making a reputation. In fact he never made any money, and he was usually suffering from financial embarrassment if not also from bad health. Yet he lived into his eighty-fifth year, and his achievements seem to me to be well-nigh miraculous.

A number of people have helped me in my task. My deep gratitude is due in the first place to Mr S.L. Dennis, for his unfailingly generous help with family matters and for lending me letters and photographs; secondly, to Mr John Murray Junior and his famous publishing house for permission to consult and use the ninety letters in George Dennis's handwriting which now repose at No. 50 Albemarle Street. Various other friends and acquaintances have helped in so many ways that I can only say how grateful I am to them all: especially to Mr Denys Haynes and other colleagues at the British Museum, the Public Record Office, the British School at Rome, and the German Archaeological Institute in Rome.

I am much indebted for constant encouragement and advice to another intrepid explorer and writer of first-class travel books, my friend Mr James Wellard. I should also like to express my thanks to my friend Mr Roger Fearon for his valiant attempts (even though they proved fruitless) to trace any signs of the Dennises in present-day Smyrna. The British Consuls in both Palermo and Smyrna likewise made unsuccessful searches on my behalf, and I am grateful to them. Finally I would like to acknowledge my indebtedness to Mr Ridgway of Edinburgh University for his help at various stages of my work.

D.E.R.

CHAPTER 1

THE EARLY YEARS — 1814 - 1839

A SPIRIT of adventurous travel is always apparent in certain members of the Dennis family in the eighteenth century. John Dennis, great-grandfather of the subject of this biography, had survived the great Lisbon earthquake of 1755, while his son George had spent many years in Canada surveying land, laying military roads and making maps for the Admiralty. This George Dennis, who married Caroletta Ravenscroft in July 1775, had five children, of whom one son, John, was born on 8 May 1779. It seems to have been in 1801 that John entered the Excise Office in London, and here he spent the whole of his working life. His father George appears to have worked there too in his later years, if he is to be identified with a Mr G. Dennis who in 1810 was First Clerk to the Receiver General of Excise. In 1810 too the Accomptant for Foreign Spirits and Tobacco was John James Catherwood, the uncle of the architect Frederick Catherwood, whom we shall meet later in this story as a close friend of George Dennis; John Dennis was Clerk to the Receiver General from at least 1816 to 1842, while in his last working years, 1844 to 1845, he was promoted to be Receiver General. From 1836 to 1845 he was also Distributor of Stamps. His name is no longer found in the official records after 1845, in which year he reached the age of sixty-six and presumably retired. He was to live almost another twenty years.[1]

John Dennis and his wife Mary (née Hull) were married at St Stephen's, Exeter, on 24 January 1809. The Dennises had many connections with the West Country, and their ancestors had for centuries held lands and property in Gloucestershire. Mary may well have been a Devonshire woman, but after her marriage she lived all her life with her husband in London, where their home was in Ash Grove, Hackney, until on his retirement they went to live at Rose Hill, Dorking. They had ten children between December 1809, and January 1825, of whom one daughter, born in September 1817, died after only one month. Of those who survived, seven were daughters and two were sons. George was their fourth child, and he was born at 5.15 p.m. on Thursday, 21 July 1814. His only brother, the youngest of the family, was John Dennis, born on 8 January 1825, who became a distinguished critic of English literature, on which he wrote many books. The daughters who lived beyond babyhood were Mary (born 1809), Elizabeth (born 1811), Anne (born 1813), Caroletta (born 1816), Maria (born 1818),

15

Frances (born 1820) and Octavia (born 1822).

When George was about ten or twelve years of age, he received the following undated letter from an uncle, the contents and sentiments of which to our modern minds are, to say the least, rather curious:

My dear George,

How big are you? Are you large enough to read Greek without a lexicon? I intended, by way of making up a parcel, to have sent you some classic, but being ignorant of the size of your mind, I send for your acceptance a corporal instrument, to wit a silver bladed knife, being sure your body must have arrived at an appleparing and peardevouring age. I should be very happy to see you in Norwich, but I shall never invite you, for a reason best known to your mother.

I was going to say 'I hope you are a good boy' — but every Uncle says this. Besides, I know you *are* good. I hope you are a lively, manly fellow, fond of skating , swimming and riding — hating arithmetic, hating lies, hating boys with dirt under their finger-nails, without gloves, dirtyshoed, without pocket-combs.

Don't fall in love with every little fellow that comes in your way and fancy him worthy your friendship because yourself are ingenuous and unsuspicious, and ashamed to do what is wrong. Depend on it, not *one* boy in a *hundred* is deserving your society: I have known, first and last, a thousand boys, and I declare from my heart I wish I had kept myself solitary, the companion of my books, my parents, my brother, sisters and dog.

Ask your father to let you keep a dog. Nobody can expect to go happily or innocently through his youth, who does not keep a dog. The animal calls forth the best affections, he draws you out to pleasant walks, he displays all the good qualities of human nature without the bad. But then he must be a handsome dog. In the lower animals the mind and body are certainly symmetrical. A cur, a yelping, stupid-faced dog is the last thing to be tolerated. And he must fetch and carry and go into the water; no dog is fit for the company of a Latin scholar, unless he likes the water. He may be fit for game or turning spits but he is totally unadapted to classic company.

Give my love to your parents; I hope your mother's arm is well. I hope your father's arms and legs are well. Give my love to your Sisters; I hope they are all in good health, hearty at bread and butter; fond of walking in the garden; not fond of catching butterflies nor drinking London Porter. Ask your Mother if there is at her house a boot tree which I must have left in her possession in the year 1814 or thereabouts. If there be, and you do not

wear topboots nor your father nor, therefore, want it, ask her
to send it by some van or coach* which passes the door. Perhaps the coach would charge too much.

    Adieu! my dear George!
      Believe me to be
        Your loving Uncle
        Robert Hull.

*immediately or I must buy one: in a week.

In 1828, when he was fourteen, his father sent him to Charterhouse, and his name appears in the list of boys in the second
division of the sixth form which was published on May 7th 1828.
Another boy who entered the school in 1827 was John Drummond-
Hay, whom George was to meet in Tangier in 1836. George's
younger brother John is not recorded at Charterhouse. George
could not have stayed at Charterhouse for many terms since his
name appears in the lists in 1828 only. Although in later life he was
to display knowledge of so many languages — Latin, Greek, Modern
Greek, French, Spanish, Portuguese, Italian, Turkish and even Arabic
— yet in his short stay at public school he was distinguished in no
way whatever, and certainly wrote none of those prize poems
which Charterhouse was so fond of publishing. George had no
chance of going to a university, for in 1829 when he was only
fifteen his father took him away from school and put him to work
as a clerk in his own office. In 1832 the father suffered a long and
severe illness, during which he wrote to George begging him to
understand that his prime duty in life was to God and to the Gospel
of Jesus Christ, without complete devotion to which no man could
be happy. 'I intreat of you to read your Bible with a devout spirit
— ask the promised influences and teachings of the Holy Spirit to
guide you into all truth — distrust your own understanding, avoid
evil communication . . . and may the best blessings of this world
and for that which is to come be showered down upon you so prays
your affectionate Father, J.D.'

George hated working in a London office, but soon he began to
take holidays away from home, even though he was earning so
little money. When he was about eighteen he went to Wales, where
he was particularly impressed with Llanberis Pass. It seems that
about this time he also went for the first time to Paris, probably in
the company of his father, who was very fond of sketching, and
who more than once visited the Louvre. Rather more than a month
before his twentieth birthday, George went alone on a walking tour
of Scotland. It was June 1834. He went to Aberdeen, then up the
Dee to Ballater and Braemar. Much of the time he was walking
across rough country with no trace of a road, sometimes sinking up
to his knees in heather and boggy grass. He realised that one could

starve to death after several days of such dangerous walking, without even meeting a single shepherd. 'W. Scott could never have seen Glen Tilt' he commented in his letter home of 8 June, 'or he would certainly have laid the scene of a novel there. I never saw a place so well calculated for banditti and so inaccessible. It was in former times celebrated for its warriors. Scenery for four or five miles above Blair highly picturesque and beautiful, stopped at a gamekeeper's cottage, and had some bannocks, cheese and milk. The bannocks are flat cakes like a pancake, of oatmeal, or barley, not exactly suited to an English palate.'

He must have walked at least forty miles that day. He walked over the Pass of Killiecrankie and along Loch Tummel to Trinfour where he was lulled to sleep by bagpipes. The next day he walked another thirty-one miles to Garviemore, where the scenery was as wild and desolate as possible, with hardly a human being to be seen.

> About three miles from Garviemore I passed a farmer's house, saw the mistress with some milk jugs in her hand, ran up and asked for a draught of milk; she asked me to walk in, introduced me to her husband and daughter and gave me some most delicious milk. She said they were just going to tea, asked me to stop, and gave me some cold goat, cheese bannocks and butter. Two sons came in to tea, and the whole party tho' very plainly clad were far more polite and well-bred than I should have expected in so remote a spot. I like the Scotch far better than I anticipated, I find them extremely civil and kind, and all classes very well informed, even the children of the peasantry learn Latin and French. I had a very interesting conversation with a shoemaker from Perth yesterday, and learnt something about the religious sects in Scotland. I think the Scotch, like the Germans, are inclined to be metaphysical.

He then walked eighteen miles to Fort Augustus, and had his first enchanting view of Loch Ness.

At Inverness he was kindly received by a friend of his father's, Mr Grandison, whose Scottish accent he found practically incomprehensible. Just over a week later, when he was on his way southwards again, he stopped long enough at Tyndrum in Argyllshire to write a long letter home. He had attempted to climb Ben Nevis. 'I succeeded pretty well in finding my way over the heather and swamps which always compose the lower part of these mountains, but on leaving the region of vegetation, I found it next to impossible to make my way over the beds of loose sliding rocks, of which the upper part of the mountain is composed. After immense labour, losing sometimes by one step what I had gained by the previous three, I succeeded in reaching the highest ridge, for peak there is none, just as the sun disappeared from the horizon'. The descent was even more dangerous and difficult, and he was greatly relieved to find himself at Banivie late at night, with a whole skin and rent breeches. On reaching Glencoe he was obliged to get a man to carry him on his back across a burn to a farmer's house where he begged shelter for the night. 'It was a farm of the most miserable description; the old man, however, treated me to the best in his power, gave me milk and potatoes for supper; an old lumber room for a chamber, with a nest of cats on the counterpane in the corner of the bed on which I dosed out the night.' He continued: 'I cannot say that my expectations of Glencoe were surpassed by the reality, tho' there is in it much that is gloomy, awful and terrible. I was not so much excited by it as by the Pass of Llanberis which I think exceeds this in sublimity. It is a scene, however, well suited for the awful massacre that took place there.' His feet were blistered and he could not manage more than '20 Scotch miles' a day. He disliked Scotch whisky intensely.

By 20 June he had reached Callender, where he was glad to receive a letter from home, and to know that his pigeons were being well looked after. 'Fanny shall be rewarded on my return if they are well attended to, and if any old ones return, she must not forget to let them into the house immediately, but at the same time must prevent the rest escaping. She must give them straw for their nests; she will find plenty in a hamper in the cellar.'

And so the Scottish tour came to an end by the last week in June 1834. The following spring, 1835, George's mother went to Devonport to stay with her daughter Elizabeth, who had just had a baby. George reported to her that Gordon (his dog) and the pigeons were very well, and that his father was proposing to come down to Devon too at the end of April. He hoped that his sister Elizabeth would not have nine children: '4 or 5 is a much more respectable number.' George himself was invited to visit Devonport too, but said that he must decline the invitation, because if he were able to escape from London during the present summer of 1835 he would certainly travel southwards. It appears, however, that he was not able to go until the following year, 1836, when in the month of May he suddenly departed from home and to the great anxiety of his parents was not heard of again for some three months. He had in fact gone by sea from London to Portugal and the south of Spain, and, all alone, had set out on his first extensive tour abroad which was to lead to the writing of his first book. Landing first at Oporto, he made his way to Lisbon, and thence to Seville, Granada and Cadiz. His father became so worried at not receiving news from him that he applied to the Foreign Office for help. The result was the following consular letter which was despatched on 1 August 1836:

Sir,

I am directed by Viscount Palmerston to request that you

will make inquiries in the Place of your residence, with the view
of tracing Mr George Dennis, an English Gentleman 22 years of
age, who has been travelling in Spain, and who has not been
heard of by his family since the 4th of June. He wrote to his
family on that day, that he was about to leave Cadiz for Xeres
and Seville, with the view of visiting the Moorish cities in the
South of Spain.

As it is possible that he may have been induced to cross over
to one of the Regencies on the coast of Africa I address this
letter to you in common with His Majesty's Consuls in the
Southern and Eastern Ports of Spain.

    I have the honor to be
        Sir
            Your most obedient humble servant
            (Signed) John Bidwell.

But George was not lost. He was extremely busy collecting notes
and impressions for the book which was published in 1839,
anonymously, by the firm of Richard Bentley. It was entitled *A
Summer in Andalucia,* and is in two volumes, with only one
illustration. Why George Dennis did not put his name on the titlepage is a mystery.

He had only a few hours ashore in which to visit Oporto. He
found 'some of the streets broad and handsome, but in general they
are narrow, tortuous, steep, rugged, and filthy, though in the last
particular, as I afterwards found, they cannot rival those of the
capital.' In Lisbon indeed, when he arrived next day, 'many of the
streets are narrow, badly paved, and execrably filthy'. In fact 'the
more I saw of Lisbon', he says, 'the less did it please me. Its
magnificent appearance from the river has deceived many a traveller;
and had I not been prepared to behold a city renowned for its
filth, my astonishment would have equalled my disgust'. An
Englishman, he felt sure, would find it hardly possible to enter
many of the streets on account of their dirt and their fearful smells.
At least Dennis had a good view over the Tagus from his windows
on the Caes do Sodre. He went to the Italian opera at the theatre of
São Carlos, where he saw the Queen of Portugal and the young
Prince Ferdinand. The Queen was making obvious efforts to conceal the fact that she was growing fat.

Dennis left Lisbon without much regret and sailed to Cadiz. Here
he was 'perfectly fascinated by the wondrous grace and elegance
floating before my eyes' as the young women of Cadiz took their
evening strolls. 'If Lisbon has disgusted the stranger with its filth,
Cadiz will no less delight him with the contrast; for its streets are
scrupulously cleansed from whatever might offend either the sight
or the smell.' In Xeres he visited the establishments of several
sherry merchants which were refreshingly cool after the dazzling

heat of the streets outside. Dennis carried a brace of pistols to guard himself against robbers, but nothing terrible ever befell him in Spain. The cathedral in Seville he found 'magnificent' and 'superb', worth any journey to see it, and the view from the tower 'most interesting'. Next he visited the Biblioteca Colombina, built over the eastern arcade of the Court of the Orange-Trees, to which Fernando Colón, the natural son of Christopher Columbus, had bequeathed 20,000 volumes. Dennis stood for a long time admiring the Murillo pictures in the cathedral. He has in fact quite a lot to say in praise of Spanish painting. The visit to Seville cathedral was, and is, 'an epoch in one's life', despite the terrible number of beggars who are always hanging about in its precincts. 'Seville has not the startling freshness of Cadiz: the houses are not as showy, nor the streets as straight and regular as in that city, but it more than counterbalances this by its venerable air and picturesque appearance'.

He made himself go to a bull-fight in Seville, but although he gives a detailed account of it he was horrified at the savage and needless cruelty. Next he went to Córdoba to see the Moorish architecture. 'The city is small; the streets narrow, tortuous, irregular, and execrably paved; and the houses low, mean, ruinous and poverty-stricken, which air is increased by the general absence of glass'. The overall impression of Córdoba was of a dull place, even though there was much that was picturesque, gardens of orange, fig and pomegranate trees, vines growing over the roofs, and a thoroughly Spanish atmosphere about the town as a whole. Roman antiquities abound in Córdoba, but even more abundant are the Moorish remains. Travelling in 1836 was still very difficult, and Dennis came to the conclusion that 'if the state of internal communication in any country be a true test of its civilization, then must Spain rank much below every other Christian country of Europe, and be classed with the semi-barbarous nations of Arabia and Egypt'.

On arrival in Granada he was met by Mateo Ximenes, 'celebrated, I may say immortalised, by the pen of Geoffrey Crayon.[2] He still acts as guide to travellers, and in that capacity, on hearing of my arrival, had come to offer his services'. Granada in its general aspect resembled both Seville and Córdoba, but 'has not the poverty-stricken appearance of the latter city, and has an air of greater antiquity, with more of the ruinous and picturesque than the former'.

Dennis devotes eight whole chapters to the description of Granada, and seems to have stayed there longer than anywhere else in Spain. He did a great deal of sketching there, and, as we shall see when we meet him in Etruria, he was no mean artist with the pencil. Later he visited Malaga and Gibraltar, and while in the south of Spain (probably from Gibraltar) Dennis crossed over for a

short visit to Tangier, where he met a young man two years
younger than himself named John Drummond-Hay, who had been
a pupil at Charterhouse from 1827 to 1832. They had no doubt
known each other at school. Drummond-Hay's father was Political
Agent and Consul General in Morocco, and the son had been there
four years when Dennis met him in 1836. For forty years
Drummond-Hay, who was later knighted, was to represent Great
Britain in Morocco, and he eventually owned a villa at Tangier.
After this meeting in 1836, he and Dennis were not to meet again
for fifty-three years, until Dennis revisited Tangier in the winter of
1889-1890. He ended his tour by returning to Cadiz and ending
his second volume with his views on the present religious and
political situation in Spain.

The book published in 1839 comprises 850 pages in two
volumes. For the first book of a young man of twenty-five this was
a remarkable achievement. He was presumably occupied with the
writing of it during most of the years 1837 and 1838, for the agreement which he made with the publisher Bentley is dated 22
November 1838 and the book duly appeared in June 1839. Between those dates three extracts from it in the form of anonymous
articles were published in *Bentley's Miscellany*, that famous periodical edited by Dickens. The three articles are entitled respectively
'A Pilgrimage to Seville Cathedral', 'Córdoba' and 'Granada', under
the collective title 'Sketches of Andalucia', and they were printed
in the issues of January, February and March 1839. There is in
existence a letter from his father, headed simply 'Wednesday',
which probably belongs to late 1838, in which John Dennis shows
some misgivings about his son's intention of publishing articles in
this magazine. He writes:

My dear George,

In the many musings of my mind since you informed me of
Bentley's decision, one fear has arisen, lest writing for him
should lead to companionship with the contributors to Boz. I
intreat you to be careful on this head, and not to engage to fur-
nish articles of that frothy character which [the] readers of
Boz require. I am most in hopes that if the Book should have
sterling merit Mr Backhouse may be able to do something for
you in this country.

Do my dear George avoid the desecration of the Sabbath;
the blessing of God will not attend those who despise his ordi-
nances and neglect the merciful provision of a day of rest.

Believe me that the supports of religion in the extreme of
weakness, in sustaining the spirits and shielding from alarm is
worth far more than the world can offer.

I can truly say I have not had one moment of alarm or dis-
quiet.

I am my dear George,
        Affectionately your Father,
            J. Dennis.
I still feel the extreme of weakness.

Already in 1838 John Dennis had suffered another serious illness. In the July and August of that year George had visited Ireland, but details of his tour there are lacking. He left Dublin on August 1st, 1838, and after a stormy passage of 63 hours reached Devonport, where he stayed with his sister Elizabeth, whom he found looking very thin and much older than when he had last seen her. He made some excursions in Devon, to such places as Tavistock and Dartmoor, and when writing home on August 6th he was still worried about Gordon the dog and the pigeons:

> I don't like Gordon to go out in the evening because there [are] so many dogs about and at this season it is scarcely safe, but before breakfast he may go with a string as often as John pleases. I hope he remembers the doves, to give them a little gravel, a little lump of salt, fresh water daily, and wheat, buck wheat and canary seed, alternately with crumbs of bread.

After this holiday it is evident that he was busy at home writing the book and the articles, for which Bentley paid him twenty-five pounds, and fifty guineas for the book six months after publication. If his father objected to his association with other contributors to Boz and his magazine, the effect seems to have been that George never again wrote articles for Bentley's magazine. But he had not yet done with visiting or writing about Spain. When his first book was published in 1839, he had an intimate knowledge of Southern Spain and Portugal, but he was only twenty-five years old, full of vigour and anxious to acquaint himself with Northern Spain. His eyes and his thoughts were also turning towards Switzerland and Italy.

On 8 June 1839, he wrote from London to his father, who had gone with his wife to spend a holiday in Dover:

> My work will not be out till next week, but it has been already reviewed in the Parthenon, Spectator, Lit. Gazette, and Court Journal. All speak very highly of it, the Spectator alone finds fault, and that with the superabundance of description in proportion with incident, manners etc. which inequality it says 'detracts from the high classical position the work might otherwise challenge, and prevents it rivalling Beckford's letters if not excelling them in dramatic (I forget what) and the art of narrating dialogue'. Bentley promises me 12 copies, and seems eager to get anything else I may write.

A Summer in Andalucia was also reviewed at length, not with complete praise, anonymously (but by Don Pascual de Gayangos) in the *Athenaeum*, no. 610, on Saturday, 6 July 1839. The *Spectator* was more lavish in its praise, declaring it to be 'the most striking and characteristic book of travels that has recently issued from the press', while *John Bull* declared: 'These volumes are both instructive and entertaining. They are evidently the production of a clever and discriminating mind'. The reviewers naturally wondered who the author could be. The distinguished Spanish reviewer in the *Athenaeum* said he would not be surprised if it turned out to be the work of Captain C. Rochfort Scott, who had in 1838 published a book entitled *Excursions in the Mountains of Ronda and Granada, with Characteristic Sketches of the Inhabitants of the South of Spain*, in two volumes. It is probable that the true authorship of *Summer in Andalucia* became known fairly soon after the book's appearance.

The first book and the first articles were a success. The job at the Excise Office in London was a bore, and the pay was poor. The young man was lucky to have travelled so much in the first quarter-century of his life. There was at this time another important factor in his life, and this was an affair of the heart. The young lady's name has not been preserved; all we know is that George refers to her father as 'Mr C.' This prospective father-in-law told George that he must be earning four hundred pounds a year or near it before he could hope to win the young lady's hand, and in fact George was earning less than two hundred. By the end of June she had taken her father's advice and decided to turn down George's offer of marriage on the sole ground that his financial prospects were so poor. The affair was over. George determined to look for a position as secretary, librarian, or (by advertising himself as the author of a book) as a sub-editor of some periodical. Above all he wanted to travel and to write of his travels.

CHAPTER 2

SWITZERLAND, NORTHERN ITALY, NORTHERN SPAIN—1839-1841

GEORGE DENNIS left home again in the middle of July, 1839, bound first for Switzerland. He crossed to Boulogne, reached Paris the next day, and thence took the diligence for Geneva. It was a very tedious journey through Troyes, Dijon and Dole. The sun was so hot in the daytime that he could not bear to touch the leather over his head. It took just over six days to reach Geneva from London, and only one of those nights was he able to spend in bed. He therefore arrived very tired. Mont Blanc was for the most part hidden in cloud, but George was rewarded with one glimpse of its peak. He was rather disappointed to find the vegetation of Switzerland so similar to that of England, with the sole exception of the vines. From Geneva he took the steamer to Villeneuve at the other end of the lake, then he went by diligence to St Moritz and so into Italy. He arrived at Milan on July 27th after a continuous journey of five days from Geneva. He wrote to his parents on July 28th:

> Milan is a handsome city, stone or cream-coloured houses with balconies and jalousies. I see it in its glory today which is Sunday, for the streets are full of people gaily dressed, with carriages and horses in abundance. I have only had a glimpse of all this on my way to and from the Cathedral, where I have spent the morning hearing High Mass and ascending the highest pinnacle. It is a superb edifice, in some respects superior, in others inferior to the Cathedral of Seville. It is adorned to excess, not simply grand, and the whiteness of its marble destroys its venerability. I thought of you often during the service which I have just witnessed. Surely all these genuflections and crossings, this ringing of bells and tossing of incense cannot be so acceptable to the Deity as the simple, silent, heart-born adoration of a Protestant Christian. I have met on my journey with many Catholic priests and some Oxford tractarians and I feel more and more opposed to Popery and anything which approaches it.

During his evening stroll along the Corso he was reminded of Hyde Park on a Sunday afternoon, with hundreds of carriages moving up and down and the pavements lined with people in their Sunday best. He was so tired that he went to bed at eight o'clock.

'All this', he told his parents next day in his letter, 'serves to convince me that however agreeable it may be to visit foreign

countries for a short time, a residence in them would not be
desirable. I am almost cured of my desire to live abroad. I think
however I should enjoy a few months' residence on one of the
lakes.'

He could not have foreseen at this stage in his career that he was
destined never again to live permanently in Britain. He wished his
father could have been with him in Northern Italy, but feared that
if he had been, he would have worn himself out with sketching, so
many beautiful scenes met the eye at every turn. His mother wrote
to him at the end of July and said that everyone seemed to be
talking about his book on Southern Spain. Its authorship seemed
to be fairly generally known in London literary circles, and most
readers were loud in its praise. Mrs Dennis told her son to take
his travelling more leisurely, while his father warned him to avoid
controversies in Catholic countries.

Early in August George reached Venice, having passed through
Vicenza at midnight and seen little of Padua, which was described
to him as 'the most ancient city of Italy'. 'It seems one great
university', he afterwards wrote. 'Cloisters, cloisters, cloisters meet
the eye wherever it turns . . . The streets are narrow, tortuous and
dreary; and altogether Padua has by far the most gloomy air of any
city I have yet seen in Italy.' (He had seen very few!) At La Mira on
the Brenta he enquired for Lord Byron's villa, but nobody was able
to point it out to him. When he reached Venice he was sorely
disappointed, even though he wrote home to his parents on
August 6th: 'Venice is a most wonderful city, picturesque and
peculiar in the extreme and no less melancholy. I passed down
the Grand Canal today in a gondola and enquired of my boatman
about each of the superb palaces which line its banks, almost all
empty or used as warehouses or the abodes of beggars.' When he
asked the gondolier about the original families who owned these
palaces, he was invariably told: 'All dead.'

He stayed at the Albergo dell'Europa, near the Piazza S. Marco
and the Doges' Palace. He feasted his eyes on the masterpieces of
Venetian painting, which made his visit worthwhile. In the article
which he later wrote he lamented: 'the flowers were faded; their
freshness and glory have departed, decay and ruin only are left. The
feelings of anxious delight which I naturally carried into a city so
renowned in history, and so peculiar in everything around. . . the
almost death-like silence which reigned over all . . . called forth a
sympathetic sadness from the soul. . . Venice is beauty in tears'.
There is here a sensitive strain of real literary merit. It should be
remembered that this sadness in Venice must have been largely due
to the Austrian occupation, which a few years later, in 1848, was to
lead to the Venetian uprising under Daniele Manin. The article
which Dennis wrote and published anonymously in *Bentley's*

Magazine was entitled 'The City of the Doge: or, Letters from Venice. By the author of "A summer in Andalucia." '[1]

The worst of Venice in August was its insects. George was almost flayed alive by mosquitoes and fleas. 'Tell Anne I wish she were here were it only to admire the spiders.'

He returned via Bergamo ('renowned for nothing but goitres'), Como and Lugano. He received no letter from home until he reached Berne. His father had given him permission to stay in Switzerland a week longer than planned. He therefore returned to the Bernese Oberland, where the scenery was the most magnificent he had seen or indeed could imagine seeing anywhere in Europe. After many storms he reached Zurich where he finished writing a long letter home: 'This morning is beautifully fine. I am now sitting at an open window overlooking the Lake of Zurich which is a sheet of gold, and the light fleecy clouds overhanging it are gradually rolling back and disclosing the town of Zurich and the white villages on the opposite shore. I am now on my way home which I shall perhaps reach as soon as this letter.'

When he came back to London, he renewed his efforts to find employment as an author or editor. In October 1839 his mother was again staying at Devonport with 'poor Elizabeth' (whose health seems always to have been precarious and whose husband was always suffering embarrassment over his business), and George told her that Bentley was only offering him twelve guineas per sheet of 16 closely printed pages of his *Miscellany*, so he had written to Chambers offering his services for his *Journal*. 'I have received an answer not very encouraging — he wishes assistance but is afraid to seek it; not one in ten suits him — though he does not like to ask me to write, lest he should not be able to insert my communication, he allows me to send him some articles on trial.'

But even if Dennis succeeded in having any articles published in Chambers's *Journal*, it is impossible for us now to identify them, since all articles in that journal are anonymous, short and undistinguished by their style and subject matter.

In the spring of 1840 George's parents went to stay at Ryde, Isle of Wight, mainly for the sake of his father's delicate health, while George stayed at home and continued to work at the Excise Office. His younger brother John, now sixteen years of age, was described as 'very delicate and weak', but must have gained strength later on, since he lived to be eighty-six. George was making his plans for his next holiday abroad, which began in July, 1840, when he travelled via Le Havre to Rouen and Paris. He studied the new collection of Spanish masters in the Louvre very carefully, and continually found himself wishing that his father could revisit Paris. On July 14th (perhaps the most important date in the French calendar) George dined on vermicelli soup, kidneys stewed with truffles, two wild

boar chops, peach fritters, a large plate of strawberries, bread ad
lib., and half a bottle of wine, for which he paid two francs or
about one shilling and sixpence. By July 19th he had reached
Bayonne, and had decided to cross over into Spain. He was
assured that conditions in Northern Spain were absolutely calm and
peaceful, and that the mail and diligences had run daily to Madrid
for months past and that no accident had happened to them. He
wanted to see Burgos because he had recently begun to take an
interest in the Cid. He told his parents: 'I never in my life saw
such gay colours on human forms as are worn by the Bayonnais
male and female, men in red, blue, brown, or white caps with tassels
of some other colour, scarlet sashes and variegated clothes, the
women in headdresses of the brightest hued handkerchiefs, crimson,
scarlet, orange, blue or yellow shawls, and gowns to match. An
assemblage of both sexes looks as bright and gaudy as a tulip bed.'

He told John to take great care of Gordon:

> I would rather he did not take him out except in the cool of
> the morning and then only for a short distance as dogs who
> are not accustomed to much daily exercise are apt in summer
> to fall into fits; which should it happen to G. would frighten
> John exceedingly, and perhaps the poor dog would be killed as
> mad by some ignorant bystanders — as I have several times seen
> occur. The new young doves he must turn into the cage with
> the old young ones, as soon as they can feed themselves, which
> will be soon after the mother has laid again. As soon as they
> are fledged, he must take out the nest and put in clean hay for
> the mother. Tell him to remember to give them all fresh gravel
> or red sand, and to leave a lump of salt and a piece of mortar
> in the cage of the old ones.

Sketching, sight-seeing and making notes made him grudge the
time he had to spend sleeping.

The well-known author of the *Handbook for Travellers in Spain,*
Richard Ford, who was eighteen years older than George Dennis,
having been born in 1796, wrote that 'the diligences, though only
introduced into Spain in 1821, were admirably managed. Travelling over excellent main roads, drawn by teams of eight, twelve, or
sometimes fifteen mules, they were lighter, more roomy, and faster
than those in France. As compared with English stage-coaches, a
traveller considered them to be more comfortable than our own,
and equally regular in their working.' He was here quoting from
A Summer in Andalucia, where, of course, George Dennis was describing diligences in the South of Spain, not the North. In July,
1840, he considered those in the North to be greatly more reliable
than those in the South had been three or four years earlier.

From Bayonne he rode to Vitoria over beautiful, mountainous
country, which in its general aspect resembled North Wales more

closely than anywhere else he had been. 'The traces of the recent wars are everywhere evident' he told his parents on July 26th, 'houses covered with bullet-marks, or battered to pieces; forts on every hill, every village with a slight rampart around it. Many houses burnt to the ground, and one whole town, Urnieta, destroyed by fire. This the British Legion had the honour of accomplishing. They are execrated by all the inhabitants of the Basque provinces as demons. The fact is they knew that they would receive no quarter from the Carlists, and they gave none.'

From Vitoria he passed over dreary, desert-like country, stiflingly hot and dusty, to Burgos, which delighted him both for its cathedral and for its relics of the Cid. On arrival in Madrid he took a room at the best inn in the principal street in the heart of the city; but 'here as everywhere else in Spain, I am devoured by bugs of gigantic proportions.'

On Tuesday, 'August something,/40', he wrote from Madrid a very interesting letter to his friend William P. Ord at Tryon's Place, Hackney:

My dear William,

It is the hour of twilight, when all the Madrileño world is on the wing to the Prado or to the Theatre — but I am seated in a balcony overhanging the street, with my back turned to the fair ones who are gliding down the street with fluttering fans on their way to the general evening rendezvous — Oxcars, many coloured *calesas*,[2] and betasselled and bebelled mules are passing below, a flock of goats is reposing for the night a little way off in the street tinkling soft music but these doings do not distract my attention — A hanging chapel of the Virgin has just been lighted up — nay more, a couple of Señoritas in a window opposite are fluttering away and waving handkerchiefs, evidently to attract my attention, and wondering from what boorish land I can have come who am totally indifferent to all their attractions and allurements. I hear them now hissing at me as I write in compliance with your request that I would drop you a line. I write in great haste and in great heat, for the nights here are little less oppressive than the days. It is but a 'continuity or contiguity (I forget which Milton has it) of shade', and I cannot touch the paper lest I should so damp it as to render it unfit for writing.

I began this at Madrid some days since but was not able to finish it. I now write from Zaragoza where I have just arrived in safety. Travelling on certain roads in this country is now reputed safe, tho' a couple of *escopeteros*[3] armed to the teeth who accompany every diligence serve to remind you that you are in a lawless land. Other roads are still so infested by factions or robbers that no one will travel on them unless pressed

by necessity. Such is the road from this city to Barcelona; and
the road from Madrid to Andalucia. Diligence after diligence
has been stopt in La Mancha since I have been in Spain. On
one occasion the robbers to the number of 15 or 20 attacked
it near Puerto Lapiche,[4] the scene of D. Quixote's windmill
exploit — but the diligence happened at the moment to be met
by a galera, or waggon, and the passengers mustering together
nearly 40 muskets returned the robbers' fire with such effect
as to put them to flight. But the marvel is that this country,
so long distracted by civil war and infested by hordes of banditti should be as tranquil as it is at present. Were it not for
the ruined buildings and the recent shot-marks which meet the
eye in almost every town north of Madrid, it would be difficult
to credit that not two months have elapsed since this land wit-
nessed the most frightful atrocities which have ever attended
a civil war. I hear accounts of battles, murders and sudden
deaths from every mouth, and the women seem to have seen as
much of the work of destruction as the men. By the by, I cannot say much for the women of Castille — they are far inferior
in beauty and grace to the Andaluzas. What little I have seen
of the Aragonesas I like better, but the Basque women bear
away the palm of beauty from all in point of complexion and
feature and they seem more virtuous and modest than their
countrywomen of the south. I was very nearly dividing my
heart between two young ladies at Astigarraga in Guipuzcoa.
They were sisters but of different styles of beauty; one of a
true Spanish cast with a full, wild, glowing eye, and a smile and
word for every one; the other like an English girl tho' as dark
as the other, and exceedingly like you know who — but withal
so pensive and sad that I felt sure she had lost a lover or met
with some misfortune in the late war — the house by the by in
which they lived was prettily sprinkled with bullet-marks. I
have not seen another girl in Spain that has interested me half
as much. By the way *in re mulierum,* I will tell you how I
returned from the Escorial a few nights since. Every place in
the diligence was taken and as it was imperative on me to return that evening to Madrid, I agreed to go per galera, which I
was told I should find very comfortable. And comfortable
enough you will think it when I tell you that I lay all night on
a new feather-bed or mattress, with half a dozen pillows for
my head; and no companion but a young lady who shared the
mattress with me and talked and sung to me all the night long.
I should have said that we left at 11 at night and did not reach
Madrid before 8 or 9 the next morning. She was unmarried
and as far as I know respectable, but I tell you this fact to give
you some idea of the freedom of Spanish women. The more

I see of them the more strongly I feel persuaded that if it be
my fate or lot to marry, it will not be a Spanish woman who
will 'call me husband' as the Irish say. I thank God I am born
of an English mother, and in a land where I have learned what
women ought to be. Delicacy seems to be unknown in Spain.
But I have told you nothing of what I have seen. Well then to
omit all mention of battles etc., of which my memory and note-
book are full to the brim, I have seen the birth-place of the
Cid, his tomb and that of his wife Ximena, and his veritable
sword Tizona with the armour he was wont to wear. I have
seen the tombs of all the Spanish Kings from Charles 5 to
Ferdinand 7 inclusive. I have seen one of the children that
Herod put to death, and one of the jars which contained
the winefied water at the marriage of Cana — I have seen the
grandest Cathedral in Spain, next to Seville, viz. that of Toledo,
and the most elaborate of all, that of Burgos. I have seen a
church hung with the fetters taken from the Christians who
were liberated at the conquest of Granada. I have seen a
synagogue built of the earth of Jerusalem and of the cedars of
Lebanon. I have seen Louis Philippe, not to be seen every day,
I warrant you. I have seen the birth-place of Martial, the
ancient Bilbilis. I have seen pictures of every school except
our own, and of superlative merit, one hundredth part of
which would put our friend Johnson on the stilts for a year
to come.

I have not seen the Queens of Spain, I have not seen a bull-
fight, nor even a bolero on the stage, nor have I seen a line
from home to tell me whether you are all in existence and
thriving. I go as soon as the office is open tomorrow to seek
letters. I have seen nothing except the climate to make me
love my own country the less. I want much to know how
you are going to dispose of yourself — and any other particulars in which I feel interest. I hope your parents will not have
left Hackney before my return. Remember me very kindly to
them and to your sister — you will sadly miss their society.
I would not be in a hurry to fix, were I you, nor would I before
trial make an agreement to take any lodgings for a long time.
You will of course read what you think proper of this letter to
my parents. I shall not therefore write to them for a few days.
I am now at a loss which way to move, whether to Pamplona,
or into the heart of the Pyrenees. My movements will depend
principally on the comparative expedition on the roads. I
knock myself down for the shortest to Bourdeaux, whence a
journey of 4 or 5 days will carry me to London. I am now
well seasoned, inured to heat and dust, and think nothing of
a journey sans cesse of 3 or 4 days per diligence. I should

ask you to excuse a letter so full of myself and own proceedings but in present circumstances it will prove more
interesting to you than were it otherwise.

Last night it was excessively hot and sultry — this morning
it is quite cool — a fresh breeze, and a cloudy sky that
obscures the sun. The cities in the north of Spain are subject
to these vicissitudes. At Burgos I found it so cold, that seated
in the sunshine at 10 a.m. I could not hold my pencil to draw.
This is a very picturesque old city, quite in decay — narrow
streets, high houses — grated windows hung with cobwebs, and
large massive buildings so gloomy and venerable that each seems
a storehouse of dark traditions. Many bear their history on their
faces, for the Zaragozanos have in very many instances preserved the fronts of their houses in the state that the French left
them in the two celebrated sieges of 1808 and 9 — i.e. riddled
with bullets. It is a curious sight to see the houses on both sides
the principal street so decorated — the shell holes have of
course been plugged up, but the bullet marks remain as memen-
tos of the unrivalled heroism of the citizens in those sieges. It
much annoys me to be mistaken for a Frenchman, as I have
been throughout the journey in Spain. It must be the dress I
have assumed — a blouse and cap — I bought the blouse in Paris
for the Pyrenees, but wear it for coolness' sake — that occasions
the mistake. My love to all at Ash Grove. You were perhaps
as much surprised as they to hear that I had reached Madrid.
You know I expressed my desire to do so, but thought it
impracticable till on reaching Bordeaux I heard of the tran-
quillity of the country. I reckon myself now safe — I have
passed thro' the most dangerous parts. In ten days or so I
shall be in London — if within a week I can cross the
Pyrenees — but I find that the communication from this city
to France is not regular or frequent. I long to hear from
home. When a man is a resident in a foreign country and has
had time to form new friendships and connexions, he may
perhaps by degrees lose much of his interest in his home, but
the solitary traveller isolated like myself from all who care for
him, feels the ties of home more tightly drawn about his heart
as his absence is lengthened. Excuse, dear W^m, this jumble
(remember I am in the land of ollas and dine on them daily).
I have written on scarcely knowing what I have said, and believe me,

Ever yours most affect^y.

G. Dennis

Remember me to Johnson. I thought much of him and of our
trip to Hampton when I was the other day contemplating the
Raffaels of the Escorial.

William, who was his closest friend at home, obviously knew the young lady whom George had wooed and lost.

So George had seen Toledo (where the heat had upset him and caused him a few days of unpleasant indisposition) and had stayed in Tudela, but had not had time to satisfy his desire to visit Segovia. His conclusion, as he told his parents before leaving Tudela, was that:

> there are so many discomforts in this land, that to escape them I shall rejoice to pass the frontier — though I am by no means tired of Spain — nevertheless this northern part is not a second Andalucia. Castile is without exception the most dreary country I ever was in. Aragon and Navarre are more tolerable and the Basque provinces are green, fertile and picturesque; but Andalucia is so infinitely superior in interest every [   ] that I cannot feel so charmed with this visit to Spain as with my former. But it is well to see both sides of the shield — and after all there is even in this part of Spain far more originality of character than in France — more to interest also in every way — I wish my father could see the gallery at Madrid — it contains some of the finest pictures in the world.

And so George reached home once again about the end of August, a few days late for the office. No letters of his from the year 1841 seem to have survived, but in that year he published a series of twelve anonymous articles on The Cid in the *Penny Magazine* of the Society for the Diffusion of Useful Knowledge, and in these articles he refers to his recent visits to Burgos and to the Royal Armoury at Madrid. The *Penny Magazine* was published by Charles Knight & Co. of Ludgate Street, and four years later, in 1845, the same firm published an enlarged version in book form entitled '*The Cid: a Short Chronicle, Founded on the Early Poetry of Spain.* By George Dennis'. It is a little book of 220 pages, and it is the first time that the author's name appears in print in Britain. He was then thirty-one, and devoting his whole time, energy and thoughts to ancient Etruria. But as yet, during his Spanish voyages and studies, Dennis was not an archaeologist; he was interested in everything he saw around him; he was a sightseer with an acute power of description as well as a remarkable gift for portraying with the pencil the scenes he saw on his foreign excursions. His object in writing his little book on the Cid was, as he tells us, 'not only to present to the British public a sketch of the life of the Cid, the great hero of Spain, but to make them further acquainted with the early poetry of that country'.

Rodrigo Diaz de Bivar, known as the Cid, was born at Burgos in 1025 and died in 1099. Since the suppression in 1835 of the monastic orders in Spain, as Dennis recounts, the convent of San Pedro de Cardena near Burgos, where the Cid and his wife now lie buried, had been uninhabited, 'save by a man who keeps it in order, and who, happily for the visitor, is deeply read in the Cid's history. It stands about six or seven miles to the east of Burgos'. 'The village of Bivar (from which the Cid took his name) lies about the same distance to the North. I did not visit it when recently at Burgos, but heard that some remains of the Cid's castle are still standing'. Thus Dennis wrote in 1841. After 1841 it seems that he did not return to the Iberian peninsula until his retirement. A new period in his life was about to open. He was twenty-seven and unmarried; he had enjoyed so far the most varied travels both in Britain and on the Continent, and had already reaped a certain literary success as a result of these travels. He was largely self-educated; he was well read in Latin literature, had studied Spanish thoroughly and had translated from that language. He was beginning to teach himself Italian, and soon he was to set out to explore ancient Etruria.

CHAPTER 3

ENTERING ETRURIA — 1842-1848

ALL HIS LIFE George Dennis was fortunate in the number and the quality of his friends and acquaintances. At Hackney he knew Arthur Ashpitel, the architect (1807-1869), who, after being crippled in an accident, left England for Rome in 1854. They were not intimate friends, but Dennis always had a high regard for Ashpitel. A closer companion was Edward William Cooke, who was born at Pentonville in 1811, the son of the engraver George Cooke. Cooke was in Tuscany in 1845, where he undoubtedly met Dennis as well as in London. He became an R.A. and an F.R.S. In later years he placed his Italian portfolio of drawings at Dennis's disposal. Thirdly, there was Frederick Catherwood, fifteen years George Dennis's senior, whom he met through Catherwood's uncle at the Excise Office. In 1832 Frederick Catherwood was in the Regency of Tunis making architectural drawings; his Tunisian notes and sketches were still unpublished when Dennis saw them in the 1840s.

But the man who was to be George's most constant travelling companion and artistic collaborator in the early 1840s was Samuel James Ainsley, the exact date of whose birth does not seem to have been recorded but appears to have been about 1810, if he held his first exhibition of paintings in the Royal Academy in 1836.

It must have been during 1841 that George made up his mind to begin exploring ancient Etruria, and with that object in mind he must have read intensively the histories of Livy and other Roman authors. He left home in April, 1842, having probably obtained a special leave of absence from the Excise Office. On the 17th he was in Lyons, while his parents had gone to stay at Brighton in order to give his father the benefit of the sea air. When his mother addressed a letter to him care of *Poste restante,* Genoa, on April 26th, she included the sound motherly advice: 'We all hope "la belle" has not stirred your heart; please not to look about for French beauties, even at *Arles*; we wish your heart to be reserved for some good English woman who will be worthy of your love — and especially please to avoid Catholic ladies.' His sisters all added their pieces to this letter, writing in very affectionate terms, but in such small and spidery hands across the top of their mother's writing as to render the whole letter now almost illegible; Mary, Caroletta, Elizabeth, Octavia and Anne all wished him well, and Anne added: 'Your little miniature is my greatest treasure and I would gladly give my services to Mrs Ibbs for a twelvemonth to possess such a remembrance of you.'

In May George was in Florence, and the family again wrote to him. His father admitted: 'We have many anxieties about you and intreat you not to expose yourself needlessly to danger by exposure to heat or rain or in slight boats on the sea. Above all take care of the miasma so prevalent on the shores of the Mediterranean or the neighbourhood of Rome.' Young John, who was now eighteen years of age and ought to have known better, made far too many spelling mistakes, but wrote to tell George that he was trying to do something about the camera lucida which George had left behind at home because it would not work properly. 'Your Doves are very well and have just brought forth two young ones which Mary has given me for taking care of them for her.' Anne wrote: 'Will you notice whether the shells are so beautiful on the shores of the Mediterranean as I have heard? You know my fancy for them and if when you are returning you have room for the *smallest* specimen of a nautilus, I should like it extremely.' She added that 'we have many kind enquiries about you and my dear little miniature must be weary of exhibition.' On May 28th his sister Maria wrote from Walthamstow:

> Your most interesting letters have been a real feast to me in my solitude, and I have devoured them again and again with a pleasure which I cannot express. I hope some record of your travels will appear in a more public as well as more lasting form. I am so glad you enjoy the scenery of Italy so much. It must indeed be most lovely and your descriptions of its beauties make me long more than ever to travel, but for a *residence* I am satisfied with the country which surrounds me here and which is the source of some of my purest enjoyments (though *you* no doubt despise my ignorance and want of taste). I am seldom happier than when rambling in the Forest with my darling children, especially at this season when there is so much to see and admire and most thankful am I that my lot is not cast in London.[1]

They were all terribly disappointed that George would miss Mary's wedding early in June, and they all repeated how devoted they were to him. Never before had he been away from home for so long.

It was probably on arrival in Rome that George joined company with the artist Samuel Ainsley. Together they were to explore Etruria, on which George had now set his heart.

When they set out on their first tour of Etruria together in 1842 Dennis was twenty-eight, while Ainsley was most probably in his early thirties. They made an admirably suitable pair for such excursions, for while Ainsley the artist of so many drawings and etchings could also write, Dennis the archaeologist and writer was also an accomplished artist; so that in all their work each complemented the other in happy harmony.

Their first tour took place in June and July 1842. All the details of their itineraries can be well studied from the catalogue of the 112 items of Ainsley's work which were bequeathed to the British Museum at his death in 1874. They spent the first month, from 7th June to 9th July, 1842, in the region of Tarquinia, where to-day the most important Etruscan museum outside Rome is to be seen; Ainsley drawing Etruscan tombs, ancient bridges, grottoes, views of the hilly countryside, scenes at Corneto and Toscanella; and Dennis minutely examining the Etruscan tombs and writing down his voluminous notes. From Toscanella they moved on to Bolsena; they were at Montefiascone from 13th to 16th July, and the following week, from 18th July to about the 23rd, they stayed at Orvieto. On the 25th they went to Bomarzo, that remote village which is still visited for its Orsini Park containing the famous grotesque statues which have even today not been fully explained, although they are known to have been carved in the sixteenth century. Ainsley drew a view of Bomarzo on July 25th, and here they ended their first tour, returning to Rome where their headquarters was the German Institute of Archaeology, which had been founded by the King of Prussia on 21st April 1829. Called at first the 'Instituto di Corrispondenza Archeologica', it published an important bulletin to which Dennis afterwards frequently contributed. Its two learned and enthusiastic secretaries, Doctors Emil Braun and Wilhelm Henzen, gave Dennis constant encouragement and support, which (as his obituary notice in the *Athenaeum* in 1898 was careful to emphasize) was more than he received from his own countrymen. Indeed he had to thank only Italian and German scholars for their help throughout these early explorations in Etruria. The English did not yet appreciate the Etruscan civilization as fully as did the continentals.

At the beginning of September 1842, George Dennis visited the lovely site of Horace's Sabine Farm. Nowadays it is a delightful day excursion to take the Sulmona train from Rome as far as the village station of Vicovaro, carrying a sandwich lunch and buying a half-litre of local wine and a kilo of grapes on arrival. The walk up the valley, between orchards of trees laden with ripe apples and pears, with rows of heavily fruited vines in between, and a rushing mountain stream on the right of the road in which we always paddle before our midday picnic, is one of the most charming outings imaginable. September is also the season when the chestnut woods are dropping their ripe fruit everywhere, while the ground under the trees and beneath the hedges is carpeted with hundreds of wild pink cyclamen. When George Dennis went there in 1842, the countryside must have been almost entirely deserted except for a few local *contadini*; and Horace's farm was subjected to none of the tourists who today come by car and leave small gratuities with the custodian appointed by the Italian Department for the Preservation of Historic Monuments.

The letter which Dennis wrote on September 4th was afterwards published in Milman's edition of the works of Horace. Addressing an unnamed correspondent, he writes:

> I write from Licenza, hard by the site of Horace's Sabine Farm, where I have spent the last week,
>
> 'Excepto quod non simul esses, caetera laetus.'
>
> I am lodged in the house of the present possessor of the said Farm, and from my window look out on the wooded crests of *amoenus Lucretilis,* on the *Ustica cubans,* and the *reducta vallis* at their feet. The spot is still, as in the poet's time, the abode of rural simplicity – a calm retreat from the heat, the dust, the noise of 'royal Rome'.

The name of his host was Giuseppe Onorati. During his stay there, Dennis saw several green snakes, and 'this morning' (September 4th) a black snake six or seven feet long slithered across his path.

He was convinced that the *Fons Bandusiae* was near the Farm. 'I have taken the trouble to trace every streamlet for several miles round to its source, and in one only can I perceive the requisite analogy; and that so perfectly answers to the description, that I have no hesitation in asserting that, if the *Fons Bandusiae* were in the neighbourhood of the Farm, the said spring is it.'

The editor, the Rev. Henry Hart Milman, disagreed with him on this point, and persisted in thinking that the Fons Bandusiae was near Venusia, or Venosa, in Apulia, where Horace was born. But of course it was Dennis who was right. Several times I have myself walked up from the Farm, through the orchards filled with peach and almond trees, along a narrow path lined with late summer flowers, past vines groaning with huge bunches of grapes, past an occasional almond or fig-tree, to reach at last that famous spring, and to drink copiously of its cold, sparkling water, to prepare myself for the long walk back to Vicovaro and the late evening train back to Rome. There can be no doubt that this enchanting spot was where Horace found his inspiration.[2]

A number of the engravings in Milman's Horace (which was not published until 1849) are from sketches made by George Dennis. They include places far away from the Sabine Farm: Aricia, Anxur (now Terracina), Formiae (now Mola di Gaeta), and Praeneste (now Palestrina).

But to return to his first Etruscan travels with Ainsley. Their second tour lasted from the end of October to November 18th, 1842, when no doubt the miserably wet weather which always sets in about that time of year sent them back to Rome. They concentrated on Lazio, that beautiful tract of hilly country to the north of Rome in the direction of Viterbo, Ainsley again doing twenty or more drawings and Dennis visiting the Etruscan tombs at Isola Farnese and the site of ancient Veii, Sutri (which has only in the 1950s been properly excavated and described by a scholar of the British School at Rome), Ronciglione on its steep hill, Castel d'Asso, which is near Viterbo but about as remote and eerie a spot as anyone could hope to find in Italy, Norchia and Bieda (Blera); and they made further visits to Bomarzo and Tarquinia. Now, at the end of their first year in Etruria, by Christmas, 1842, Dennis and Ainsley could claim to have a thorough acquaintance with those parts of Etruria between Rome, Viterbo and Orvieto. On returning to Rome for the worst part of the winter, George took lodgings at No. 130, Casa Tarpeia, on the Capitol, and here he was still living on January 7th, 1843, when he wrote a long letter to his father in London. There had been trouble at the office, and his father said he had been made 'really ill' over it. But the trouble concerned other employees, and not George directly. Mr Backhouse, an influential friend of Mr Dennis senior, was in Rome, and was at all times exceedingly kind to George.[3]

> I went with him a day or two since to the Gregorian, or Etruscan Museum, and he writes me word that he derived such advantage from my company on that occasion, that he proposed yesterday to Lord Lifford that I should be his cicerone also, and was about to bring L. Liff. up to the Capitol to introduce me to him, when his Lordship remembered he had a special engagement. I have now no time, unfortunately, to see anything of Rome. I seem not to have half seen it yet. I leave for England in a day or two as soon as I can get my passport and everything ready for departure. You may expect me in less than three weeks from this date.

George had been planning a tour of Greece, but had had to cancel it. He had been absent from London for nine months, and there was naturally some danger that he might lose his post at the Excise Office. He knew he was returning to 'the same pittance I have received for 14 years', but it was his only source of income and he could not ignore it; at the same time he feared his father would not wish to recommend him for promotion, which might look too much like favouritism.

So George arrived home by the end of January, Ainsley having come back earlier. But they were out in Italy again by the beginning of the following April, 1843, when their third tour started at the famous Etruscan site of Cerveteri, between Rome and Civitavecchia. Between April 11th and July 13th, they worked hard, Ainsley making the most delightful drawings and an occasional water-colour, while Dennis explored the Etruscan tombs and made the most industriously detailed notes about them. They went to

Bracciano, Nepi, Falleri, Civita Castellana and Todi, before arriving
about the end of the first week in May at Perugia. Here they met
Giovanni Battista Vermiglioli, the grand old man of Perugian history and letters.[4]   From Perugia they went to the important
Etruscan city of Volterra where they made many sketches. Ainsley drew the island of Elba from Populonia on May 27th. They
were at the ancient site of Vetulonia on the first day of June.
Sovana was another important site where they spent several days,
and then they travelled to Chiusi and Cortona. Finally, they made
their way up to Florence, stopping at Arezzo and visiting the
Etruscan remains of Fiesole, where the tour ended on July 13th.
By October of this same year, 1843, Ainsley had published in the
Gentleman's Magazine an article on 'Tombs at Savana in Tuscany'.
This he wrote from Portland Place, Lower Clapton, his London
home.   It is likely that he and Dennis had both arrived back in
London about August.

Although the three tours of Dennis and Ainsley ended in July,
1843, they were both in Etruria regularly between then and 1847,
though not, it seems, together. Dennis begins his book with the
words 'This work is the fruit of several tours made in Etruria between the years 1842 and 1847'; and he refers to Ainsley as 'my
erstwhile travelling companion'. Ainsley, on the other hand, was in
Viterbo in November, 1846, when he drew and signed there part of
an Etruscan pediment. He also drew sketches of more than one
tomb at Cerveteri which had been discovered only as late as 1845
and even 1850. There is an album of forty-five pencil sketches by
him bearing various dates from 1842 to 1857. His visits to Italy
must have been almost annual events, even after the publication of
Dennis's great book.   Ainsley held a second exhibition of his
paintings at the Royal Academy in 1844 and died thirty years later,
in 1874. He and George Dennis did not quarrel after 1843, but it
was presumably felt that their collaboration in Etruria had achieved
all that it had set out to achieve, and Ainsley probably had other
commitments and interests, while George continued to dedicate his
whole energy and intellect to the minute study of ancient Etruria.

Ainsley in his article described Sovana as the greatest variety of
sculptured tombs he had seen anywhere. 'Views of them will
appear', he wrote, 'in a work I am about to publish'; but nothing
seems to have come of such a work. However, all his drawings and
water-colours of Etruscan sites are now in the Department of Prints
and Drawings at the British Museum.

Dennis and Ainsley had now completed three tours covering all
the major sites of Central and Southern Etruria. They had come at
a time when the Italians themselves had just made some of the most
exciting of all Etruscan discoveries. In 1840, for instance, one of
the finest known Etruscan tombs was found at Ponte San Giovanni,

near Perugia, which is now the railway junction for Todi and Umbertide. It is the Ipogeo dei Volumni, probably dating from about 150 B.C. Then in November 1842 an engineer had discovered an ancient city at Magliano in the Tuscan Maremma. George Dennis, when he was in Florence in 1844, visited the site and decided that it was most likely to have been the original Vetulonia. As for the most important Etruscan city of all, Corneto-Tarquinia, it was sporadically excavated in the 1820s and 1830s. There is the well-known story of the warrior stretched on a bier found in a tomb on the necropolis of Tarquinia in 1823: when fresh air was let in he crumbled away to nothing. The oldest tomb of all on the site of Cerveteri, the Regulini-Galassi Tomb, was discovered intact in 1836.

When George returned to London in the summer of 1843, he approached John Murray, the publisher in Albemarle Street, with a view to arranging publication, and Murray evidently agreed at once, so that George was able to spend all of the following autumn writing the first volume. On 29th January 1844 he wrote from Ash Grove the first of his many letters to Murray which have survived:

Dear Sir,

Being about to depart for Italy in a few days, I return you the accompanying plates, with many thanks for the loan.

I would have sent you the portion of my work which is written out, but I have determined to take it with me to verify its correctness. Very soon after my return I hope to bring out this half of the work, which treats of the southern division of Etruria, following it up more leisurely by the northern part, which together, I flatter myself, will form a complete guide to the extant antiquities of that land.

I think the following would be a more appropriate title than that I showed you on our last interview:

'The Cities and Cemeteries of Etruria'

Believe me, Dear Sir,

Yours respectfully,

Geo. Dennis

So the title of the great work was decided upon in January, 1844. George left London once more on February 3rd, and in crossing France he found the whole countryside under snow as far as Lyons, and travelling conditions far from comfortable. By February 10th he was still only at Marseilles, where together with three other Englishmen he took a berth in a French man-of-war to sail to Leghorn. On arrival in Rome he found a long letter from his parents, in which his mother repeated how happy she would be if only she could help him to find the right girl to marry.

On 28th March, 1844, in Rome, George wrote his first communi-

cation in the form of a long letter to the German Institute of Archaeology. This was immediately printed, and occupies three pages of
small type. The letter is addressed to Dr Emil Braun, and, curiously
and erroneously, Dennis is described as an architect. He writes:
'Having recently visited the Etruscan necropolis of Sovana, which
my friend Mr Ainsley discovered last May, and finding that no-one
else has made further researches in the meantime, I am induced
to offer some observations which refer to the latest report made
by my friend'. This letter and the article by Ainsley in the
Gentleman's Magazine of October, 1843, give a complete account
of Sovana. Then in the Bulletin of the Institute for 1844, we read
that at the meeting on 22nd March the members heard how Mr
Dennis, 'returning from one of his scientific voyages through at
least thirty cities of ancient Etruria, reported on a most important
discovery in November 1842 in the Tuscan Maremma between
Magliano and Orbetello'.

By May of the same year, 1844, he was back in London, for on
the 23rd of that month he wrote from Ash Grove to Dr Henzen in
Rome, apologising for not having sent a number of Latin inscriptions which had come from Africa. 'Next week,' he said, 'I expect
to see Ainsley at my house, with my friend [i.e. Frederick Cather-
wood].' This was the English architect whose uncle, as we have
seen, worked in the Excise Office in London.[5] By the following
April 11th, 1845, the Institute in Rome had received these Latin
inscriptions which Catherwood had copied in the interior of the Regency of Tunis, and Dr Henzen was able to communicate them to
the members. Dennis afterwards mentioned them in his book on
Etruria.[6] He and Catherwood were close friends until the latter's
untimely death by drowning in 1854.

In 1845 Dennis (now aged thirty-one) published his first important article in a British journal on his Etruscan expeditions. It is
seventeen pages in length, entitled 'On an Etruscan city, recently
discovered, and probably the Vetulonia of antiquity'. It appeared
in the periodical *Classical Museum*. The city was of exceptional
importance, near the sea, but it had only been unearthed just over
two years when Dennis wrote about it, and little was known of its
true history. In his letter to Dr Henzen of July 16th, 1845, he
complained that the article had for a time been lost, but had later
turned up and had just been printed. He also said that no diplomas
had arrived, although they had apparently been sent from Rome.
He said too that business was keeping him in England while his
friend Ainsley was about to go to Rome. But he did not explain
what this business was: presumably the Excise Office.

It seems that Dennis's conjectures about the exact site of
Vetulonia were wrong, for from 1880 onwards the researches of
Isidoro Falchi on Poggio Colonna, to the right of the River Bruna

between Giuncarico and Grosseto, officially established the true site of Vetulonia; and Dennis had thought it to be somewhat further to the North.

In his letter of November 25th, 1845, he sent to Dr Henzen some more inscriptions from Tunisia. Having spent the whole of 1845 at home, George felt it necessary to go back to Italy for a lengthy stay during 1846. Accordingly on February 1st, 1846, he wrote from Ash Grove to Murray:

My dear Sir,

Being obliged suddenly to go to the South of Europe, I have determined to take up my quarters for the winter at Rome, taking my MS. with me to correct on the spot, and have the benefit of the society of the Archaeologists whence I hope to profit much in the way of accuracy. You have a sufficient number of my sketches to be progressing — ere those are finished I doubt not to be able to transmit to you the rest. Many I think might be done in outline alone — without any attempt at the picturesque, such as mouldings etc. — which will be necessary to the full comprehension of the work. Those with the inscriptions I think I can do myself on the copper when I return — I have a number of little maps also, of cities — which must be done on wood. Accuracy there is the sole requisite. The map of the country is progressing nicely. Mr. Walker has nearly completed it in outline, and a few weeks only will be sufficient to add the names of places etc. I have a copy of it with me, which I shall revise. Perhaps you will be good enough to put my Father in communication with the artists who have my sketches in hand — He understands what I want and mean. Address to me as usual and he will open the note; I expect to return in the spring with the MS. ready for the printer — for I shall give my undivided attention to it.

Believe me, My dear Sir,
Yours very truly,
Geo. Dennis.

But he must have known that he would not be ready to return in the spring! By February 11th, 1846, he had once more reached Marseilles, and was anxious to be in Rome as quickly as possible in order to find cheap lodgings before the Carnival began. On the way he spent a day in Genoa, and from Leghorn paid a quick visit to Pisa, arriving in Rome by the 20th. In Rome, among other English acquaintances, he met Edward Cooke and his sister. 'He is far from well,' George told his father in a letter, '—the air of Rome does not seem to agree with him, and he talks of soon leaving for the coast — but he has made some beautiful paintings in oil, on the spot, and sketches innumerable'. Ainsley was there, as kind and amiable as ever.

George stayed first at an inn where he had to pay three times as much as usual, on account of the huge numbers of visitors who had already swarmed into Rome for the Carnival. He asked his father to find out what would be the expense of sending a portmanteau of books and clothes to Rome. 'Ainsley tells me the charge is enormous, yet when I received the alabasters I was surprised at the moderate charge. If it be moderate, it would be better to send than for me to purchase clothes etc. here which I shall otherwise be obliged to do. I shall want my frock-coat, 6 shirts, stockings both fine and grey for walking, pockethandkerchiefs and collars. Of trowsers I have abundance. Boots I must have, 2 or 3 light pair, and a stout pair newly soled. Of books I shall want particularly Muller's *Etruskar*, Smith's Dictionary of Antiquities, 4 thin vol[s] of Pompeii, in the Ent[s]. Knowl. series, 3, 4, and 5 vol[s] of Livy, Suetonius, Silius Italicus, Plinii Epistolae in 1 vol., a Greek grammar, John's school one w[d] do best — a little book, sewn, of Latin abbreviations. I do not know in what part of the book-case it is. If I go to Sicily I sh[d] like Brydone[7] — it is a pamphlet — and a little work in Italian, bound, *Viaggio in Sicilia*, among the books I put on one side — and if there be room I should like Niebuhr 3 vols [and] Hobbes' Thucydides. I think my portmanteau will be too large — perhaps it would be well to buy a smaller, which may be done for 25/- or 30/- or to exchange this — taking off the brass-plate with my name.'

Then at some length George explained to his father his desire to visit Naples and Sicily. His friend Edward Cooke, who found the air of Rome quite unsuitable, intended to leave for the South, and George thought it would be an excellent idea for him to accompany Cooke, especially as he wanted to see Paestum, whose walls and tombs should throw more light on his subject. He felt that a tour of Sicily could be accomplished in six weeks, but he emphasised that he would not dream of going if his father had any objection, or if it would prove too expensive. Indefatigable as ever, he wanted to compare Greek monuments with Roman and Etruscan; but he had another motive too: 'I might add notices of that Island to the selected portions of my second work on Spain, which is completed but not sufficiently extended, and so form an attractive couple of volumes.' (Had George then written a book on Spain which was never published?) He felt sure that such a tour of Sicily would not interfere with the work on Etruria, because Murray had assured him that this could not in any case be published before Christmas, 1846. 'I should have the advantage of Cooke's society, which is very desirable, as he is a most interesting man, ever cheerful, ever pleased, yet with excellent taste and discriminating powers, stored with information, and full of enthusiasm — and I flatter myself that I might also be of service to him from my experience in travel and knowledge of the language.' There was an ulterior motive as well: 'When I have finished my work, if no permanent situation presents itself, I shall endeavour to travel with some nobleman or gentleman and Cooke, from his connection with the Barings etc. might be of service to me. Such a tour would then be an additional recommendation.' But all depended on his father's permission, since George was still employed by the miserable Excise Office.

In Rome he next took a room on the banks of the Tiber, 'commanding the finest possible view of the Castle of St Angelo and St Peter's, with the Monte Mario in front and the Pincian on my right. Here I pay only ½ what I have been paying at the hotel — and am living — bed and board alone considered — at the rate of about £45 per ann. After the Holy Week I shall be able to live even at a cheaper rate — for lodgings are everywhere double their usual price.'

For the time being he stayed in Rome, making occasional trips with Cooke into the Campagna. He reckoned that three or four months more of hard, dedicated work would see his book on Etruria to its conclusion. Cooke and Ainsley were very good friends, but in his letter home of March 12th, 1846, George (now nearly thirty-two) let slip a sentiment which showed that he desperately missed a female companion: 'Beg John to congratulate "the dear bewitcher" for me on his marriage. James too I see is married — Will my turn ever come?' He had to be patient still. An occasional joke is met with in his letters: 'My love to Aunt Dennis also — and do not tell her, what I have before remarked but never expressed — that she is remarkably like his Holiness Greg^y. XVI.'

In a day or two he was intending to move back to his old quarters on the Tarpeian Rock, there to remain as long as he stayed in Rome, and to devote his time wholly to his work. When this was published, he told his father, he thought there ought to be a full-time occupation for him in Rome:

> There is room for a professional antiquary, who may accompany English parties about the city to point out its antiquities not in the superficial, blundering way of an ordinary cicerone, but to satisfy those who wish to be more fully informed than the common herd of travellers, and to obtain that acquaintance with the objects in question which they would seek in vain from the Guide Books. Of course some study would be requisite to fit me for this but at the Institute I have all the materials at hand. It is deemed a very gentlemanly occupation here. Nibby, who has written much on the antiquities of Rome and its neighbourhood, used, when alive, to do much in this way. There is now no Englishman in this line, tho' a Swiss and an Italian I believe are in the field. When you consider the crowds of English nobility and gentry who flock

to Rome every winter, and who scarcely know how to get
rid of their money fast enough, and who whether they care
for antiquities or not, care for fashion, and will have anything
which may be in fashion — you may imagine that if a man
could get his name up as an antiquarian-guide, he would be
pretty sure of a good recompense. However, it is a thing I do
not wish to be talked about; I do not wish it said that I am
going to do so and so — because it is impossible to foresee
what may come to pass to prevent such a step; I merely mention it to show you that I am fully alive to the necessity of
looking about for some new course of life, and I shall be
willing and happy to avail myself of any means of rendering
myself independent, that I may be able to embrace. A man
who takes up his residence in Rome, i.e. for the winter and
spring, may find other means of making money — the most
simple would be to take a house and let it out in separate
stories. The sums paid by the English for apartments at this
season are enormous. Then the superintendence of excavations offers another field for exertion — but these are mere
hints of what *might* be done. My course however at present
is clear enough — I must fulfil my engagement with Murray
ere I enter on any other. That I hope may be the means of
introducing me to something else.

He moved back to his old rooms on the Tarpeian Rock. The
view was not so pleasant, but there was an orange-tree laden with
fruit just outside his window, and, although it was only March, the
air was mild and the sun was delightful. He wished that his dear
parents would decide to spend a winter in Rome; they were both
delicate, and it would do them so much good. As it was, they
seemed to go no further than Brighton.

In his next letter home, of March 23rd, 1846, he expressed
some opinions which to us today may well seem intolerably narrow-
minded:

You quite mistake if you think I am in danger of acquiring
'tastes for everything foreign' — I never was less in love with
foreigners — or more desirous to be at home than now. Take
from Italy its climate, scenery, arts and antiquities, and it has no
charms for me — as to the natives I know and see and care less
about them than ever. I have not one Italian acquaintance —
save among antiquaries. I am glad I have not, like Ainsley, a
passion for music. That would lead me into society and into
expences I could not afford. As it is I have nothing to draw me
from my studies. I rise at dawn of day — and the first object my
eyes rest on, while yet in bed, is the grey crest of the glorious
Alban Mount, towering above the mingled ruins and foliage on
the Palatine Hill opposite. I then sit at the open window, not

exactly enjoying the scene, for I am otherwise engaged, but
with it at my elbow — till 8 when I breakfast — then to work
till the middle of the day, when if Tooke[8] calls for me I
accompany him to some or other of the lions, and after dinner
return to work till I am taken captive by Morpheus. Or if
neither he nor any other friend calls, I step out to dine at 2
and return for the rest of the day. So that I am happy as it is
possible for an exile, a bachelor, a light-pursed and heavy-
worked man to be. I have not yet learned the *dolce far
niente*. My only female acquaintances are Miss Cooke and
Miss Heath, and I shall lose both in a few days.

Poor George! Ainsley was ill and could not go to Naples and
Paestum, so George remained in Rome too. The Cookes left, and
soon there was scarcely anyone English whom he knew. By May
the sedentary life he had been leading for the past two months
had brought on inflammation of the kidneys; when at last he went
to a doctor he was told he had gout: and he was only thirty-one!
So he decided to leave Rome and go on an expedition into the
country, combining work with physical exercise. The weather was
not yet hot enough to forbid walking in the sun. He told his
mother in May:

It is the most delightful season of the year for Italy — the sky
gloriously bright — heat equal to that of our hottest summer
days, yet (to me) very genial, and endurable at all hours — the
vegetation brilliant and fresh, and flowers in profusion. It is
our June in fact, roses in abundance, peas and strawberries almost going out (figs threatening soon to come in), haymaking
in the Campagna. Musquitos too hardly yet in, so that you
may still leave your window open at night with impunity, but
fleas — they are never out all the year round — their courage is
never cooled, their ardour never damped. I have learned however almost to disregard them — always out of their reach at
night, and not much exposing myself to attack by day. If I
indulge them at all it is with pasture between the shin and the
ankle. North or South of that is forbidden ground.

He continually asked after the family. Elizabeth had several
children by now, and Mary was having a difficult confinement.
How is John? What is he doing? He ought to be rubbing up
his Latin as well as German. Tell him if he lets what he
knows slip thro' his fingers, he will surely have cause to regret
it. I sadly regret having neglected the classics on leaving school.
Latin I have now more than recovered, but in Greek I feel my
deficiencies greatly, and can do that only with difficulty which
I might have accomplished with ease, but for my neglect.
However with the daily practice I now have I hope soon to
make more way. Half an hour's reading a day would serve for

him to keep alive what he knows and to add to it. . . Of books
I have almost everything I want in the Library of the Institute
and can get access to anything else in the Vatican and other
public Libraries — so that I find there will not be the necessity
I imagined to forward my books — and as to clothes I may
manage to get on pretty well to the end of the year with the
purchase of a few shirts, which will cost me far less than the
freight etc. of the package. . . I brought only 8 shirts with me,
and only 4 of them good — so that I cannot make this slender
stock answer till my return. I am as badly off for socks — and
everything of this description is very dear at Rome — as it all
comes from abroad. Silk handkerchiefs, too, which should be
cheap enough, seeing that Italy is the land of mulberries — are
extremely dear. It is an article of the highest luxury a silk
fazzolletto [sic] — I have seen many a marquiss or Count in the
Pope's Guard of nobles, which only musters on high state
occasions, pull out of the pocket of his splendid uniform-coat
a dirty cotton wiper which a servant would be ashamed to use
in England.

Dr Henzen and Dr Braun of the German Institute were exceptio-
nally kind to Dennis; not only did they allow him full use of their
library and make him a member of the Institute, but in June, when
he set out for Florence, Dr Henzen gave him a letter of introduction
to Professor Migliarini which is still preserved in the Museo Archeologico of that city, although slightly damaged by the floods of
November, 1966. Arcangelo Michele Migliarini, born in Rome on
Christmas Day, 1779, and therefore sixty-six when Dennis was
introduced to him (the same age as George's father), had settled
in Florence in 1820, and was Professor of Archaeology and Director
of Antiquities for Tuscany.[9]

One of George's main reasons for going to Florence was that he
had some shares to dispose of; but he also studied many books not
available in Rome, and he walked for many miles through the countryside of Etruria, revisiting old sites, even though 1846 had one of
the hottest summers for many years and to go anywhere on foot
after the beginning of June must have been exceedingly trying.
Yet on one of those days he walked twenty-seven miles with a
heavy knapsack on his back. The Arno was already reduced to a
mere trickle. He arrived in Florence only to find that his shares
were not negotiable there, and he was desperately low in funds.
He then went to Leghorn, from where he wrote to his father on
July 5th, telling him that by far the biggest expense in travelling
was that of passports; for there were constant fees and taxes to be
paid whenever anyone moved from one city to the next. Much of
this letter is taken up with a lengthy account of a German gentleman at the Institute in Rome who was starting up a profitable

business in bronzes made by electrotype, and had the idea of spreading his business from Rome to England. George began to think that this might be a very lucrative opening for himself. First, however, the great book must be finished. 'You ask me what I have done towards finishing my work' he answered his father.

I have done by far the largest and most difficult portion — those cities most frequently mentioned in history — as well as Rome itself; and I have now only to write out the chapters on the cities of Tuscany, for which I have been getting materials at Florence — and to finish the Introduction, which is only in skeleton, but which is a very difficult part. I shall introduce into it however a great part of the article I wrote for the *Westminster*. This I cannot finish till all the rest is done, and then it will be comparatively easy. I have to wade thro' a great mass of matter at Rome, and to write sundry disquisitions for which I gather material as I go along and also to verify my authorities — this last I shall do as it goes thro' the press, but I wish to have the whole written out before any is printed, as I shall therefore save expence in the correction of the press, which Murray says is of great importance.

He was quite sure the book would sell well at Rome and in Germany; and he had met four or five dons from Cambridge who had showed much interest in the subject. 'But it is impossible to make it a work of great fireside interest in England', he admitted. Murray had already advertised the forthcoming work as the result of two tours through Etruria: George now asked his father to ask Murray to change 'two' to 'several' in future. He enquired after all the family and his friends, especially William Ord, who was now married: George's mother wrote to tell him that William had recently been presented with a daughter.

On returning to Rome, he wrote to John Murray on August 6th, telling him that although the temperature was about 100° he was working very hard:

I am anxious to have the book out as soon as possible on sundry accounts, one of which is that Mrs Gray has brought forth, I hear, a fourth edition, and I would fain put a full stop to her erroneous progeny. . .

If Professor Milman made use of those notes I sent you about Horace's farm, I should like to see a proof before publication, for I wrote as a superficial describer, not as an antiquary; besides I think I am out in my botany.

He was still at Rome on October 6th, when he told Murray in another letter that he had delayed writing for some time in expectation of receiving a proof of the Horatian epistle, 'but as it has not yet arrived I conclude it was not possible to send it. . .'

So the year 1846 came to an end: the year in which George

Dennis had probably worked harder than in any other of his
thirty-two years, despite one of the hottest summers in recent
Italian history and the ever-gnawing embarrassment of a very nearly
empty purse. Towards Christmas he came home.

Another young English traveller, named Edward Falkener, who
was almost exactly the same age as George, writing home to his
father in London from Naples on 20th December 1846, said:

> I expect a Mr Dennis will call on you. His father holds a
> situation in the Excise Office. Mr Dennis Junr has been at
> Rome for some time writing a work on Etruria. It is now com-
> pleted, and (he) is about to return to England to have it print-
> ed. He is a talented man, very quiet, and gentlemanly, and
> therefore I should be glad if you would shew him any atten-
> tions in your power — you can shew him my sketches, draw-
> ings, and memoranda, but do not allow him to copy any of
> the inscriptions.

The meeting between Dennis and Falkener in 1846 was the beginning of a friendship which was to last throughout their lives.
Falkener had already made drawings in Pamphylia,[10] and later,
from 1851 to 1853, he was to edit *The Museum of Classical
Antiquities.*

George was at home in London during the spring of 1847, but
was busy sending reports for publication to the German Institute
in Rome.

It is not possible to reconstruct very clearly his movements
during this year of 1847, since no letters have survived except one
to John Murray written from Ash Grove on April 15th. Later in
the year, however, he paid his first visit to Sicily, having been denied
the chance the year before; and it seems clear that he had already
persuaded Murray that a handbook for that island was badly needed
by the English-reading public, since Sicily was most imperfectly
known.   So far from having exhausted himself on the terrific
labour of the book on Etruria which he had just finished, he proposed to start work at once on the Sicilian guide-book.   This guide-
book did not in fact see the light of day until many years later, in
1864, but the slow unfolding of its history is worth studying in
some detail, and will be recounted in its due place.

Meanwhile various reports of his were published during this year
in the Bulletin of the German Institute in Rome. At the meeting
of 15th January 1847 he described how he had come across the
site of an ancient city near Ponte Felice, and at the meeting of 12th
March he published an account of an ornamental bas-relief which
must have been used to decorate the columns of an ancient portico
or to close up the spaces of some window.

In the March Bulletin he wrote twelve pages on his travels in
Etruria, concentrating on Santa Marinella and Cerveteri. In May

1847 was printed the result of the meeting of January 8th of the
same year, at which he reported on the site of Graviscae; and after
Vetulonia he described how he had visited the site between Civita
Vecchia and Santa Marinella, called Puntone del Castrato, where
in 1840 the Duchess of Sermoneta had carried out extensive excavations. These transactions of the Institute do not indicate that
Dennis was present in Rome in 1847; instead, he must have com-
municated them by post and his papers and reports must have been
read for him, some of them being translated into Italian for publication.

And so we come to the year in which George Dennis's vast work
on Etruria was at last published — 1848. He had up to now been an
indefatigable traveller in Europe. His great achievement of 1848 was
destined only to lead him straight into a series of new adventures
and much longer journeys, and, in every sense, into a New World.

During the late summer of 1848, John Murray had written to
ask Dennis if he would contribute an article on pottery to Mr
Marryat's book.[11]   George's reply, dated September 22nd, ran as
follows:

> My conditions are simply that the authorship should be
> acknowledged, and that I should be remunerated for my
> labour. It would give me great pleasure to write you an article
> unconditionally, as I did for the Horace, and as I have done
> for certain periodicals, but 'tempora mutantur'. I have had
> more of Fortune's frowns than smiles of late, and am obliged
> to turn my time to account; and were I to send such an article
> to the Westminster Review or some similar publication, I
> should certainly be remunerated. If you wish, I could write it
> at once instead of proceeding with 'Sicily'.

By December 21st however he had made up his mind to reject
the invitation to write the article, because his future had now been
decided. Three days earlier he had sent a copy of his first book,
Summer in Andalucia, to John Murray suggesting that it might be
suitable for abridging and reprinting in a new edition.

But there was to be no more writing for George Dennis in London for the time being. He had had to find a new job. He had been
interviewed by the Colonial Office, his appointment at the Excise
Office having come to a not very glorious end. He had been offered
a position as private secretary to a Colonial Governor in a remote
corner of the world, and he was due to sail from England on
January 17th, 1849.

CHAPTER 4

'THE CITIES AND CEMETERIES OF ETRURIA'

THE GREAT BOOK was published by John Murray in two volumes, at a price of two guineas, towards the end of 1848. The British Museum's copyright copy was received on 18th January 1849. A modern Etruscan scholar writes:

> It was George Dennis, a British consul in Italy, who wrote the most valuable of these accounts of journeys [off the beaten track] made through districts which were still half-wild. His book, *The Cities and Cemeteries of Etruria*, appeared in 1848 and went into several editions. This success was amply merited, for Dennis, a cultured amateur, contrived to write an account full of life and humour, and to unite the most minute and detailed observation with an amiable and lively style. Even now, there is no better introduction to the study of ancient Etruria than the reading of this little masterpiece; its charm and its value remain undimmed after a century.[1]

But it is scarcely a *little* masterpiece. The first edition has a total of 114 pages of preliminaries and 1,085 pages of text, almost every page heavily footnoted and dense with facts. Such a book might well have taken an average man a lifetime to write; but Dennis was only thirty-four when it appeared, having previously written one other long book, one short book, and several articles besides, and having taken up his Etruscan studies only six or seven years before. It was a prodigious and monumental achievement.

Before Dennis, Etruscan studies were practically unknown to the English reading public except for the works of one woman, Mrs Hamilton Gray (Elizabeth Caroline Gray). This lady published a book of 500 pages in 1840 entitled *Tours to the Sepulchres of Etruria in 1839*, and a second edition came out in 1841. The book was well-known to Dennis, who refers to it several times, not always in an entirely complimentary way. He knew that Mrs Gray had not even visited all the sites she describes. Her book was not received very favourably. An anonymous writer in the *Edinburgh Review* wrote in 1849:[2]

> Mrs Hamilton Gray, whose lively and amusing work on the sepulchres of Etruria had the merit of first attracting the attention of the English public to the subject, had the misfortune on beginning her Etruscan studies to fall into the hands of Italian *letterati* of the ultra-national school: and she appears to have imbibed their prejudices so deeply as to have been

unable subsequently to extricate herself from their dominion, or listen to the dictates of more sober and impartial criticism. These defects have rendered her work of comparatively little value to the scholar; and we certainly cannot congratulate the traveller who should put himself under its guidance.

George Dennis was not quite so scathing, but declared that his intention was to fill in the gaps and add more details to Mrs Gray's account. She herself was not deterred by criticism, for she went on to write and publish a *History of Etruria* in three parts, which came out in 1843, 1844 and 1868.

The *Edinburgh Review* began its long article by praising Dennis's 'long-promised work', which shows that the public must have known, through Murray's notices, for some time that it was in preparation. The reviewer declared that Dennis's scholarship was 'at once accurate and extensive', and was 'enlightened by a sound and rational spirit of criticism; and the natural enthusiasm with which he regards the subject of his long-continued researches is rarely permitted to mislead the calmness of his judgment'. He goes on:

It is not the least pleasing feature of Mr Dennis's very pleasing book, that it bears throughout the impress of a kindly feeling towards the present occupants of the lands through which he has been wandering.[3]   Neither time nor labour have been spared in verifying his descriptions. We have rarely met with descriptions of Italian scenery, at once so striking and so characteristic, as those with which Mr Dennis has interspersed the drier details of antiquarian topography.

It is one of the circumstances which greatly enhance the value of such careful details and accurate descriptions as those of Mr Dennis, that much of what he has here recorded may no longer be found when some future antiquary shall re-visit the locality.

The paintings in the tombs at Tarquinii, which have attracted more attention than any other Etruscan relics, are already familiar to many English readers, in the lively pages of Mrs Hamilton Gray. All therefore that can be said for Mr Dennis's descriptions of these objects is that they are more complete and accurate in their details.

The reviewer believed that Dennis might have taken more pains with the Etruscan language:

We cannot but take this opportunity of expressing our regret that in this, as in many other cases, Mr Dennis has not given the literal inscriptions which he had copied on the spot. These omissions will be keenly felt by the scholar; accurate transcripts of existing Etruscan inscriptions being at present one of the chief desiderata for the study of the language. It is true that he had already published them in the Bullettino dell' Instituto for 1847; but that work is accessible to comparatively few persons; and if he was afraid of 'heartily wearying the general reader' (see vol. ii, p.44) he might, at least, have given them a place in an appendix to the chapter.

In Dennis's defence one can but say that he *did* copy out and print quite a large number of inscriptions, as well as giving a long discourse on the Etruscan language in his introduction; moreover to have printed every inscription he found would have been to make a very long book much longer. Another factor is that he was not primarily a philologist but an archaeologist.

A careful reading of *The Cities and Cemeteries* in its first edition of 1848 tells us several useful details about Dennis's life which we have not hitherto been told. For example, he had been to Holland, for he says (vol. II, p.205n.) 'I have seen a similar urn in the museum of Leyden'. We do not know when, but it must have been before 1848, by which year (aged thirty-four) he had been in France, Spain, Portugal, Switzerland, Italy, Holland and probably parts of Germany too.

As for Italian acquaintances, we have already seen that Dennis met and talked with the aged Vermiglioli in Perugia. In Florence he met Cavaliere Francesco Inghirami (vol.II, p.133), who was born at Volterra in 1772 and died in Florence on 17th May 1846. Dennis reports that Inghirami had his own printing-press at Fiesole. His most important work was *Monumenti Etruschi*. Dennis describes him as 'the patriarch of Etruscan antiquities'; he must have been over seventy when Dennis met him, probably in 1844 or 1845. Dennis's own declared intention in writing the book at all is revealed in a letter which he wrote on November 6th, 1848, to a certain Rev. Philip Smith, who had lent him a copy of Steub's book:[4]

> As you have on a former occasion made enquiries about my work on Etruria allow me to mention that it is now finished, but will not be published till the commencement of the new season, at Christmas. It is of a very different character from Steub's work — propounds no new theories on the origin, language, or arts of the Etruscans, but gives a plain, unvarnished tale of extant local monuments. It has been written also in the hope of interesting that 'many-headed monster', on whom no German literatus condescends to waste his midnight oil, and therefore I trust it will meet with due indulgence from scholars, and be tried by the low standards it has assumed.

Dennis's style in *The Cities and Cemeteries* is frequently lyrical, not to say sentimental, especially when he is comparing an Italian scene to the countryside of his native land. At Nepi he tells the traveller that:

> it is one of the few portions of central Italy that will remind him, if an Englishman, of home. Those sweeps of bright green

sward — those stately wide-armed oaks scattered over it, singly, or in clumps — those cattle feeding in the shade — those neat hedge-rows, made up of maples, hawthorns and brambles, with fern below, and clematis, dog-roses, and honeysuckle above; they are the very brothers of those in Merry England. The whole forms a lively imitation of — what is most rare on the Continent — English park-scenery; and it requires no stretch of fancy to conceive himself journeying through Surrey or Devonshire.

Then again, the Ager Faliscus, that country between Mount Soracte and Monte Cimino, on the way to Viterbo, consists of plains covered with oaks and chestnuts — grand gnarled giants, who have lorded it here for centuries over the lowly hawthorn, nut, or fern — such sunny glades, carpeted with green sward! — such bright stretches of corn, waving away even under the trees! — such 'Quaint mazes in the wanton groves!' — and such delicious shady dells, and avenues, and knolls, where Nature, in her springtide-frolics, mocks Art or Titania, and girds every tree, every bush, with a fairy belt of crocuses, anemones, purple and white cistuses, delicate cyclamina, convolvuluses of different hues, and more varieties of laughing flowers than I would care to enumerate. A merrier greenwood you cannot see in all merry England. . .

Dennis is carried away on flights of poetic fancy, but he is down-to-earth and reasonable enough when describing the Etruscan tombs. He is always most impressed by the antiquity of things around him; and this sense of age reaches its climax at Cortona:

Traveller, thou art approaching Cortona! Dost thou reverence age — that fulness of years which, as Pliny says, 'in man is venerable, in cities sacred?' Here is that which demands thy reverence. Here is that, which when the Druidical marvels of thine own land were newly raised, was of hoary antiquity — that, compared to which Rome is but of yesterday — to which most other cities of ancient renown are fresh and green. Thou mayst have wandered far and wide through Italy — nothing hast thou seen more venerable than Cortona. Ere the days of Hector and Achilles, ere Troy itself arose — Cortona was.

It is worth noting that Dennis's book soon reached India, where in March, 1850, a long anonymous review-article praised it highly.[5]

Some thirty-five years after the book's first appearance, that urbane, fantastically energetic traveller and eminently readable writer Augustus Hare was able to declare that George Dennis was the one great exception in English travel books which do not tell us nearly enough about the more remote parts of Italy.

In studying this delightful work, [writes Hare], and even in the few extracts given in these volumes, the reader who knows

Rome will seem to feel again the fresh breeze from the Sabine and Alban hills sweeping over the Campagna, laden with a scent of sweet basil and thyme, and he will enjoy again in their remembrance that glow of enthusiasm which the real scenes brought into them. The great volumes of Dennis are too large to be companions on the excursions themselves, but in preparation for them will be pleasant fireside companions for Roman winter-evenings.[6]

'The great volumes of Dennis' certainly seems a more appropriate description than the 'little masterpiece' of Raymond Bloch's account.

How has *The Cities and Cemeteries of Etruria* survived the test of time? Here is what the greatest modern Etruscan scholar, Professor Massimo Pallottino, has said of it: 'As a work of reference on the topography, history and archaeology of the cities and sites of Etruria, G. Dennis' *Cities and Cemeteries of Etruria* (third edition, 1883) would be difficult to replace, for its descriptions, its erudition and its considerable literary merits.'[7]

Such a judgment is true enough. The work cannot be bettered, even now, for its unrivalled wealth of accurate detail. Perhaps only on the linguistic side, by not making a concerted effort to interpret the Etruscan language and hence to decipher the inscriptions, can Dennis be accused of failing to reach the goal which he had set himself as the first real interpreter of the Etruscan civilization to the English-speaking world. But the generations of Etruscan scholars who have followed him have never ceased to be baffled by the mysteries of that language, and they have made very little true progress in its decipherment in the past century. Dennis never tired of continuing and perfecting his descriptions of the Etruscan cities and tombs; as will become clear later in this book, he worked hard to improve his masterpiece through not less than thirty-five years after its first publication. The edition of 1878, published when the author was well over sixty years of age, was the climax of his wonderful achievement on the art and the life and the death of the Etruscan people.

CHAPTER 5

SOUTH AMERICA AND SICILY — 1849-1863

A FEW DAYS before leaving England, George Dennis wrote to the publisher Bentley:

> Ash Grove, Hackney.
> 12th January 1849.

Sir,

In reply to your letter of December 16th offering to resell to me the copyright of the 'Summer in Andalucia' for the sum of £25 I beg to inform you that I am now ready to repurchase it for that sum, and will call tomorrow (Saturday) morning to pay you, when I will thank you to leave with your clerk the original agreement between us, by which I transferred the copyright to you, and also a receipt for £25 — which should state that this sum is the repurchase-money of the said copyright.

I am, Sir,
Your obedient servant,
G. Dennis.

Richard Bentley Esq.

P.S. I thought I had already made over to you a regular assignment. If so, this should also be returned to me.[1]

The reason for this desire to obtain the copyright of the Spanish book back from Bentley was that the author hoped to persuade Murray to publish a second edition of it.

On January 17th, 1849, he entered the Colonial Service. He knew Southern Europe well, he knew Spanish, Italian and French; yet he was appointed Private Secretary to Sir Henry Barkly, the Governor of British Guiana; and so he set out for one of the remotest and most unhealthy spots in the British Empire, where his gifts and his knowledge would be of no advantage to himself or the community. When in February, 1864, back in London, he wrote the preface to his *Handbook for Travellers in Sicily,* he apologised for the delay in publication, which was due to 'avocations of a totally foreign character in one of the hottest and most insalubrious climates of the globe'. The miracle was that service in British Guiana did not rob him of the strength or the will to write or even to think of Sicily. Nor did it turn him sour.

The British had captured the three river colonies of Demerara, Essequibo and Berbice in 1796, temporarily losing them again to the Dutch, from whom they recaptured them in 1804. It was not

until July 21st 1831, that Berbice was added to Demerara and
Essequibo, and placed under British government to become the
colony of British Guiana. The name Demerara, however, continued
to be frequently used to designate the whole. Henry Barkly
arrived as Governor on February 13th, 1849, and stayed there until
May, 1853. George Dennis probably sailed on the same ship.[2]
Although a contemporary writer described Georgetown as 'the
prettiest town in the West Indies', it was in fact almost insufferably
hot, fever-ridden and humid to an uncomfortable degree, full of
flies and other insects, and, of course, completely devoid of culture
in the shape of books or libraries. George Dennis was of a tough
enough constitution, but he must have felt sadly removed from his
beloved Etruscan, Latin and Greek studies.

He nevertheless made the best of a bad lot, and in over fourteen
years of service in the colony he was at least able to pay several
return visits to Europe, not only home to England, but also to Italy
and especially to Sicily, which he visited in 1852 and in 1857.

After he had been about four months in the colony, he wrote to
John Murray:

Demerara,
19th June /49

My dear Sir,
    I find it impossible to spare time to complete the Handbook
of Sicily. I therefore return to you by this mail the MSS and
books you lent me, regretting much that I did not resign them
into your hands before I left England, but I expected to have
had abundance of leisure. My duties, however, official,
domestic, and social, consume the greater part of my time.
I do not send you what I have written of the Handbook as it is
but a fraction and is made up chiefly from the materials you
gave me. The abridgment of Andalucia gets on but slowly, but
I know you are in no hurry for it. We hear here little of the
literary world at home. Politics, sugar, rum and the weather
(not to mention scandal) are the staples of conversation.
Catherwood, who was a great acquisition here, has just left for
England, and there is not a man in the colony (barring the
Governor) who cares for literature, art, or antiquities. It is a
dreary residence for one who loveth the lands of old. My
Genius must have been irate when he cast my lot in the far
West. I hope he soon intends to transfer me to a fairer land
than this region of mud, molasses, and musquitoes. I envy
Layard returned to the East to bring Nineveh to light. If there
were a chance of such occupation for me, I would return
incontinently. I should like a copy of Layard's work — if you
will be kind enough to send one to my Father he will forward
it. If of the 1st Edition tanto meglio.

Should there chance to be a Review of Etruria in the Quart-
erly, perhaps you will send that also. If you or Mr Cooke can
spare time to drop me a line, I shall receive it with great
pleasure. Remember me to him. I see by the papers that Mr
Ford has lost his wife — how is he, and what about?[3]
I hope Mrs Murray and yourself are well.
　　　　　Believe me. . . .
　　　　　　　Geo. Dennis.

Already, then, after four months he was weary of British Guiana,
its terrible climate, its sad lack of intellectual company, and its
complete isolation from culture. Yet he was destined to stay there
for nearly fifteen years.

Standards of education were not high in British Guiana, and in
1850 a Board of Council of Education was appointed to work out
a better system. In June, 1851, George Dennis, aged thirty-seven,
was promoted to be Inspector of Schools for the colony: somewhat
surprising an appointment, we may suppose, for a man who had not
even a university degree, let alone a teacher's training. He must have
been held in high regard despite his lack of qualifications. To quote
a contemporary writer:[4]

The more effectually to carry out his duties, Mr Dennis visited
nearly all the great educational establishments in the United
Kingdom; and on his return to the colony, reported the result
of his labours, in a document remarkable for elaborate research
and sound reasoning, in which he recommended that the system
pursued by the British and Foreign School Society or that of
the Irish National Schools should be adopted in the colony.

Dennis presented his long and well-written report to the commis-
sioners appointed to enquire into the education system of British
Guiana, but they did not accept or carry out many of his proposals.
He nevertheless continued in the same work for the next ten years.
As he wrote in 1864, these duties in South America left him 'neither
time nor energy steadily to fulfil literary engagements', but in 1852
he visited Sicily and continued to make notes on its history and
antiquities. Again in 1856-57 he was on leave in Sicily, where he
made archaeological researches on behalf of the British Museum.

Sir Henry Barkly only remained as Governor of British Guiana
until May, 1853. The local Gazette wrote that he had 'administered
the colony with such tact, skill, courtesy, and firmness, that his
diplomatic ability was the subject of unreserved admiration'. The
new Governor, P.E. Wodehouse, arrived on March 23rd, 1854 and
remained until May 9th 1861. Dennis served in the colony for rather
more than the terms of office of both these governors.[5]

George was back in London at the end of 1851, living temporarily
at No. 9 Cornwall Crescent, Camden Road Villas. In 1849 his father
had reached the age of seventy, and it must have been about that

time that he moved with George's mother from the home at Ash
Grove, Hackney, where the family had lived for so long, to a new
house at Rose Hill, Dorking. But all too soon, on February 1st,
1851, George's mother died. Most of his sisters were now married,
and his brother John, who also married and had five children, lived
for many years at Hampstead, until he in his turn retired into the
country at Crowborough. While George was on leave in London in
1851, he resumed work on the handbook on Sicily, and asked
Murray to let him have fifty pounds for his expenses on it. He
wished to visit Sicily again before he was obliged to sail back to
Demerara; but Murray's terms were not sufficiently generous to
allow him to do this. At first he had thought of visiting the United
States, but this idea, too, came to nought because he could not
afford it. If he could not revisit Sicily, he felt he could still produce
a guide-book to the island which would be the best in existence, but
it would necessarily be shorter and less ambitious than if he were to
go there and make many more notes on the spot.

The fairly short tour of Sicily was made possible for him in the
spring of 1852, and he arrived back at Georgetown on May 12th,
as he wrote to Murray on May 25th:

Georgetown, Demerara,
May 25th, 1852.

My dear Sir,

I arrived here on the 12th after a favourable passage across
the Atlantic in the new steamer Parana. The yellow fever which
has been raging for some months past, has now somewhat
abated; its ravages have been chiefly among the shipping, yet
the town has suffered also, and there have been two victims
at Government House. One vessel which came in with a crew
of 15 men, has lost them all — another which had 24 sailed a
few days since with only one man of her original crew on
board, all the rest being either dead or in the hospital. We are
expecting much benefit from the heavy rains and a thunder-
storm with which we have been visited of late.

I can hardly set to work on Sicily in earnest, till I receive a
box of books, local guides, histories etc. which I picked up
there, and forwarded to Liverpool from the Mediterranean.
When they arrive I shall lose no time with the Handbook. I
have to thank you sincerely for your goodness in furnishing
me with Serradifalco and the other works I asked for, which
will prove of great assistance to me.[6]

I should like a copy of Etruria for the insertion of notes I
made in Italy, with a view to a 2nd edition, should that ever be
demanded. If you will be kind enough to send a copy to:

Andrew Johnson Esq., Shacklewell Green, Middlesex
who will take charge of it for me, I shall feel much obliged.

If you have a hot-house attached to your new residence, and would like some orchids or other tropical plants, it would give me great pleasure to send you some. I have many opportunities of collecting them in my excursions into the interior.

Believe me

My dear Sir,

Yours faithfully,

Geo. Dennis

This Andrew Johnson was probably the school-friend with whom George had visited Hampton Court many years ago, together with William Ord.

And on the following October 21st, 1852, he sent to Murray an abridged version of his first book, the *Summer in Andalucia*. Murray actually got as far as advertising in print the second edition of this book, but for some reason it was never published. Meanwhile he made slow progress on the Sicilian handbook, for the box of books had still not arrived, and George had had a brief attack of fever, which he managed to throw off quickly by taking double the normal quantity of quinine.

He confessed to Murray that he was desperately anxious to leave Georgetown:

I am glad to see that Mr Ford has some diplomatic appointment — the papers do not say what — under the present Ministry. Yet what can it be but Minister at Madrid? Should vacancies occur in his consular staff, I hope he will not forget me; and if you would remind him that there is such a person, who has long had the ambition of holding such a post in the Mediterranean, and especially in Spain, you would do me a very great favor. Such a post was promised to me again and again by Mr Backhouse, when Secretary under Lord Palmerston, but he died before I was considered old enough. At the mature age of 37, however, no such objection can be raised. The truth is I am anxious to leave this land, where everything, mind as well as body, rots at a fearful rate, and a few years' residence renders me utterly effete — in fact, it is a most unfortunate land for authorship, as the process of decomposition goes on much more naturally and rapidly than that of composition.

By the next mail I will send you a short preface to the 2nd edition of the 'Summer', and also a line or two to wind up the book, instead of the prosy dissertation on politics which formed the original ending. Being obliged to leave town in a hurry, I have not had time to enclose them with the MS.

I remain, My dear Sir,

Yours sincerely,

Geo. Dennis.

So George was spending every available moment of leisure thinking and writing about Sicily and Spain, although as things turned
out the Spanish efforts were wasted. But anything that could take
his mind off the uncongenial surroundings and the sticky, unhealthy
atmosphere of Demerara was worth attempting. He seems to have
stayed in the Colony uninterruptedly from May, 1852, to the summer of 1856, when he was again able to visit Europe.

After 1849, when he first went to South America, we find no
more of his letters home, and indeed the only letters of his to have
survived from the decade 1850-1860 appear to be those to John
Murray and one isolated letter which is now in Florence. There is
no more news of his family in London or Dorking, except for one
letter from his father of 1857, sent to him in Sicily, and we have no
more intimate glimpses of his friends. He becomes at once a much
more solitary, impersonal figure than he has appeared to us hitherto,
and we have to imagine him at work as a lonely colonial servant in a
far-distant and uncomfortable land, with only his books and his
writing to console him.

On June 9th 1854 George Dennis wrote the following letter from
Georgetown to Professor Migliarini in Florence:

My dear Sir,

I should apologize for writing in English, but it is so long
since I had the opportunity of writing or speaking Italian, that
I fear to address you in that language.

I beg to introduce to you my friend Mr Holmes,[7] who is on
his way to the Ionian Islands; and I shall feel greatly obliged if
you will kindly put him in the way of seeing to advantage the
antiquities under your direction.

I was in Florence for one day only in January, 1852, but the
Museo was closed, and I thus lost the pleasure of renewing my
acquaintance with you. I was then en route to Sicily, to
investigate the local antiquities of that island, in which, as
respects the tombs, I find great analogies to Etruria.

I had tidings of you recently from mutual friends, and rejoice to hear of your continued health.

I am,

My dear Sir,

With great respect,

Yours faithfully,

Geo. Dennis.

This letter is preserved in the Museo Archeologico at Florence.

In September of the same year, 1854, Dennis's friend Frederick
Catherwood was drowned in the Atlantic, but it was probably
several months before the news reached him at Georgetown.
Catherwood had accompanied John Lloyd Stephens on his voyages
of exploration of the wilds of Central America, and afterwards had

worked on the first railway to be built in British Guiana. Here he had renewed personal acquaintance with George Dennis, the two having known each other in London many years earlier.

When eventually George was able to return on furlough to London, in September, 1856, he made the first of several stays at No. 7 Queen's Road, St John's Wood. Here he lived until Christmas, working for Murray on Sicily. On Thursday, January 15th, 1857, he was elected a Fellow of the Society of Antiquaries of London. It was his first British honour, and a fitting reward for his mammoth work on Etruria.

It was also on this European furlough that Dennis's long, and not always happy, connection with the British Museum began, for he was to carry out certain excavations for the Museum on the trip which he now undertook. He once more left London for Italy at the beginning of January, 1857, while Western Europe was suffering a particularly hard winter. Even at Florence there was frost, fog and snow, and Naples was cloudy, wet and cold. About the 24th of January he reached Palermo, where at last it was warmer, although raining every day. Roses were in full bloom, and peas, cauliflowers and artichokes in season. He wrote to John Murray on the last day of January and told him that there were very few English at present in Naples or Sicily, since fear of political disturbances had kept them away. But he himself experienced no difficulty in getting his passport stamped with a visa for Sicily, and he even managed to carry his notebooks to Palermo without being questioned. He told Murray:

> The disturbances in this island are completely suppressed — and hitherto only one life, that of the Baron Bentivegna, has been forfeited to the offended majesty of Bomba.[8] It is the fashion in this part of the world to testify great joy by the consumption of gunpowder. Great must be the happiness his subjects enjoy under his paternal rule, when they seek to express it by explosions on the grand scale of powder-magazines and steam-frigates. The greater part of the Mole of the Naval Harbour at Naples is level with the waves — and at the mouth of the port a topmast rising from the water shows where the Carlo III was sunk. Naples is in daily expectation of similar catastrophes. When I was there a French frigate came in and saluted the royal flag — great was the consternation among the citizens until the cause of the firing was ascertained. As the people here have no newspapers thro' which to express their sentiments, they give vent to them by chalking the walls with treason.

So great was George's energy that while passing through Northern Italy he had made many notes, which he now sent to Murray to use on another guidebook. Having heard that the Consul at Naples had just had a stroke, he decided to apply for the post, although the salary was only £400: but anything to save him from having to go back to Demerara!

He stayed at Palermo until nearly the end of March, working for the handbook on the western part of the island. He studied the Sicilian school of painting, which was quite unknown even in Italy, let alone England.

Before completing Western Sicily, he left Palermo for a tour of two or three weeks, and then planned to move his headquarters to Messina. If he heard that he had to go back to Demerara, then he would have to be back in England by the beginning of June; but if not, he would stay in Sicily until about August, and then stop in Rome and Florence on his way home. 'I must visit Rome', he told Murray on March 24th, 1857, 'to make a new catalogue of the articles in the Museo Gregoriano, and to see certain sites in Etruria, where excavations have been made of late years; in order that I may have the latest information for the 2nd edition of the *Cemeteries*'. Sicily, he reported, was now perfectly tranquil, and travelling there was safer than in England.

In fact he fell ill at Palermo, and was unable to leave there for Messina until the middle of May. There was no letter awaiting him on his arrival in Messina, and he still did not know whether the Colonial Legislature had decided that he must return to Demerara; if they had, he was due in the colony by July 25th. All the time he was making as fast progress on the Sicilian handbook as he could, but in country districts, he said, progress was of necessity slower, since 'the entire day is spent in creeping from place to place on muleback'. The weather was now delightful as he prepared to set out for Catania and Syracuse. 'In many parts the whole face of the country is covered with flowers of the most rich and varied hues — living and fragrant Turkish carpets. This is certainly the most charming season for the South of Europe.'

At Messina he received a letter from his father written from Dorking on May 8th. 'This day', wrote John Dennis, now a lonely old widower, 'I complete my 78th year and that I have attained it surprises me. I cannot be too thankful while I see old friends and acquaintances at ages greatly short of mine going to the grave with little warning — not that I have had any special loss of friends of late, yet persons of whom I had been in the habit of hearing and of comparing as neighbours and acquaintances now from my rare visits to town (once only in the quarter) finding on enquiry that they are gone with little expectation.' Octavia was the only one of George's sisters now at home, and she sent him her fondest love.

As it turned out, George obtained leave of absence from Demerara until the end of October, and so he remained in Sicily until early in July. He wrote to Murray on July 6th from Messina:

I am about to leave Sicily, and shall certainly turn up in London before the end of the month. Next week, however, is the grand festa of Sta Rosalia at Palermo, which I cannot afford to miss, but I shall run northwards immediately it is over. I am afraid I shall not be able to take Rome on my way home. I wrote, however, long since to Santini, ordering a cameo of the Bacchus & Semele, which ought to be finished by this time. It will be easy to get it thro' McCracken if I do not fetch it.

Poor Douglas Jerrold! I shall never cease to thank Robert Cooke for the delightful reminiscences I have of him.[9]

I have obtained leave of absence till the end of October, but I do not know if I can afford to avail myself of it, for the alternative is Demerara and £750, or England and nothing!

This sojourn in Sicily, which was just coming to an end, had lasted about six months. Apart from the voluminous notes which he had made for the handbook, and apart from a certain amount of archaeological work carried out on behalf of the British Museum, there was yet another side to Dennis's tireless activities. He had written long reports on the terrible state of Sicilian prisons as he had heard them from witnesses. The Bourbon governors of the island kept the gaols filled with wretched political prisoners in conditions of indescribable horror, for they were said to be verminous, stinking and largely subterranean. In Palermo there were the three prisons named the Vicaria, the Castellammare and the Arsenale, while at nearby Monreale were some dungeons, not less horrible, called the *dammusi*, where many men were kept in irons. The infamous and brutal Inspector of Police was a certain Leopoldo Sferlazzo whose reputation for barbarity almost passed all belief. George Dennis was determined to collect and publish as much information as he could gather on these terrible prisons.[10] He had published none of it yet, but fully intended to do so in Britain. Meanwhile he had to return home, and was in London or Dorking until the following December 16th, when he left for Southampton and the ship back to Georgetown. He had been in Europe for fifteen months, far longer than he could have dared to hope, and although not to be finally relieved of his colonial sentence for some years to come, he was nevertheless in many respects very lucky, and had made much progress towards his book on Sicily. On arriving back in British Guiana, he made many journeys through the interior of the colony, where he had official reports to write on education and other aspects of local life about which he felt he knew nothing.

He told John Murray in a letter from Georgetown on June 24th, 1858:

Since my return to this land I have been unsettled — without any fixed habitation, having made several removes, and [am]

writing at last from an hotel. Only yesterday I succeeded after
many efforts in obtaining a house, which I could only ensure
by taking it for three years. My friends being out of power, I
have no hope from Downing Street, and can only look forward
to my own exertions to better my position. I have next month
to conduct a public examination, and to enter my new abode —
then commences my leisure, and then I trust that nothing
will interfere to prevent me from finishing Sicily. It is not,
as you suppose, that I am slow at composition; I can sit down
and knock off an article for a newspaper *currente calamo*,
but to write a handbook requires reference to a number of
books and notes which I, being conscientious, find a tedious
process, and can only accomplish when I have my materials
all around me, and have nothing to distract my attention.
My new abode is some miles from town, and I shall not often
be disturbed by visitors, so that when once settled down I
hope to make almost as much progress as I did in London.
I sent you some time since Mr Gladstone's Journal, which I
hope you returned with my compliments and thanks. Now
I send you a few extracts from the same to be put in type, and
which I shall feel much obliged if you will forward to him for
approval. The 'ascent of Etna' you may consider too long
for the Handbook — but it is so good, and his name will give it
such interest, that it will be a sin to omit it, if he will allow its
publication. Apropos of Etna, this day last year I stood on the
verge of its cauldron of smoke and sulphur — and here I am
gasping for breath in this steaming swamp, even harder than
when I first reached the crest of that almost precipitous cone.
We have been deluged of late by rains of unprecedented heavi-
ness, and were it not for occasional sunshine, our land of mud
must by this time have melted into the waves, and have disappeared from the list of British possessions — an event I should
hardly regret.

Lord Derby was Tory Prime Minister in 1858-59, and the men
whom George Dennis here calls his friends (which does not imply
that he knew them personally), and who were out of power, were
the Whigs Lord Palmerston and Lord John Russell. It was in 1859
that Palmerston returned as Prime Minister.

In December 1858 or January 1859 British Guiana received a
visit from the enthusiastic and tireless traveller Anthony Trollope,
who later wrote of it in his book *The West Indies and the Spanish
Main*: 'I never met a pleasanter set of people than I found there, or
ever passed my hours much more joyously.'[11] If ever he decided to
settle in the colonies, Trollope said, he would choose British Guiana.
George Dennis would certainly have helped him to change his mind,
but there is no record that the two ever met. Trollope's visit lasted

less than a month, and he had no idea what it meant for an Englishman to be stuck there year after year in lonely exile.

There are none of Dennis's letters from the year 1859, but several
of 1860. On July 7th, 1860, he wrote to Murray and admitted that
his progress on the Sicilian book had been very slow:

> What with official duties, farming avocations, and the lethargic
> effects of the climate, I had made but small progress, till this
> glorious revolution stirred me up; tho' of late I have devoted
> all my leisure time and spare energies to the completion of the
> work. Like Garibaldi, I have mastered all the interior of the
> island, and want only the east coast with the cities of Messina
> and Catania to complete my conquest, though I fear it will yet
> take me more time to hand Sicily over to you than that illus-
> trious chieftain will require to place the island in the hands of
> Victor Emanuel.

For Garibaldi, who incidentally was just seven years older than
George Dennis, had with his band of redshirt volunteers captured
Palermo after three days' fighting, even though it had been guarded
by 20,000 troops with artillery and by the Neapolitan fleet in the
harbour, while Garibaldi and his thousand North-Italian volunteers
were assisted only by a band of poorly armed Sicilians.[12] Such
news as reached British Guiana of these momentous events of June,
1860, filled Dennis with renewed inspiration to complete his book.
He was afraid, however, that what he had written already about
Palermo would be immediately out of date, as so many churches and
palaces must have been bombarded, and who could tell what works
of art destroyed? But he felt sure that the sacrifice of Palermo was
worth it to deliver Sicily once and for all from 'the most atrocious
tyranny of modern times'. Murray had warned Dennis to avoid
politics and religion in his handbook, and this he promised faithfully
to do. Yet he felt he could not omit all mention of Garibaldi when
describing such places as Marsala and Calatafimi.

By July 21st he had to admit to Murray in another letter that he
had been so incensed by the atrocity stories of Sicilian prisons that
he had written another small book about them. He begged Murray
to send him a recently published pamphlet by a Frenchman, Charles
de la Varenne, called *La Torture en Sicile*. George was thinking of
calling his own new work 'A Recent Chapter in the History of
Sicily, with an Exposure of the Abuses that have led to the Present
Revolution in that Island'. He now revealed that while in Sicily in
1857 he had sent several long letters or reports to the Foreign
Office, and that extracts from them had on several occasions been
used in the House by Lord Palmerston and more recently by Lord
John Russell. The facts were horrible, but Dennis had gathered
them all on the spot, and he knew them to be authentic. He was
sure that the British public were now, in 1860, so interested in the

liberation of Sicily that his little book would be sure to sell.

By August the little book had swollen to something considerably over one hundred closely written foolscap pages, and he had not finished expanding it yet. He knew so much about Sicily, ancient and modern, that he did not know where to stop writing in either of the two books. He decided to cut down the title of the modern work to 'A Recent Chapter in the History of Sicily'.

'What sad havoc L. Napoleon is making with your Handbooks', he remarked to Murray on August 22nd, 'You already want new editions of France — North Italy — Switzerland and Savoy — and will soon want one also of North Germany.'

But John Murray did not take kindly to the little book on the Sicilian prisons right from the beginning. On October 12th he wrote and told Dennis that if it treated only of torture it was unsuitable for publication. Dennis replied on October 23rd that although torture certainly played a part in his story, its main theme was Neapolitan misrule: it was as much historical as political. Murray thought it would have no interest for the British reading public; Dennis thought this was absurd.

Meanwhile George went on another official tour of Demerara for a few weeks, and had to put his pen aside for the time being. He promised to complete the handbook as soon as he settled down again, having now received from Murray the plans of the bigger Sicilian cities for which he had asked. He reminded Murray: ' "Travels in Sicily" will soon be issued in large numbers by newspaper correspondents and others who have taken part with or followed Garibaldi; and mine, tho' possibly more diffuse on the art and local monuments of the island, will be eclipsed by the brilliant feats of arms and stirring incidents which these campaigners will have to record.'

Early in November, 1860, he sent Murray his little book on Neapolitan misrule, minus the last chapter which was not quite finished. He suggested that a dedication to Gladstone might be appropriate.

Murray refused to publish the book, and in January 1861 George had to write to his brother John in London, requesting him to collect the manuscript from Murray and try its luck elsewhere. But it was never published, and the manuscript seems to have disappeared.

George's health had been deteriorating during the year 1860 in British Guiana, and he felt less than ever able to contend with the enervating climate. Nevertheless, towards the end of his residence in Demerara he made an excuse to carry out anthropological and ethnographical researches in the country which, many years later, bore fruit in one of his most original articles. For in 1861 (when he was forty-seven) Dennis volunteered to take the census of the Indian population of the River Essequibo, and thus he had to visit every

Indian settlement throughout the length of that great river and its tributaries. He began to speculate on the origin of the aborigines of South America, and he came to the conclusion that it was probably the Phoenicians who had in ancient times set foot on South American soil and left traces of their physical aspect in the blood of the Indians. At the same time, he was obliged to admit that the natives of British Guiana showed remarkably Mongoloid features, and concluded that they must have originated from the Eastern coasts of Asia. Dennis employed a native Guianan boy whose face was so oriental that many people believed him to be a Chinese.

Dennis was a sincerely religious man, as his report on education in the colony shows. The following passage also emphasises this: 'I have often attended Sabbath services at the various Missionary stations, and have been struck with the deep interest the Indians took in the proceedings, and surprised to hear that they often came forty or fifty miles in their canoes to attend these services.' [13]

On one occasion while travelling in the interior of the country he has this to say:

> In one tribe far up the river Essequibo, the women fortify their mouths with a double row of thorns, four or five inches long, from the stem of a species of palm which bristles at intervals with these defences. They pierce both lips with these thorns, which stand out like a double *chevaux de frise*, rendering it impossible for a lover, however ardent, to steal a kiss from his enchantress. My wife, who was with me on this occasion, made the experiment of handing a paper of pins to one of these fair Indians, who seized it eagerly and retired hastily into the forest, but soon returned to display herself.

This episode is important because it is the first time we have been informed that George Dennis was, at last, married. He does not give the date of his marriage, nor has it been possible to discover it, but it seems that it must have taken place between about 1858 and 1862. Next to nothing is recorded about his wife, except that her name was Nora. They never had any children. He never again refers to her in his published writings, but constantly in his letters from now on he concludes with the words 'Mrs Dennis joins me·in sending you best wishes', or some other phrase that is equally unrevealing. She appears to have been a woman who never enjoyed the most robust of health, and she predeceased her husband by ten years. Occasional glimpses of Mrs Dennis are given by later writers who met her in Sicily and in Asia Minor; but throughout her life with George she remains very much in the background.

Dennis's passion for antiquity led him to make researches on certain mysterious inscriptions found in a remote corner of British Guiana. He writes: 'Before crossing the Atlantic, I had taken some interest in Punic inscriptions and had visited several Museums in

Europe where such inscriptions were preserved, to ascertain if there
was any affinity between the Punic and Etruscan letters.' He then
made rough copies of some inscriptions found on a rock on the
Essequibo river, 'which I forwarded to the late Dr Samuel Birch,
then Curator of Oriental Antiquities in the British Museum. Not
having preserved a copy, I regret that I can offer only this vague
description to my hearers.[14] Dr Birch, in his reply, informed me
that he could not recognise any Punic *words,* but acknowledged the
general resemblance of the characters to Punic letters . . . If these
rock-cut characters are really Punic, they prove that in very early
times some Phoenician or Carthaginian vessel must have visited
these shores'.

Another feature which struck him as very significant was the
Indians' habit of including Greek frets, or meander patterns, in the
decoration of their baskets and other hand-made goods; and he
thought that this idea must originally have come from Europe or
North Africa. No one can deny that there is the possibility of some
truth in Dennis's theories. To this day, however, they remain to be
proved.

In the spring of 1862 George Dennis once again came on leave
to London, and lived at No. 6 Fitzroy Street, off Fitzroy Square.
On June 30th he sent Murray the extracts which he had made from
Mr Gladstone's Journal, with a request to submit them to him for
approval. He thought that Gladstone's account of the ascent of Etna
the best that anyone could have written, and proposed to include it
in full. He apologised for taking so long over the Sicilian handbook,
but said that no one who had not been to British Guiana could ever
understand what an enervating effect residence there had on the
writer. He longed to get back to Europe, not to live in England, but
to explore the sites of ancient cities in Sicily, Greece, or even Asia
Minor, when, he declared, all his old Etruscan energy would quickly
return. 'I only want a Mercury to deliver me from the mud and
steam of Demerara.' Then on July 11th he wrote the first of the
fifty letters to Henry Layard, M.P., which have survived. He had
been trying to obtain a personal introduction to Lord Russell, with
the object of asking his permission to take extended leave of absence
from South America and go to Sicily to excavate; but having found
direct access to Lord Russell impossible to gain, he wrote to him
at the suggestion of the Duke of Newcastle, who, says Dennis, 'as
well as Lord Taunton, has offered to bear high testimony in my
favour'. He ventured to mention Layard's name as one who was
aware of Dennis's claim to notice as an antiquary, and hoped he had
not taken too great a liberty. From now on, Layard was destined to
be asked all manner of favours by Dennis, all of which he graciously
endeavoured to fulfil. The regulations of the Colonial Office were
that Dennis could not obtain extended leave of absence without

revisiting the colony. Accordingly he had to sail once more for British Guiana by the mail which left England on July 17th, arriving there at the beginning of August. 'But I shall return at once', he told Layard, 'if Lord Russell should be pleased to view my pretensions favourably, and if permission to excavate can be obtained from the Government at Turin.'

On August 22nd he wrote to John Murray:

Demerara
22nd August 1862

My dear Mr Murray,

I did wonders with Sicily on my passage out, and hope to do as much more on my way home. On my arrival I must have it at once put into type, to take it with me to Sicily for correction, for I have just heard from Lord Russell that he will give me a trial this winter at the scavi, and has placed a sum of money at my disposal for that purpose. I hope to have this by the next mail, but I have had a fierce fight for it. Conceive my astonishment on landing there to learn that our new Governor had proposed to the Secretary of State during my absence that I should be removed from the post I have filled for the last 11 years, and whose duties I have discharged to the satisfaction of previous Governors, and of Secretaries of State, and be placed in one of much inferior emolument. He confesses he has no fault to find with me but ill-health, yet he actually refuses (or rather at first refused) to grant me leave to recruit unless I would at once consent to this degradation. Of course I refused indignantly; and have appealed to the Duke of Newcastle for justice. The reduction proposed would be from £750 to £625, but as there are travelling expenses in the one case and not in the other, I would not so much object to this as to the fact that my claim for a retiring pension would be reduced in proportion, which is a most serious matter to me, for should I obtain another post under Government, I shall still retain my claim to this pension, but if I retire from my present post it will be one-sixth larger than if I retire from that which is thrust upon me.

Governor Hincks is brother to Dr Hincks of cuneiform reputation — was a dealer in a small way, a supercargo, a Radical editor, and afterwards a rebel in Canada, where a price was set on his head. He was then prime minister of the same colony, next Governor of Barbadoes, and now here, where, tho' he has been only a few months, he has already made himself most unpopular, by his attempts to upset all existing arrangements to display his zeal and sagacity, and by his 'hoc volo, sic jubeo' way of carrying his point. He will not listen to argument but seeks to bear down all opposition by the weight of authority. If His Grace will only look into the matter himself, I am safe, but he is obliged to leave much of the colonial business to his subs, and if he does so in this case, I am lost, for the rule of office is in every possible case to uphold authority. A word to His Grace to interest him in the matter would save me. It is not patronage or favour I ask of him, but mere justice. I want to be allowed to hold my own post until I have at least had the opportunity of re-establishing my health by a temporary absence from the tropics. Meanwhile I must endeavour to earn a consular appointment by my success in excavating, so as to avoid the ugly necessity of returning again to this colony.

With my kind remembrances to your cousin Cooke, I remain,
My dear Mr Murray,
Yours very sincerely,
Geo. Dennis.

P.S. If Mr Gladstone is willing to serve me he has now the opportunity of doing so with very little trouble, for a word from him to his intimate friend the Duke would ensure me justice — if it is not trespassing too much on your kindness to manage it for me.

This is perhaps the most depressing and pathetic letter that Dennis ever wrote. Written in red pencil at the head of it are the words: 'What can be done more to help this poor man? J.M.'

It is the last of his letters from South America which we have. In September of that year, 1862, having been Inspector of Schools for the colony since June, 1851, he was made Receiver-General and Government Secretary for the Colony of Berbice. This was, however, a very short-lived appointment, for a month or two later the Dennises left South America for good, George having to his immense relief obtained permission from Lord Russell to proceed to Sicily and begin digging at Girgenti and Terranova. They must have sailed back to Europe during the winter, for in March, 1863, they were already in Sicily. There were no regrets at saying goodbye for ever to the exile and the evil climate of British Guiana.

CHAPTER 6

SICILY AND NORTH AFRICA — 1863-1867

THE DENNISES lost no time on arrival in Sicily in the early spring of 1863. It was George's fourth prolonged stay in the island, which he now knew extremely well. From Terranova on March 17th he wrote to Charles Newton, the Keeper of Greek and Roman Antiquities at the British Museum, whom he had recently visited while in London. Newton had asked him to report on a collection of Greek vases and Sicilian coins belonging to a certain Signor Cambolo, who was bankrupt. If this man's creditors openly declared him bankrupt, there would have to be an auction sale, and Dennis felt he would be virtually alone in the market for the vases. If the British Museum did not purchase them, he was even prepared to find the money himself, although he was far from well off. He thought the creditors might be satisfied with five hundred pounds for the entire collection. He sent this letter to Newton with a covering letter to John Murray, together with a tracing of a lecythus, or coloured vase, which he had found: as these all remained in Murray's possession, it is uncertain whether they were ever passed on to Newton. George had heard many accounts of the abundance and beauty of the vases in the various necropoleis of Cyrenaica, and openly declared how anxious he was to explore them, if only he could break off his connection with the Colonial Office and devote his time to exploring on behalf of the British Government, especially the British Museum. But such an idea needed money which was not likely to come his way. Meanwhile he began to dig at Girgenti and, being very disappointed at what he found there, moved on to Terranova, all the time trying not to attract the attention of the Italian Government to his activities and feeling forced to conceal from them his official connection with the British Government. During the following summer he wanted to try Selinunte, where nothing above the surface betrayed the existence of ancient tombs, but where he was convinced that many must lie hidden. By March 26th he had not heard from Newton, and felt that until he did so he could not leave Terranova. He had sent Newton a catalogue of more than eighty figured vases, but there were besides many more unfigured pieces, all belonging to Cambolo. He told Murray that his health had improved greatly in the mild climate of the Sicilian spring, but his sight had suffered so seriously from his last attack of fever in South America that he could no longer do any writing by candlelight. Digging suited him admirably, and although he was making quite a nice little

collection of pieces, it was very rarely that he ever found a vase un-
broken. He told Murray on March 26th:

> There are more difficulties attending excavation here than in
> Etruria. To say nothing of impediments thrown in my way
> by local authorities, who forget they are no longer under the
> Bourbons, the tombs here do not so well repay research. While
> a tomb in Etruria will have several chambers, each full of vases,
> in all it may be from 20 to 50, here a 'monument' rarely has
> more than 3 or 4 — and as the tombs lie much nearer the sur-
> face, they are more frequently rifled than in Etruria. Then
> there is less treasure in the shape of gold or jewellery, no
> bronzes, no reliefs in terra-cotta — nothing but vases of terra-
> cotta, or alabaster. But some of the vases I have seen here
> are among the most exquisite specimens of Gk ceramography
> for simple and chaste beauty not to be surpassed. You may
> imagine the intense interest with which I extract them, often
> piecemeal, from the soil in which they have been embedded
> for the last 23 or 24 centuries, and removing the dirt or tartar
> with which they are encrusted, disclose their beauties one by
> one. I have always fancied myself an ardent admirer of ancient
> art, but I now seem never before to have thoroughly apprecia-
> ted those 'glorious Greeks of old', and the reverence for them
> inspired by my excavations, in which I am brought face to
> face with them, is breaking on me almost like a new sense. I
> have heard such accounts of the abundance and beauty of the
> vases in the cemeteries of the Pentapolis of Cyrenaica that I
> am most anxious to try my spade in that corner of the Hellenic
> world, and if I can only cut my connection with the Colonial
> Office, I would, after doing Sicily, cross the Mediterranean to
> that 'dry nurse of lions' — a phrase Ford facetiously applied
> to Mrs Starke. No systematic excavations, I believe, have ever
> been made in the necropoleis of those cities. I wish they
> would give me the consulship at Benghazi. I am working at the
> Handbook every morning, and would have done much more
> to it by this time, had I been able to write at night. Consider-
> able alterations are necessary in the chapter on Palermo.
> Some of the pictures have been removed to other churches
> since the bombardment in 1860. Such changes have taken
> place in the Museum, that I have had almost to rewrite that
> portion.

But for the next three weeks he could do no digging, being
prohibited under the threat of force. So all he could do was to
press on with the handbook.

If in later years he thought back on this wish of March, 1863 —
'I wish they would give me the consulship of Benghazi' — how
ironical it must have seemed, and how he must have regretted it!

He wrote to Layard from Terranova on April 10th:

> I tried the cemeteries [at Girgenti] both on the south and west
> of the ancient city, first attacking some of the mounds near the
> so-called Tomb of Theron, and the slopes beneath the tem-
> ples. I found sepulchres in abundance but no *roba*. I met
> with no better success in the necropolis on the heights to the
> W. where the ground teemed with tombs, but all thoroughly
> rifled. Having asked no permission of the authorities, I went
> to work as quietly as possible to avoid attracting attention,
> and I confined my operations to the necropolis to escape the
> strong opposition which the discovery of statues or bas-reliefs
> would be sure to call forth; or I should have attempted certain
> spots within the city, where I doubt not much remains to be
> discovered.

Failing at Girgenti, Dennis's thoughts had naturally turned to
some of the sites of Greek cities which had been desolate since their
destruction by the Carthaginians; but two considerations put him
off camping out: the island was overrun with bands of ruffians who
had escaped from Girgenti prison, and the weather was bad. So he
had gone to Terranova, further east along the south coast, which
changed its name back to Gela in 1927. The ancient city had been
founded by Rhodian and Cretan Greeks in 689 B.C. and was destroyed by the Carthaginians in 405 B.C. It had enjoyed its greatest
prosperity under Hippocrates from 492 to 485 B.C. Dennis knew
that the site had yielded vases of great beauty, and since excavations
had been made there for some time past, he was not so afraid of trespassing or incurring any kind of trouble as where excavations had
not been officially allowed. But there was more disappointment:

> I was going on very well here, and was making a nice little
> collection of Siculo-Greek vases, when my proceedings were
> suddenly arrested by the authorities at Palermo, and for the last
> 3 weeks I have been idle, waiting for permission to proceed.
>
> This interruption came at an unfortunate moment. I had
> been waiting for certain crops to be cut to open up ground of
> great promise. I had entered into agreements with the owners,
> and was to have begun on the following week. Now I have
> lost my chance in some of these fields, for the barley has been
> reaped, the ground ploughed and re-sown with cotton. There
> are still a few fields, however, which remain open, and which I
> shall attempt directly I obtain permission. I need not tell you
> that it is not in a day that one can learn the comparative pro-
> mise of this or that field, especially where not a trace of sepul-
> ture appears above the surface. Every necropolis has its own
> peculiarities. I have now been here long enough to have as-
> certained the character of the ground in the several portions of
> this ancient cemetery, and have learned to judge, from the

nature of the soil and the surface, from the position relative to
the ancient city, from the aspect as regards the points of the
compass, of the quantity and quality of the *roba* likely to be
found — above all I have ascertained what fields have, and
what have not, been excavated in modern times, and can pronounce with some degree of certainty on the prospect of
success in the several parts of this necropolis. It would be very
vexing, therefore, after acquiring this experience, to be debar-
red from reaping the advantage of it. Should I obtain permission to go on, unfettered by such conditions as deterred
you at Girgenti, I intend, after finishing here, to try Selinus
or Heraclea, whose cemeteries have been untouched in our
days. The country is now much safer than it was, and the
warm weather approaching will enable me to live in a tent if
I can find no habitation in the neighbourhood. Should I fail
to obtain permission to continue my researches in Sicily, I am
most anxious to try the Greek cities of Cyrenaica [little did
he realise how disappointing they would prove too!] where
Lieuts. Porcher and Smith found the beautiful Apollo and
other statues now in the British Museum, and whose cemeteries have never been systematically explored.[1] There at
least I need fear no such opposition as I have here encountered. I should confine myself to the sepulchres, unless I saw
something to tempt me strongly to try some more important
monument. The cost of such an expedition would be trifling,
as the expense of a journey expressly from England would be
saved, which after all runs away with much more money than
the excavations, and as living and labour are cheap enough on
the African coast.

Another long cherished scheme of mine, which could not fail
to be attended with most interesting results, as enabling me to
verify the asserted connection between Lydia and Etruria, is
to open the 'tombs of the kings' at Sardis. The tomb of Alyattes has been attempted, but its vast size makes its exploration
a work of much difficulty. But the 1001 tumuli near it offer
a most interesting field to antiquarian research — the more so
as we have no sepulchral furniture from that land.

In case I am not allowed to continue my labours in Sicily, I
trust His Lordship will permit me to transfer them to Cyrene
or Sardis — Libya or Lydia — and I shall have to beg your good
offices and influence with him to sanction whichever of these
expeditions you deem the most important and promising.

I have applied to the Duke of Newcastle for an extension of
leave of absence, which he will doubtless not refuse me, if Lord
Russell should be pleased to continue to patronize my diggings.

A picturesque vision of the Dennises at work at Gela is given us by the well-known Italian archaeologist Paolo Orsi:

> About 1860-61 [he presumably refers to their work of 1863]
> George Dennis, British Consul General at Palermo, came to
> Terranova and was welcomed with deference and enthusiasm.
> He excavated with splendid success at Capo Soprano, carrying
> away about forty boxes full of vases, which must be now in
> the British Museum.
>
> The good citizens of Gela of half a century ago remember
> the characteristic figure of Mrs Dennis, sitting on a field-chair
> and shading herself from the sun with a huge red parasol,
> taking a most active part in this new kind of sport, helping
> assiduously with the excavations, and hiding under an enor-
> mous crinoline the most precious pieces which gradually came
> out of the tombs. The Dennises, made the object of the
> greatest regard, and distributing very few tens of pounds, took
> away from Gela hundreds of vases of great value.[2]

In May 1863 the Dennises had to return from Sicily to London,
and took up residence for a few months at No. 7 Queen's Road, St
John's Wood. Here, despite a severe attack of pleurisy, he worked
hard on his *Handbook for Travellers in Sicily,* which he finished in
time to write the preface to it in the following February. On
October 1st, 1863, he received the appointment of Vice-Consul at
Syracuse in Sicily, being thus transferred from the Colonial to the
Foreign Office. But the appointment did not materialise, for
Dennis begged Lord Russell to grant him a few more weeks in
England as he was in the last throes of the *Handbook to Sicily,*
and wanted to see it into the world before he again left England.
He went to the British Museum to see the ailing, sixty-five-year-old
Principal Librarian, Antonio Panizzi, who told him that he had
heard from Layard about Castellani's collection of vases at Naples,
and thinking that as Dennis had accepted the post at Syracuse he
was about to go to Sicily immediately, Panizzi asked him to look
at this collection as he passed through Naples. Panizzi wanted to
obtain the collection for the British Museum. But Dennis got his
way, and remained in London until the spring of 1864. He wrote
to Layard on October 21st, 1863:

> Mr Newton left England on the 13th for Rhodes, via Trieste
> and Corfu. Mr Berkeley Wodehouse, resident at Ithaca, is
> reported to have made a good collection of antiquities in that
> island, which C.N. is anxious to secure. There is surely much
> to be done in those islands, not perhaps by digging, for the
> Greeks are too jealous to allow that, but by collecting articles
> already found. In the Greek islands, however, that belong to
> Turkey there is a grand field for excavations, especially in
> Crete and Cyprus. I hope you will not forget, when an
> opportunity occurs, to transfer me from Syracuse, where I

am comparatively of little use, to a sphere where I can explore for myself, and turn to account my acquaintance with the cemeteries of the ancients.

On December 9th 1863 Dennis was appointed to be Vice-Consul at Benghazi instead of Syracuse, and on the same day wrote to Layard to thank him for influencing Lord Russell; he had called on Layard the previous day, but Layard was not at home. Dennis hoped that in going to North Africa he would be able to make new and valuable discoveries for the British Museum, although he had little hope that the Trustees would finance his researches. He wrote and told Panizzi of his new appointment, and asked whether the Trustees at their next meeting the following Saturday might at least consider making him a grant towards his expenses.

On December 19th 1863 George wrote to Earl Russell acknowledging his appointment to Benghazi at a salary of four hundred pounds a year, with an allowance of one hundred pounds a year for office expenses.[3] Full of eager expectation of the new life ahead in North Africa, Mr and Mrs Dennis sailed from England on January 18th 1864, and reached Malta on the 27th. While waiting there for a connection, George received a despatch from Her Majesty's Consul-General at Tripoli, directing him to come there first in order to receive his instructions. They sailed from Malta on H.M.S. Icarus and arrived at Tripoli on February 9th and at Benghazi on the 29th. There was dissension felt by the Maltese inhabitants of Benghazi, and one of George's first tasks was to dispel it if he could. Thus he entered upon the consular duties which he was to carry out in different countries for the next twenty-four years. At Benghazi he also acted for some time as Consular Agent for Austria. He settled down quickly, but soon realised that Benghazi was not going to be a very fruitful spot for antiquarian exploration or even a comfortable one for ordinary living. He wrote to John Murray on March 20th to acknowledge receipt of a revise proof of the introduction to the Sicilian hand-book which had been sent to St John's Wood after his departure. Already he had to admit to Murray:

Such a dismal place, this Benghazi! A collection of low windowless hovels, with stable-yards as interiors, on a spit of sand surrounded on three sides by the sea or salt-lakes, and on the fourth by a grove of date-palms, the only trees in that direction for the next 200 miles. Inland a bare stony desert stretches to low table heights, which bound the horizon to the east, some 15 m. distant. Not a blade of grass in or around Benghazi — a wide belt of sand strewn with dead dogs girdles the town, above whose mud-coloured walls rises one white minaret, and here and there a lonely palm.

'Oh the dreary, dreary moorland!
Oh the barren, barren shore!'

The level line of the latter is broken on both sides of the harbour by huge black mounds of salt, ready for exportation. A tail-less lion in relief over my doorway, as quaint in style as those at Mycenae, and a flag-staff, alone distinguish my abode as that of H.M. representative. I hope I am not doomed to a long exile in this Ulubrae, but for the present it has more attractions than it would possess for most other people, for I have already established diggings tho' on a small scale, and hope when the hot season is past to make a good haul of antiquities. So long as the Museum supplies me with funds I must dig for them, but when they cease to assist me, I can do something for my friends. The best vases here would please you greatly. The art is not so simple and severely beautiful as that on the vases of Sicily, but it is richer and more developed, and the forms of the vases are more varied and more elegant than those I excavated last year. This site has been pretty well ransacked by De Bourville, but there are others on the coast which have been little worked.[4]   So I hope to do something by and by.

The preface to the *Handbook for Travellers in Sicily* is dated 'London, February, 1864', and so it must have been thus dated by Murray himself. The book was published in the early spring. It is a long book of over five hundred pages of small print, with a map and plans. Dennis is only described as the editor, but he must be considered its author. It would have been published some years earlier but for his enforced residence in South America, where he was totally cut off from the old culture of Europe and from all books of reference, yet where, as we have seen, he never ceased to do all possible work on it. The miracle is that such a book was completed at all, and that the finished product should be so good. Dennis thanks Mr Goodwin, H.M. Consul at Palermo, and Mr W.E. Gladstone for the use of the journal which he had kept on his tour of Sicily in 1838. The book is particularly valuable for its descriptions · of the Greek temples in Sicily. It went through several later editions.

George sent Murray a list of names of friends to whom he wanted a complimentary copy of the new book to be sent. It included, of course, Mr Gladstone, and Mr Goodwin, the Consul at Palermo; also a Miss Holloway of Palermo, the Rev. J. Gough Clay of Messina, and Mr Alfred Oates, Vice-Consul at Girgenti. (It will be noted that there are no Italians on this list.) When a copy of the book reached him at Benghazi in June or July, he remembered to ask also for another copy to be sent to Mr George Lenox Conyngham, who was his agent at the Foreign Office and who sent him *The Times* every week via Malta. In his letter to Murray of July 15th, 1864, George declared that in everything but climate Benghazi was greatly inferior to Demerara: while living in

Georgetown, he would not have thought such a thing possible.
No fevers — ophthalmia and dysentery are the prevalent dis-
orders, but these are greatly owing to the dirty and careless
habits of the people, and were it not for these and the bad
water, there would be few diseases in Benghazi. . . The heat is
oppressive only during the 4 months of summer and has hitherto never reached the ordinary heat of Guiana, save when the
Ghibly or S.E. wind, the Simoom, the Hamseen, as it is called
in Egypt, blows, and then it is intolerable — the very breeze
is fire — and your only remedy is to close all doors and
windows as against a hurricane, and remain in your close
rooms till it changes. Some weeks since I visited an Arab camp
and on my return was overtaken by the Ghibly in the Desert,
where I could obtain no shelter, except from my horse. I was
well-nigh suffocated, and for several days did not recover my
speech.

His official duties, though not light, were much more to his taste
than those which he had had to perform in Demerara. The principal
duties were magisterial and judicial. At first he felt very much out
of his element, but trusted to common sense. He had on hand in
July a defamation case on which he had already sat fourteen times
and heard some forty witnesses, and another case of an attempt to
bribe to commit burglary and murder. He felt sadly in need of a
guide to English law. His 'subjects' were chiefly Maltese traders,
shopkeepers and artisans, a few of whom were very bad characters,
and all of them litigious. He felt, however, that he was gradually
getting them in hand.

He wrote at length to Layard on July 21st 1864:
I came here to dig, but as yet I have done little in that line.
I reached Benghazi at a season rather inopportune for such
operations, as the labourers since my arrival have been engaged
in the harvest, and as the excited state of my Barataria has
required my undivided attention and constant presence at my
post.[5] The recent affairs of Benghazi, insignificant as the place
is, can hardly have failed to reach your ears, but as they have
probably acquired a French gloss in the passage, I venture to
give you an English version.
The matter originated in a dispute between the priests here
and the French Vice Consul, who, as is often the case in the
East, endeavoured to substitute government for protection.
The Maltese, who form almost the entire Christian population,
took the part of their pastors though in no way aggressively or
offensively, the English Vice Consul supported the Maltese,
naturally enough when he found them undeservedly attacked,
and thus was inaugurated the Batrachomyomachia of Benghazi
. . . At this crisis the French Vice Consul's wife left his house on

account of his ill-treatment, and took refuge at this Vice Consulate, and though Mr Reade would not receive her but handed her over to the priests immediately, yet her having sought shelter here, and afterwards in the house of a Maltese, gave M. Bacquerie a handle to charge Mr Reade and the Maltese with getting up 'scandalous and seditious plots against his official authority'. His complaint was backed by M. Botta, at Tripoli, who took all he stated *au pied de la lettre*. Scurrilous libels on the honour of the Maltese women then made their appearance, complicating affairs and aggravating the excitement. Yet in spite of these provocations the Maltese were never guilty of any breach of the peace. The only infraction of it that took place was caused by the French Vice Consul, who, pretending to be threatened, marched thro' the streets with armed cavasses, who struck and insulted an Italian, almost the only person they encountered. At length Bacquerie was ordered to Tripoli (not to return) and Reade to Scutari, and the storm in the puddle began to calm down, but old scores had to be paid off, and it is the settlement of disputes arising out of this excited state of things that has chiefly occupied my time since my arrival.

There may have been faults on both sides, but, the 'fons et origo mali' was undoubtedly Bacquerie – a low, mischievous schemer, who having no 'subjects' of his own, gathered around him a small clique mostly of bad or doubtful character, who set themselves in opposition to the rest of the Europeans, and availing themselves of the known misunderstanding between the Consul-General and Vice Consul Reade, and finding support at Tripoli from other quarters, brought about all this imbroglio with their intrigues. This in a few words is a correct sketch of the 'cosas de Benghazi' during the 3 or 4 months preceding my arrival.

I have not wholly neglected excavations since my arrival, for I have tried various points in this necropolis of Berenice, but find nothing to repay research, it having been well ransacked, chiefly by M. de Bourville. Fragments of vases however in a beautiful style which I have seen, make me anxious to prosecute researches in the cemeteries of Teuchira and Ptolemais, which have been little rifled. I shall shortly commence operations there, and hope to inform you of my success.

I have borne in mind your injunction to ingratiate myself with the Arabs. So far as I have yet had to do with them, I think I have succeeded. I visited the camp of a powerful tribe the other day, and spent some days with them. They welcomed me in characteristic style – 5 or 600 horsemen came down on

me at a *pas de charge*, brandishing their long guns over the
heads and shouting a wild welcome; then they conducted me
to their tents, where they honoured me with races, firing of
muskets, and feats of horsemanship the rest of the day.

I am now on very good terms with the Pacha, although at
first he urged inadmissible claims to jurisdiction over British
subjects and endeavoured otherwise to interfere with my
authority, but when I withstood him firmly, he withdrew his
pretensions, and we have since been on excellent terms. I
begin to understand these orientals — I wish I could say as
much of their languages.

I was pleased to make M. Botta's acquaintance at Tripoli.
He was then much of an invalid, but I hear his health has improved of late. I fear, however, he has hung up his shovel and
his hoe. Had I the opportunity I should cultivate his acquaintance; he hardly seems to be appreciated by Col. Herman.

I ventured to send you the other day a copy of my handbook on Sicily, which I hope may prove useful, when you
carry out your intention of again visiting that beautiful island.
I hope this proof of my acquaintance with Sicily may assist
my pretensions to succeed Goodwin, when he retires.

So already George was casting longing eyes towards the Consulship at Palermo.

On August 5th 1864, George's father, John Dennis, died at his
home at Rose Hill, Dorking, at the age of eighty-five. He was buried
in the little churchyard of Holmwood with his wife, who had died
more than thirteen years before him. They had been lonely years
for the poor old man, nearly all of whose children had left home,
and he had seen very little of George throughout that time. He had
had many illnesses, and had not been expected to survive for so
long. Perhaps one of his most precious comforts was his younger
son John, who was married with five children, living at Hampstead,
and beginning to make a reputation as a critic. In the following year,
1865, John the Younger was to publish his book *Evenings in Arcadia*
(he was then forty-one), to be followed by *English Sonnets: A
Selection* in 1873, *Studies in English Literature* in 1876, *Heroes of
Literature* in 1883, *The Age of Pope* in 1894, *The Realms of Gold*
in 1899 and *Dr Johnson* in 1904, as well as editions of Scott,
Shakespeare, Southey, Jeremy Taylor and Aubrey de Vere.

Throughout their long lives, the brothers George and John kept
in close touch by letter, although there is no further mention of
their many sisters in the extant correspondence from and to George.
This is hardly surprising, as his letters which have survived after
1857 or so are not family ones. But John was always doing favours
for George in London, such as calling on Mr Murray when necessary,
and keeping George posted through the Foreign Office.

On November 10th, 1864, George wrote a report to Edward H. Walker, the Acting Consul-General at Tripoli, twenty-three and a half folio pages of handwriting, mainly about the disgraceful conduct of the French Vice-Consul at Benghazi. He reported that trade had flourished very well at Benghazi in 1864, and this report on trade and commerce was printed.

His real interests, as always, lay in the prospect of future excavations.

Since there was nothing of interest to excavate at Benghazi itself, Dennis began in March 1865 to look eastwards along the coast towards the other ancient sites of the Pentapolis of Cyrenaica. He had already paid an official visit to Tripoli, and wanted to start digging between Benghazi and the Egyptian frontier. As he wrote in 1867:

> When excavating under the auspices of Earl Russell in Sicily, in the necropolis of the ancient Gela, now Terranuova, I have often seen my daily labour rewarded by the discovery of several well-furnished tombs.[6] But my labours in Sicily were abruptly terminated by the Italian authorities. It was at Terranuova that I met a French itinerant doctor, who had visited Ben-Ghazi a few years before, and he gave me so exciting an account of the painted vases he had seen taken from the tombs there and sold for a mere trifle, that, when I found all further research in Sicily was prohibited, I begged Earl Russell to send me to the Cyrenaica. His Lordship was so good as to comply with my request, and at the beginning of 1864 I left England to undertake the office of Vice-Consul at Ben-Ghazi.

Benghazi itself was such a dull and boring place, that Dennis wrote later of it:

> The traveller will be struck with the dreary position of the town on a narrow strip of sand between the sea and a salt lagoon, its crumbling castle, a solitary minaret, and a grove of date-palms, being the only distinguishing features that rise above the monotonous line of low red walls which compose the town. On entering, he will note the extreme wretchedness of the streets and houses; the former filthy to a degree unknown in the worst European cities, and the latter constructed of unhewn stones cemented with red mud, which, dissolving in the heavy rains, often causes the rude piles to disintegrate and sink in confused heaps to the ground. Nor is the country around Benghazi more attractive than the town. For some 20 miles inland it is an undulating, arid waste, for the greater part of the year unrefreshed by leaf or blade, shrub or wild flower. It is hard to believe that this dreary, sandy, barren shore can ever have possessed such attractions as to deserve the reputation of a Paradise.

And yet this had been the site of the ancient Garden of the Hesperides!

So in March 1865 Dennis went to Teucheira (still called Tocra by the Arabs), forty miles to the east of Benghazi and the first of the five ancient sites of the Pentapolis which he intended to excavate. He then travelled on to Cyrene, where, he said, 'the necropolis is far more imposing from the multitude and grandeur of its monuments than any other ancient cemetery I have seen'. These were only preliminary visits, for Dennis was obliged to pay a visit to Malta from May 16th to July 17th in order to seek medical advice, and was unable to return to Teucheira to start work until November. From Malta on June 29th, 1865, he wrote to Layard to tell him of the exploratory expeditions which he had made during the spring. At Cyrene his few helpers had deserted him for the barley-harvest, so he had decided to wait for the close of the harvest, when 'being suddenly attacked by an old and dangerous complaint, I obtained leave from Tripoli to visit Malta for medical advice. My health being already much improved, I hope to return to my post in the middle of next month, and shall start for the Cyrenaica without delay, if I can obtain labour, for the harvest being this year extraordinarily abundant the labouring classes, who are greatly enriched thereby, are not likely to be willing to work. To be prepared against such a contingency, I am contemplating to take some hands with me from this island.'

He went on to say that Cyrene was a glorious and wonderful site.

Never have I seen a Greek city occupying so commanding a position, and with so varied, well-preserved, and abounding a necropolis. Smith and Porcher fail to do it justice in their work; their illustrations not being well selected, nor characteristic, nor even always faithful. I have satisfied myself by excavations in various parts of the necropolis that there is nothing to be done there. Smith and Porcher left untouched a few masses of ruins outside the walls, which are likely to repay research, but in my own particular province, the cemetery, there is no prospect of success; all the tombs above ground, in which alone art-treasures were deposited, having been rifled ages since.

It is at the coast-cities alone that sepulchral riches are to be discovered. Something is to be done at Teuchira, which yields beautiful vases in the fine style, though the site has been well worked already — much more at Ptolemais and Apollonia, whose cemeteries are almost intact. But Apollonia, the more promising of the two, owing to the want of water, can only be attacked from the sea, and I must relinquish all thought of it, until I have some craft at command, as a base of operations. I intend therefore at present to confine my labours to Teuchira and Ptolemais, and I feel confident of finding beautiful relics of Greek art in the cemeteries of those two ancient cities.

I have no firman, as you know, empowering me to excavate, but the present Pasha of Benghazi, who alone has a right to demand it of me, is not likely, I think, to interpose this obstacle, unless indeed the future French consular agent should suggest to him such a course. The inferior authorities are obedient to the Pacha; the Arab sheikhs are indifferent; and the only quarter from which I fear opposition is the Senoussy Convents of brotherhoods, which are scattered along that coast, and keep alive the fanaticism and intolerance of the lower Arabs to a dangerous pitch. Twice in my tour was I threatened with extermination as 'a Nazarene dog', and at Ptolemais I escaped only by displaying my *exequatur* with the Sultan's signature. I do not despair, however, of overcoming these obstacles. A spice of danger lends relish to the search for antiquities, as well as to the chase of living game.

I shall not fail to keep you informed of the progress and results of my labours.

I venture to send you a leopard's skin, the only one I have been able to procure at Benghazi. They are not uncommon at Tripoli and Tunis, but are rarely to be obtained at Benghazi, since the caravans from the interior have ceased to approach that town.

Dennis returned from Malta to Benghazi on July 20th, and on September 18th wrote a long letter to Layard which deserves to be quoted in full because of its importance in showing Dennis's attitude towards his post, his career, and his future prospects.

Private   Benghazi,
                                   18th September 1865

My dear Sir,

Your letter of 24th July was very welcome and encouraging. I have been compelled to defer operations till now in consequence of the superabundant and protracted harvest, but I have at length made a beginning with the necropolis near Benghazi, thinking it advisable to feel my way and give the local authorities the opportunity of interposing obstacles if they are inclined to do so, before I commence operations on a more extended scale at Teuchira and Ptolemais, for which I am meanwhile making preparations. I expect little success here, where I have been forestalled by De Bourville, Crowe, Werry and others, but if I don't meet with it at Teuchira, I shall go on to Ptolemais, and work as long as the weather permits, or as I can keep my hands together. Many thanks to you for offering to make the most of any papers I may send you. I will not fail to report my progress. People in England expect great results from any operations of this kind. Few, like you, understand

the difficulty of conducting excavations in the Desert, where
you have to carry everything with you — labour, shelter, food,
and even water — and where your base of operations is some
50 or 60 miles distant. They don't comprehend that a regular
campaign is necessary to overcome the natural difficulties
attending such an expedition. My friends at the Museum are not
very liberal this year, but if, as you say, I can interest them
with the sight of a few precious relics of antiquity, they may be
induced to slacken their purse-strings in future.

Should Lord Somers be inclined to pay this coast a visit
next spring I shall be delighted to be his cicerone to Cyrene,
where he will find much to interest him both as an antiquary
and an artist. I don't think I mentioned to you that at Apollonia
there are numerous large columns of cipollino, relics of X^n
churches, close to the shore, on which the Turks set no value,
but which would be prized in England, either to adorn a public
building, the new National Gallery to wit, or the portico of a
church.

Excuse me if I now direct your attention to a different
subject. You may remember that the post I have the honour
to hold is only a V. Consulate. In pay, however, in the powers
conferred on me by H.M.Commission — in everything save
rank, I am on a par with a Consul. I am persuaded it would be
of advantage to the public service if my post were placed on its
right footing, and raised at once to a Consulate.

Formerly it was consistent enough that the British authority
at Benghazi should be a Vice Consul, but his position relative
both to his immediate superior at Tripoli, and to the local
authorities, has so altered of late as to render a change of title
desirable. Before H.M.Commission was granted to my predecessor, he was in all judicial matters dependent on Tripoli, and
unable, save in cases which could be treated summarily, to
pass a sentence, being compelled to submit the evidence taken
at every trial to the Consul General for his decision. Now I
exercise jurisdiction independently of Tripoli, and correspond
on such matters with the Judge at Constantinople.

Until the appointment of the present Pacha some two years
since, the Governor of this province was a mere *Kaimakam*
under the mushir of Tripoli. Halil Pacha, however, was not only
appointed a *mutessarrif*, independent of Tripoli, but he has
recently been elevated to the rank of a *beghlet-begh*. No question that may now arise between us can be settled, as formerly,
by reference to Tripoli, but while H. ExcY. transmits his dis-
patches, via Canea, to Constantinople, I have to send mine to
Tripoli, a 3 weeks' journey in the opposite direction, so that
my version cannot possibly reach the capital for at least a

month after the Pacha's — a great inconvenience to the public service.

While the chief of the local Government was himself but a Lieut. Governor, it was consistent enough that the British consular authority should be of the lowest grade, but the disparity of rank between us is now so great as to tempt any Turkish Pacha in that position to presume on his vastly superior standing.

The raising of my post to a Consulate, I am persuaded, would give me consideration with His Exc.Y. when I have to resist his aggressions on the rights of H.M. subjects; it would add weight to any words of warning or advice I may feel it my duty to offer, when he threatens to enforce his pretensions, or to carry out measures that appear prejudicial to British interests, and it would lend me authority when he condescends to consult me on matters in which the general welfare of the community is concerned. In a word, as my relations with him partake much of a diplomatic character, and as my isolated position throws me greatly on my own resources, I feel it desirable that my little imperium should be placed on the footing best calculated to ensure it respect, and enable me to resist his aggressions with effect. It is true that my colleagues of France (when there is one) and of Italy hold no higher rank than myself: but the former has not a single French subject under his protection, while he of Italy, who is unpaid, has not more than a dozen of his countrymen under his control. Of British subjects and protégés there are between 3 and 400, and among them are the wealthiest and most influential merchants of Benghazi.

As yet there is no steamer to Europe, and the only regular communication between Benghazi and the rest of the world is a camel-mail to Tripoli, which takes 3 weeks in the transit. It may be necessary therefore that in official matters I should continue to correspond with Tripoli. But a steamer is about to be shortly established between this, Malta, and Canea, and I shall then be brought almost necessarily into more direct communication with the Foreign Office.

I beg you will understand that I do not seek this change in order to be freed from the control of the Consul General. I feel it desirable to be able to look for guidance to someone of more experience than myself in Oriental matters and consular duties, but this advantage, it appears to me, need not be lost by the elevation of my post to a Consulate. Nor do I ask for an increase of pay. The only expense the alteration would entail on the Government would be the allowance to a second cavass, which I have hitherto been obliged to pay out of my own pocket, but of which I should in that case ask to be relieved.

My predecessor, Mr Reade, equally with myself, felt the awkwardness of his position, and wrote to Mr Murray on the subject, though I am not aware that he made a formal application.

I do not know if I am in order in writing to you, even privately, on this subject. But if so, and you approve of my request, may I solicit your kind offices in forwarding my views.

> Believe me, my dear Sir,
>> Most respectfully and faithfully yours,
>>> Geo. Dennis.

But alas! Dennis could not have his way, for in faint pencil at the head of this letter, presumably in Layard's hand, is written: 'No chance of making him Consul — nor would it be expedient to make him independent of the Consul General.' A Vice-Consul he was to remain for another six years.

In November 1865 Dennis returned to Teucheira, and stayed there nearly a month. The results of his excavations were on the whole a disappointment to him. He had to show as the fruits of his labours 'only a few painted vases, some small glass bottles, and *unguentaria* or ointment-pots of alabaster, some fragments of bronze vases, and strigils, with a number of disks or mirrors of the same metal, a little sham jewellery, bracelets of lead, and necklaces of terracotta gilt, with some good specimens of the terracotta statuettes for which these Cyrenaic cemeteries are distinguished'. At one tomb at Teucheira Dennis

> lay for hours clearing away the hard clay from around these terracottas until the fifth figure, with the Italian head-dress, alone remained to be extracted. The sun had gone down, and I was working by the light of a lantern. Heartily weary, I sat up awhile to rest. The overseer of my gang, who had been watching my operations, with good-natured officiousness offered to relieve me. I refused, but ultimately yielded to his solicitations, cautioning him particularly about the head. Hardly, however, had he taken knife and trowel in hand than the head rolled off its shoulders to the loose earth at the bottom of the tomb. He handed it to me in triumph, but the lovely Greek features were obliterated for ever.

Dennis was still at Teucheira on Christmas Day, which he spent bargaining with the Arabs for a collection of Greek pottery which they had found. He succeeded in securing the entire lot, which he carefully packed and conveyed to Benghazi on camels. He was convinced that further excavations on this site were likely to produce better results, so he wrote to the British Museum that he wished to explore the ground in similar localities all round the city, especially outside the principal gates. Mr Charles Newton, the Keeper of Greek

and Roman Antiquities, wrote back and gave Dennis every encouragement to proceed. More than that, funds were found by
Newton to enable Dennis to carry on with his work; and this scheme
had the backing of Layard, who in 1866 had just become Queen
Victoria's Under-Secretary of State for Foreign Affairs.[7]

During this winter George had another attack of rheumatic gout
which kept him more or less confined to his house for three or four
months. It was a complaint which was to recur in later years.

On March 1st, 1866, Dennis wrote another long letter to Layard:

Benghazi,
March 1st, 1866

My dear Sir,

    I should have sent you an account of my excavations immed-
iately on my return from them in December, but for two
reasons — that I was not eager to report my want of success,
and that I had learned from the papers that you were travelling
in Italy, and thought it probable you would not return before
the meeting of Parliament. As you have condescended to
express interest in my proceedings, I feel bound to report
them to you, although I have reaped little fruit as the reward
of my labours. I have indeed been sadly disappointed in the
cemeteries of the Cyrenaica. In the spring I tried that of
Cyrene — in the autumn those of three other cities of the Lib-
yan Pentapolis — Hesperides (Benghazi), Tauchira and Ptolemais. That of Cyrene, as I think I informed you, has been
thoroughly ransacked in ancient times; that of Hesperides in
our own days by French and English Vice Consuls at Benghazi.
Though the necropolis of Tauchira also bore traces of extensive
excavation, I thought there might still be room for enterprize
on my part. I found tombs in abundance — not a few intact —
many also rifled, some in ancient, others in modern times; but
very little sepulchral furniture of value or interest. Such tombs
as I opened on this site, so carefully constructed and securely
closed by ponderous blocks, would, in Italy or Sicily, if intact,
be certain to contain figured vases, rich bronzes, or perhaps
jewelry. Here the only fruit of my labours would be a large
amphora, with smaller vases of common red ware, or at the
best of black varnished pottery, with an unfigured mirror, or a
strigil of bronze, and perhaps some sham jewelry of lead or
terra-cotta gilt. The only way in which I can account for the
poverty of these sepulchres is this. The necropolis of Tauchira
embraces a series of low hills extending East and West of the
city walls. The crests and upper slopes of these eminences are
full of tombs, all ransacked. There remained to be explored
only the lower slopes, and the ground at the base of the heights.
Here it was that I worked, and the tombs I opened must

either have been those of the poorer citizens, or must have
belonged to a late period, when the art of vase-painting was in
extreme decadence, and such decorations were no longer in
fashion for sepulchres while the tombs on the higher ground,
which had yielded beautiful painted vases and elegant statuettes
to De Bourville and others who had preceded me, must have
been of earlier date, or the resting places of the aristocracy of
Tauchira. I incline to think the difference is that of antiquity
rather than of class. The only portion of this necropolis which
yielded me any articles of interest was at the very foot of the
city walls, where the tombs contained some Panathenaic
amphorae, and a few other painted vases, which I have forwarded to the Museum.

I experienced even greater disappointment at Ptolemais, for
knowing its necropolis to have been little explored in modern
times, I had formed lively anticipations of success, which proved
utterly delusive. Here was a city of more than ordinary size,
and whose monuments proved it to have been of great wealth
and magnificence, yet its tombs, of which I found many
intact, contained even less of value and interest than those of
Tauchira. I tried its necropolis on all sides, and always with a
similar result. The poverty of its sepulchres I can only ascribe
to the late date of the city. I knew that it did not become one
of the cities of the Pentapolis until the time of the Ptolemies,
when it took the place of its parent-city, Barca, but I also
knew that as the port of Barca, it must have had an origin
coeval with that city, which dated from the middle of the 6th
century B.C. so that there was reason to believe that the sepulchres of the port, if not of the city, might illustrate in their
furniture all the best styles of Greek art. My researches, however, tend to prove that in the first period of its existence,
Ptolemais, or whatever may have been its name, could have
been but a mere shipping-place, with very few inhabitants.
None of its monuments and few of its tombs, in that case, can
be earlier than the Ptolemies.

Only two days before I left Ptolemais, I made a discovery
which confirms this view. On the brow of the mountain overhanging Ptolemais, I discovered the remains of an ancient
Greek city, which from its position can have been no other
than Barca, although that city is generally placed at Merge,
many miles inland. One glance at Merge, however, satisfied me
it was not a Greek site, and I was persuaded that Barca must be
sought in the mountains between Merge and the sea. The site
I have now found agrees with what we know of Barca in every
respect but distance from the sea, for it is much less than '100
stadia' inland, though on the other hand Merge cannot be less

than 200 stadia. Its proximity also to Ptolemais explains how the two were often spoken of in Roman times as identical. If I had the necessary classics at hand I would write a short article on this subject, which is one of interest, since Barca is the only one of the Five Cities whose site has ever been open to doubt, and since its history is so well known from the pages of Herodotus, while its name, no longer attached to any particular site, still survives as that of the whole mountain region of the province of Benghazi. Had I made this discovery earlier, I should have hesitated to excavate at Ptolemais. I should have concluded from the proximity of this ancient site to the sea, that Ptolemais, during the flourishing days of Barca, could have been nothing more than a port to the parent-city, and I should have confined my explorations to the necropolis of the latter, where, if anywhere in this neighbourhood, we should look for the sepulchral treasures which I sought in vain in the plains around Ptolemais.

In short, I have been grievously disappointed with the results of my excavations. I have laboured two months to little purpose. I have spent double the grant, and have little to show for it. It has not been my good fortune, though it is my ambition, to hit upon a Vulci or a Camirus. The best chance of a virgin necropolis in this land is, I think, at Apollonia, the fifth city of the Pentapolis, and the port of Cyrene. But without some vessel as a base of operations, nothing can be done there, owing to the want of water: all the old wells being rendered brackish by the encroachments of the sea. If a gunboat could be spared to lie off this spot for a few weeks during the coming summer, I would gladly essay that necropolis, which shows no traces of excavation in modern times, and from its tombs being all below the surface, is not unlikely to have escaped the attention of the barbarians who of old rifled the sepulchral monuments of Cyrene.

Seeing that there is but a narrow field for research in this land, I have petitioned Lord Clarendon to be removed; if possible, to some other part of the Hellenic world, where my services may turn to better account. I have ventured also to renew my application for the reversion of the Consulship of Palermo, when it falls vacant, which I first made to Lord Russell at your kind suggestion. But meanwhile I hope to be removed from Benghazi, both because I am anxious to find a more promising field for my enterprise, and because I am heartily tired of my dreary exile in this Desert, where I am not only cut off from society and medical assistance, but am further removed from Europe and civilization than I was in the swamps of Guiana. Could I be of further service to the Museum here I should be content to remain, but as my prospect of usefulness is the chance of a gunboat, I feel entitled to apply for removal; and, if you will add to the many kind favours you have shown me your powerful assistance in this matter, I cannot doubt of success. My aspirations tend to the Greek Archipelago and the coast of Asia Minor. Crete and Cyprus too, glorious fields for antiquarian research, have been often vacant of late. Should vacancies occur again, I beg you will kindly bear me in mind. But it is not for me to suggest. I shall be content with any post where in your opinion I can be usefully employed.

During my absence from Benghazi, last year, first at Cyrene, and then at Teuchira and Ptolemais, in all nearly 3 months, I left the Vice Consulate in charge of Mr Antonio Aquilina, formerly Vice Consul at Derna. If I had been absent on private affairs he would naturally look to me for remuneration. As it is, he has a claim on the Government for a recompense, but does not know in what quarter to urge it. Had I met with great success, I should not hesitate to throw this burden on the Trustees of the Museum, to whom it properly belongs, but I fear they will think they have paid dearly enough for the few antiquities I have sent them. Is there any fund at the disposal of Government from which Mr Aquilina might receive some remuneration for his services?

With many apologies for the length of this letter,
I remain,
My dear Sir,
With much respect yours faithfully,
Geo. Dennis.

P.S. Lest the skin I sent you last summer should not have reached you I venture to send you another by this opportunity, and hope it may be worthy of your acceptance. It is not so bright in colour as I should like, but I have no choice — such things being very rarely obtainable here, since the caravans from the far interior have ceased to touch at Benghazi.

And on March 25th, 1866, Dennis wrote to Layard the last of his letters from North Africa to have survived:

My dear Sir,

Your letter of the 14th February, this day received, was very welcome, as assuring me that my efforts in the cause of the Museum tho' far from satisfactory in their results, are appreciated by you, and not less so as opening to me a prospect at no distant period of removal from Benghazi.

You will probably ere this have received a letter from me, in which I have troubled you with some details of my excavations. It was my intention, as soon as Ramadan was over, or about the middle of February, to return to Tauchira, and work out that vein of tombs around the walls, of which I have already reaped the first fruits. Rheumatism, however, led me to defer operations in the first instance, and since the beginning of the present month, affairs have been too unsettled at Benghazi for me to entertain a thought of leaving my post. The Christian residents have been kept in a state of excitement by repeated insults offered by the Arab population, which culminated at length in an attack on the Catholic Church by a fanatic, who entering unexpectedly demolished all its furniture in a few seconds.

The Maltese could see in this only the prelude to a general massacre of the Europeans, and urged me to telegraph for a man-of-war. But seeing no ground for their panic, and knowing that the Pacha was sincerely endeavouring to maintain order, and had abundant force at his command, I would not comply with their request. The result has proved I was right. Their alarm has in great measure subsided, yet for some time to come I feel it will be my duty to remain at my post: especially as the only two Maltese whom I could at ordinary times venture to leave in charge of the Vice Consulate happen at present to be absent.

Some 2 or 3 months hence when all danger of storms on land or at sea is past, I may beg the Admiral at Malta to allow some gunboat, when on a cruise, to convey me to Apollonia, both to obtain the measurements of the columns, and to experiment on the necropolis of that ancient site. If Sir R. Smart is still in command he is not unlikely to accede to my request. If it be Lord Clarence Paget, as my application could not be official, I can hardly expect him to assist me unless, indeed, you could drop him a hint to that effect before he leaves England. My visit to Apollonia was so hurried, that I did not even take a note of the number or size of the columns. As they belonged to two or three distinct churches, they can hardly be uniform in point of size. As far as I can recollect they are about the size of the columns in the portico of the Temple of Antonius and Faustina in the Forum at Rome. But I may be deceived, as such masses appear larger when prostrate, than when erect. There can be no difficulty in rolling them to the water's edge, with hands enough at command, where they might be shipped on board a flat-bottomed lighter. If the Romans could convey them to that site, surely we can have no difficulty in carrying them away. I anticipate little or no difficulty with the local authorities. Indeed, I see no occasion to ask permission. They set no more value on these columns than on the masses of other stone which cover the site. I doubt if they are aware of their existence. You will be able to judge

if they are worth the transport when I send you a detailed
description of them. However, before I revisit Apollonia I hope
to finish my labours at Tauchira, where I am very anxious to
follow out the vein which appears so promising.

I find from a letter from Mr Newton this moment received
that I have to thank you, which I do most heartily, for obtaining for me from Lord Clarendon, a grant of £200 to carry on
my excavations, which I shall resume as soon as I can venture
to absent myself from Benghazi.

Believe me, my dear Sir, with much respect,
Yours faithfully,
G. Dennis.

Nothing more was ever heard of the scheme to remove the
columns from the North African shore, and there they remained.

At the beginning of August, 1866, Dennis was able to return to
Teucheira to resume his researches. He was again disappointed to
find that most of the tombs had been ransacked by others before
him, but he found some more good terracotta figures, and the
most important haul in the end turned out to be six Panathenaic
amphorae. No ancient necropolis in Italy or Sicily, he concluded,
had yielded more Panathenaic vases than Tocra. His painted vases,
large and small, numbered about forty, and some of these treasures
he gave to the British Museum between 1866 and 1868, while the
Museum paid him for others. The amphorae were prizes bestowed
on the victors in the annual public games at Athens, and so it was
rather surprising that they should turn up in North Africa. They
belonged for the most part to the fourth and third centuries B.C.
Dennis also worked at the site of Ptolemais, twenty-five miles or so
further east along the coast.

On November 28th 1866, Dennis asked the Foreign Office for
six months' leave in order to re-establish his health, if possible in
England. Early in March 1867, however, he again went to Malta and
on the 15th wrote to Henry Layard in London:

My dear Sir,

I have not written to you for some time, knowing that during the recess you were wandering through Italy. Now that
you have returned to your parliamentary duties I venture to
trouble you with a line.

In the excavations I resumed last year at Teuchira, where I
thought I had hit on a vein of aristocratic tombs, to work out
which you so kindly obtained me a grant from Lord Clarendon,
I have been grievously disappointed. I devoted five weeks last
summer to exploring the ground around the walls and outside
the gates and with very inadequate results. As the grant was
made for this special purpose, I persevered until I had probed
the ground beneath the walls all round the city, and was

convinced of the futility of further research. The tombs I discovered had either been rifled long ages ago, or contained nothing of value and interest. Having now tested the cemeteries of 4 of the cities of the Cyrenaic Pentapolis, I am in a position to state that further researches in that land must prove fruitless, unless the necropolis of Apollonia, unexplored in modern times, should have escaped the rapacity of the ancients.

You may remember that you advised me to confer on this subject with Lord C. Paget, and I have done so since my arrival in this island which I have been obliged to revisit for medical assistance.[8] You may remember also that you requested me to ascertain the dimensions of the monolithic columns of cipollino lying on that site. I have had no opportunity of doing this, but I mentioned this also to Lord Clarence, and informed him that there were other columns of the same material lying on the beach at Lebdah, not far from Tripoli, which with those at Apollonia might be useful in adorning the new Foreign Office or the National Gallery. His Lordship informs me that he cannot move in the matter, without instructions from the Admiralty, and that if I wished to test the eligibility of Apollonia for future excavations, he cannot, in any case, despatch a ship to lie off that coast earlier than May. Now if these columns are likely to prove serviceable in the manner indicated, no time should be lost in ascertaining their precise dimensions and condition, and this might be done in a day, without incurring any risk, as no vessel would approach the shore unless in moderate weather. I write to you, presuming that as this is a subject of national interest, you may still, tho' unconnected with the ministry, be able to put it in train for me.

As regards excavations at Apollonia, the Museum is the proper quarter through which to apply, but I am reluctant to do so, lest the authorities there should wish to keep me at Benghazi until I have worked the site, supposing I find it to be promising. I am desirous, therefore, if possible first to ascertain this fact, and if on a visit I contemplate to England this summer I succeed in my earnest desire to be removed from Benghazi, I shall not anticipate much difficulty in obtaining permission to excavate at Apollonia. In any case I must leave my Consulate in other hands while I do this. If you can help me in this matter also I shall feel greatly obliged. I told Lord Clarence that I would write to the Museum authorities, but for the reason I have given I think I had better not.

I am now about to return to Benghazi. Be so good as to address me to the care of Mr Staveley.

I am, my dear Sir, Respectfully and faithfully yours,
Geo. Dennis.

Layard must have been too busy to accede to all Dennis's requests, but nevertheless they remained on very friendly terms, and Dennis was always expressing his warm gratitude to Layard for favours received from him.

In the following month, April 1867, the Dennises were back in England, and took up residence at No. 53 Brompton Square, London. On April 26th George wrote to his friend Edward Falkener:

> My dear Falkener,
>
> Many thanks for your kind invitation, of which I shall be delighted to avail myself in due time. It will be better for Mrs Falkener and baby that I should defer my visit till the latter is at least one month old. I gather from your silence that both your household duties are progressing favourably. I sincerely hope this is the case.
>
> You may perceive from my address that I have returned to the quarters I occupied during my short stay in England during the last Exhibition year. I have not yet been able to see any one of the magnates to whom I seek access. Newton is in Sicily, but he is expected back immediately, and as he is as much interested in my removal from Benghazi as I am, I have thought it best to await his return. Any application from me is far more likely to meet with success if endorsed and seconded by him. If Panizzi were in his old place, I would not wait for Newton, but the present Librarian knows nothing of me, and would not move, I am sure, without him.[9] He will not even open a case of antiquities I have sent, before Newton's return. Did you know that a man named Wood has been excavating at Ephesus for the Museum? He has sent home only 2 small Roman ash-chests — I hear from Smyrniots I met at Malta, that the same Wood is a very self-sufficient individual, who is always abusing you, or rather your work, while Hyde Clark, a much better judge of such matters, upholds you stoutly. Wood is voted a humbug, I am told, at Smyrna. I want to go there myself. All that coast of Asia is a grand field for sepulchral researches. With my best respects to Mrs Falkener,
>
> I remain,
> Ever yours sincerely,
> Geo. Dennis.

This letter of April 26th 1867 is written on paper with black edges, but it is not known for whom he was in mourning, unless it was still for his father, whose death had occurred two and a half years before.

Only four days later, on April 30th, Dennis again wrote to Falkener:

> My dear Falkener,
>
> I must renew my thanks to you for your friendly invitation, but I must not think of accepting it for the present. Newton

1. Sutri: drawn by Samuel Ainsley

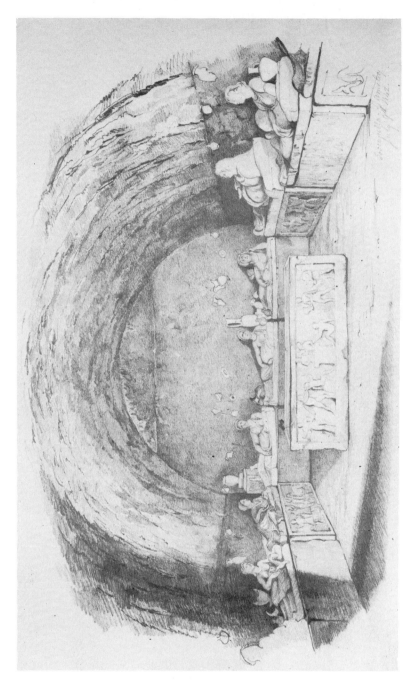

2. Etruscan tomb at Toscanella: drawn by Samuel Ainsley, July 1842

3. Castel d'Asso: drawn by Samuel Ainsley, November 1842

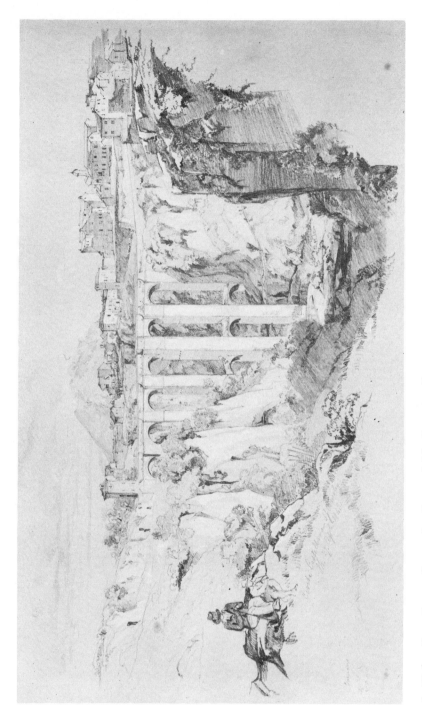

4. Civita Castellana: drawn by Samuel Ainsley, April 1843

5. Vermiglioli's tomb, Perugia: drawn by Samuel Ainsley, May 1843

6. The Gate of Volterra: drawn by Samuel Ainsley, May 1843

7. *Top:* View of Volterra: drawn by Samuel Ainsley, 21 May 1843
8. *Bottom:* Interior of an Etruscan tomb at Volterra: drawn by
Samuel Ainsley, 21 May 1843

9. Fiesole: drawn by Samuel Ainsley, July 1843

10. Etruscan tombs at Castel d'Asso, near Viterbo, still being excavated, 1967

11. Entrance to an Etruscan tomb at Blera, near Viterbo, 1967

12. Edward Cooke, R.A., 1864

13. Edward Falkener, about 1890
or 1895

14. George Dennis, about 1875

15. Henry Layard by G.F. Watts,
no date

17. Aphrodite carrying Eros (second century B.C.) from Centorbi, Sicily. Acquired by the British Museum from George Dennis

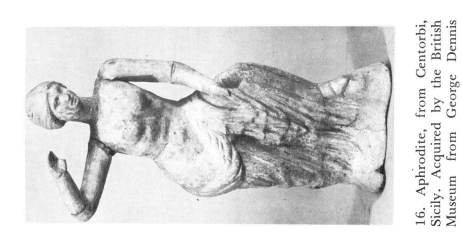

16. Aphrodite, from Centorbi, Sicily. Acquired by the British Museum from George Dennis

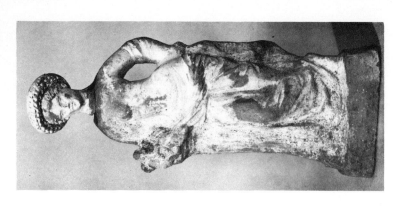

18. *Left*: Plaque: Eros (second century B.C.) from Centorbi, Sicily. Acquired by the British Museum from George Dennis
19. *Right*: Greek statuette of Aphrodite (third century B.C.) from Cyrenaica. Acquired by the British Museum from George Dennis

has just returned, and I must lose no time in putting matters in train either to secure removal to some other Consulate, or to obtain a roving commission to explore Asia Minor. He speaks of Gregory, M.P., as one much interested in excavation, and especially in mine. Therefore I must make his acquaintance. I want to try the tombs of Ephesus – not such as those which Wood has found – but the true Greek sepulchres, which Wood does not seem to know how to find – or the tumuli of Sardis. But there must be multitudes of sites in Asia Minor whose cemeteries have escaped rifling in ancient times, for we know that nothing has been done in our own. What books are there on the antiquities of Asia Minor, save Hamilton, Fellowes, Texier and Falkener? I am much amused with Wood's letter, just received. His 'prowlings' for 3 years do not seem to have been very profitable to himself, or 'beneficial to the public', judging from what he has sent home – only 2 small Roman 'ash-chests', and a few Greek inscriptions in fragments – nothing in the way of Greek art. He certainly bears strong testimony to the correctness of your site for the Temple, though he refuses to accept the obvious conclusion.

'Tomb of St Luke! known by his emblem, the bull' – probably nothing more than the boucranion often introduced in Roman architectural ornamentation even of sepulchres, as, if I remember right, on the tomb of Cecilia Metella. I am greatly inclined to vote the man a humbug, as the Smyrniots do. I will return his letter, but not till I have looked at your work, which I can see in the British Museum.

With my best respects to Mrs Falkener, of whom 'no news is good news'.

I remain,
Ever yours sincerely,
Geo. Dennis.

William Gregory, M.P. for County Galway, became in 1860 Chairman of the Committee to enquire into the organization of the British Museum under Lord Palmerston's Government, and in March 1869 he was best man at the wedding of Henry Layard and Enid Guest. It does not appear that George Dennis met him, even though he so much desired to do so. As for the architect John Turtle Wood, whom Dennis and Falkener thought such a fraud, he had been sent out in 1863 by the British Museum and the Society of Dilettanti to look for the Temple of Artemis at Ephesus. It took him six years to locate it below the hill of Ayasoluk in 1869, by which time Dennis himself knew Asia Minor well. Dennis probably disliked Wood and his methods sufficiently to avoid meeting him whenever possible.

On May 31st, 1867, Dennis wrote to Lord Stanley to ask for three months' special leave as he had to have an operation. This was

granted on June 6th. The operation could not have been a very
serious one, for on July 10th of the same year he gave a long lecture
to the Royal Society of Literature in London. It was entitled 'On
recent excavations in the Greek cemeteries of the Cyrenaica', and
three years later, in 1870, it was published in the Society's
Transactions. The paper made it quite clear to his listeners that
Dennis had been for the most part very disappointed with the results
of his efforts in North Africa. He had set his mind on beginning
explorations in Asia Minor, and thus he visited the British Museum
(which during 1867 and 1868 was still acquiring terracottas and
vases from him, some by purchase and some by donation) and he
succeeded in obtaining from the Treasury a grant of five hundred
pounds to spend on excavating the ancient cemeteries of the parts
around Smyrna. He also implored the Foreign Office to find him a
suitable transfer from Benghazi to Turkey, but at the time there
was no vacancy and he was forced to remain on the Benghazi staff
until 1869. To us examining this situation a century later it may
seem curious that a man could openly ask for a transfer because he
wished to carry out archaeological research somewhere else. The
answer today would be that his Foreign Office duties came first, that
archaeology was a private, spare-time occupation not to be undertaken in official time, and that he would go where he was sent. In
the Victorian period of a hundred years ago, however, a gentleman
could evidently tell his superiors and his employers that he wished to
devote a good portion of his time to explorations even though he
was responsible for consular duties overseas.

The Dennises left England on October 15th, 1867, and returned
to their station at Benghazi, where they spent a frustrating winter
and spring. The stormy weather along the North African coast cut
them off from the civilised world, and they scarcely saw an English
newspaper for six months. No wonder Dennis later called his residence at Benghazi a 'banishment from civilization'. It was extremely
difficult for him to wind up his affairs before leaving Benghazi. He
had to sell his horses and his furniture, and he was more than usually
hard up himself. The Arabs would normally have given him sixty
pounds for a good mare, but he obviously could not receive pay-
ment in their normal currency, which was camels, and they had
been almost totally deprived of money by a poor harvest and a
rapacious Governor General. Therefore George received about one
quarter in cash for his goods of their real worth, and for one of his
best mares he was paid thirteen pounds. He had borrowed money
from John Murray, but was unable to pay it back for many months.
He had had to pay for the upkeep of his house in Benghazi during
his long absence, and when after waiting for nearly six months for
a ship to leave there, he had to pay most extravagantly for his wife's
and his own fares.

He and Mrs Dennis eventually left Benghazi, not without a sigh of relief, about the end of April, but were delayed in Malta almost a month waiting for a ship for Smyrna. This added to their expenses.

At last they set sail for Turkey and reached Smyrna on June 3rd. Here they had to look for a house and pay a year's rent in advance. George had virtually no money left at all. But he was happy with anticipation, and it was the best time of the year. Turkey promised to be more exciting even than Sicily had been.

CHAPTER 7

FIRST EXPLORATIONS IN TURKEY – 1867-1870

ON ARRIVING at Smyrna, they were delighted with the beauty of the country, 'contrasting so gloriously with the dreary desert of Bengazi', as George told Edward Falkener in a letter written on the following August 18th. Mr and Mrs Dennis took a pretty little cottage in the picturesque village of Bournabat, six miles from Smyrna, where they had an orchard of orange, mulberry and apricot trees, and a corner railed off in which Mrs Dennis kept gazelles, while her husband had stables for his mares. Not until early August did Dennis visit Ephesus for the first time. He told Falkener:

I have been greatly interested, not so much in the existing remains, although you have done so much to render them intelligible, as in the ancient topography. I had previously informed myself of the various opinions held as to the site of the temple, and had arrived at the conclusion that the concurrence of ancient writers was undoubtedly in your favour, the sole passage in Pausanias, which seems to have staggered you, appearing to me quite in harmony with your view as to the site. I take him to say that the tomb of Androculus was shown on the road which runs from the Temple (of Diana) by or near the Olympeium, and at the Magnesian Gates, i.e. the tomb was at the said Gates.

More than this, I think I can see in the marsh the very spot you point out as the site, dry and bare when all around is green with reeds, and, if I mistake not, showing signs of substructures. I had no opportunity of going to it to inspect it, but saw it from the slopes of Pion through my glass. I shall take an early opportunity of returning to verify the matter. At what season did you visit Ephesus? If it had been summer you could not fail to have remarked this patch of brown in the green marsh. You once showed me a letter from Wood, in which he speaks of some sunken columns. I should feel obliged if you would copy what he says, and send it me. I cannot ask him, when he returns. I remember you replied that what he had said was confirmatory of your view. He has recently disinterred the gates supposed to be the Magnesian, and has found some inscriptions which I hear Newton thinks will be likely to lead to the discovery of the temple.

I have been to Sardis, and am aghast at the vast size of the tumuli. My intention is to select one or two of the smallest and dissect them entirely till I find the chamber, and then apply the knowledge so obtained to the large mounds. It will be a dreary life in that Lydian desert. I shall begin operations about the first week in October. Meanwhile I am occupying my time in travelling. Have seen everything on and off the two railways — and am about to start for Pergamos, visiting the cities on the coast, Phocoea, Cyme, Myrina, Grynium, Eleaea, and Pitane, besides several inland sites on my return. . . I intend excavating the Temple of Cybele at Sardis — give me the benefit of your calculations as to the height of the columns, and any hints which you may think useful. Remember I have never dug at a Temple. Did you see any signs of reliefs among the ruins of that temple? The depth of earth which overlies it will have preserved the remains, although increasing the difficulty of disinterring them. I have been much interested also in the ruins of T. of Diana Leucophryene at Magnesia ad Meandrum, but the reliefs have been almost ruined by exposure. Are you aware if any of them have been removed to Paris? The style of art is not first-rate — many of the Amazons have stumpy figures, as in the Phigaleian marbles, but there is nevertheless much vigour and spirit in some of the scenes so far as one can judge from the mutilated reliefs. Give me your idea of the dates of these two temples.

Mrs Dennis unites with me in kind regards to Mrs Falkener and in friendly remembrances to yourself — and with our cordial wishes for your health and happiness.

I remain,
Yours very sincerely,
Geo. Dennis.

Remember me kindly to your sisters, who I trust are in good health. Address me to care of T.G. Staveley, Esq., Foreign Office.

The kingdom of Lydia came into existence some time after 700 B.C. and was at its height under Croesus, its last king, whose name is synonymous with wealth. In 546 Croesus was defeated by the Persians near Sardis and Lydia became subject to Persia. The Lydians invented the art of using gold and silver coinage. Their capital, Sardis, was situated at the foot of Mount Tmolus, on the banks of the river Pactolus, which flows into the Hermus, that greater river whose sands, according to the ancient poets, were covered with gold. Sardis withstood many sieges, only to be destroyed by an earthquake in the reign of Tiberius, who ordered it to be rebuilt.

Sardis, represented by the modern village of Sart, lies about fifty miles to the north-east of Smyrna. Dennis had obtained special leave from the Foreign Office in order to work at Sardis,

and it was quite easy for him to get there from Smyrna, provided
that the Hermus river was fordable, which meant not during the
heavy winter rains.

It was in that same year 1868, when Dennis first worked at
Sardis, that the brilliant young German Heinrich Schliemann,
working further north in Turkey, concluded that Hissarlik was the
site of ancient Troy.   From then on, Dennis knew that in the
Germans he would have serious rivals, and so it proved when at last
he returned to work in Turkey in 1879.

On September 18th, 1868, George wrote a long letter to John
Murray, the first for many months, and told him:

> I have been exploring the country, and visiting all the ancient
> sites on or near the coast between Pergamus and Ephesus. I
> have discovered some sites not hitherto recognised as ancient,
> and have been enabled to determine the exact locality of
> several Greek cities, on which even Texier has thrown no light.
> Let me observe, *en passant*, that the notices of the Greek
> cities of Asia Minor given in Smith's Dictionary are open to
> improvement, even tho' written by such men as Geo. Long
> and Lord Schmitz.   Of the Aeolian cities, for example, they
> place three on one and the same site, altho' the site of each is
> well determined.   In other instances they assign no site, or
> state that it is 'uncertain', although it is well ascertained. Should
> you contemplate a second edition of that work I shall be very
> happy to give you the result of my researches on all the ancient
> sites I have visited in this land.   I have not met anyone here
> who knows anything of antiquities in general.   Anyone who
> made a collection of ancient objects did so, it seemed, only in
> order to get as much money for them as possible.

During the winter of 1868-9 Dennis spent most of his time digging
at Bin Tépé, the site of the royal tombs at Sardis.   To James Murray,
Under-Secretary of State at the Foreign Office, he wrote on January
18th, 1869:

> My dear Sir,
>   Before I left England, you warned me that I should find it a
> thankless office to work for the Trustees of the British Museum.
> I was then unwilling to believe this, as up to that time I had
> had no reason to complain of their treatment of me.   But I
> have now better cause to remember your warning, and to regret
> that I ever offered them my services.   They forget that I am
> labouring for them without any hope of remuneration, so far
> as they are concerned, enduring a great inconvenience and
> hardships, risking my health by exposure in camp at this cold
> and stormy season, in my endeavours to serve them — con-
> siderations which should ensure me at least justice, and
> courtesy at their hands.   But in fact they treat me as though

they did me too much honour by allowing me to labour for them, snubbing me at every turn as though I were a clerk in their pay, and, worse than all, they refuse me my legitimate expenses, because, placing myself entirely in their hands, I did not bargain for justice beforehand. I now find myself some £250 out of pocket in consequence of this expedition, although the claim I make on them, and which they refuse to accept, is only about £100 — the balance being accounted for by the sacrifices I had to make in selling my effects at Bengazi, and by the higher cost of living at Smyrna. You may be assured that I am not ambitious of continuing my connection with them, and would gladly exchange it for some new consular appointment, to which I trust my 5 years' exile at Bengazi, to say nothing of my services under the crown in the Home, Colonial, and Foreign Offices since February 1829, may be considered to entitle me. I am not in a position to hear of vacancies, but should one occur in any consulate in the Mediterranean which you think me competent to fill, I shall feel very grateful for a word from you in my favour.

     Believe me
       My dear Sir,
          Respectfully and faithfully yours,
           Geo. Dennis.

He received a letter from Falkener, who was planning to take his wife and son to Switzerland the following summer, and he replied in a letter of February 28th 1869:

I heartily wish you could extend your tour this summer from Switzerland to Smyrna, and join me in exploring the temple of Cybele at Sardis. If you could do so, I think I could get funds for the work. I am quite convinced that so important a work should not be entrusted to a mere excavator like myself, but requires the presence of one well up in classic architecture. Pullan some years ago obtained a firman for that temple, but has never been able to obtain funds for its excavation. I should be happy to join him, if I could, but should greatly prefer your assistance. As to digging on my own account, that is out of the question, since I am sent here expressly in the interest of the Museum. I should inform you that hitherto I have met with no success at Bin Tépé. I have had great difficulties to contend with, that of procuring labour being the chief. Though I have been at work more than 3 months, I have penetrated the secret of only 2 mounds, and though neither showed any external sign of disturbance, I found I had been forestalled in both, in ancient times. I have a 3rd mound, more promising than the others, in hand, but have not yet found the chamber, though I feel persuaded that when discovered

it will prove to be intact. These are some of the smallest
mounds, carefully selected for their integrity. Each is constructed on a different principle. It were a hazardous
experiment to attack one of the 3 giant tumuli which tower
over the rest, unless with unlimited command of funds. That
of Alyattes has been rifled ages since. The sepulchral chamber
it contains, tho' 50 metres distant from the centre, is, I now
believe, the royal tomb, tho' at first sight that appeared very
improbable. One of its compeers is promising, as bearing no
traces of excavation on its surface. I wish I could give you
full particulars of my labours. I can only say that hitherto,
I have discovered nothing at Bin Tépé which throws light on
Lydian history or art, save the admirable masonry of these
sepulchres and the fragments of pottery and alabaster they
contain. I have however secured a most archaic figure, which,
when you see it, you will pronounce, I think, one of the
earliest works of the chisel in existence. It will hardly reach
the Museum for a month or two. Newton is coming out very
shortly to inspect my diggings and Wood's. I know nothing
of what the latter has done; I have not even seen him. But if
he is clearing the road eastward from the Magnesian Gates, as
I hear, he may work long I think before he finds the Temple.
I have found a nice spot for it on the other, that is, your side
of the city, and not far from the site marked in your plan, but
nearer the heights of Coressus. I have carefully paced the distance from what I take to be the city-walls on this side and
find it nearly the right distance. But my researches at Ephesus
have been limited to a day. There may be other spots to the
west of the city which are still more promising, for aught I
know.

Pullan has been exploring the T. of Minerva at Priene, with
what success I know not, save that when I met him in December he said the reliefs were better than he had anticipated.

I was greatly grieved to hear of Ashpitel's death — I had
known him for more than 30 years — he was alway's an invalid,
so that when I heard he was confined to his bed, I had no
apprehension that he was near his end. I shall miss him greatly. At my time of life men do not readily make new friends,
and cling more closely than ever to those of their youth.

Mrs Dennis unites with me in kind regards to Mrs Falkener,
and love to Lyon — may he ever be rampant!

> Believe me
> > Ever yours sincerely,
> > Geo. Dennis.

As the spring advanced Dennis grew more worried about his dwin-
dling funds: the Treasury had only given him five hundred pounds,

and this was now disappearing at a rather alarming rate. So on March 27th, 1869, he wrote a long letter to the Earl of Clarendon, describing the work he had done so far in Asia Minor, and stressing his need for more funds. Then on April 8th he wrote the following letter to Layard, who was still in London but was shortly going to take up his new appointment as Ambassador to Madrid:

Smyrna,
April 8th, 1869

My dear Sir,

I must apologize for troubling you again with my affairs, but I am somewhat in a fix about my excavations. I have not yet met with the success I had anticipated, having found myself forestalled in ancient times, but I have a mound in hand which I have explored to such an extent as to be satisfied it has escaped violation, and I have every reason to believe from the pains taken in its construction, and to conceal the sepulchral chamber, that this when found will contain something rich and rare. The fragments of pottery found in the mound, mark it also as of very early date. My funds, however, are now running short, and as Mr Jones continually warns me not to exceed the limits of the grant of £500 made by the Treasury in 1867, I may be compelled to abandon my work just at the moment when I am on the point of grasping the prize. Apart from this, as I have come to this land with a view to explore its ancient cemeteries, it would be a great pity, in the interest of archaeology and of the British Museum, if I were compelled to leave it before I have accomplished my mission. But unless I get additional funds I shall have no alternative but to return to Bengazi. In 2 months' time I must turn out of the house I now occupy, and either take another, paying a year's rent in advance, according to the custom of the country, or return forthwith to Barbary. This would be a great inconvenience and expense to me, seeing that the Trustees throw on me the cost of removing my family. Having incurred the expense of coming to this land I am naturally desirous to remain here, until Lord Clarendon sees fit to promote me to Palermo or elsewhere. I have written to his Lordship, asking him to continue me here for a while, on the same terms as heretofore, and also be pleased to assist me with funds, as, through your kind offices, he was so good as to do for my explorations in the Cyrenaica. One way of fixing me here for a time would be to give me a consulship *in partibus*, at Aidin for instance, as you kindly proposed to Lord Stanley, but whether that would now be practicable I know not. If you will kindly speak to Lord Clarendon on these subjects, you will add to the many favours for which I am indebted to you.

Mr Newton has recently arrived, and is now gone to Priene to see what Pullan has been doing there this winter. He postpones his visit to my diggings until the Hermus is fordable, but thinks with me that it would be greatly to be regretted that I should be compelled to abandon my work and declare my expedition a *coup manqué,* when a little more money might enable me to bring it to a successful issue.

Should means be found to retain me for a time in this land, I see no reason why I should necessarily renounce the visit to Marsa Sousah proposed by Lord John Manners, if I can be of service to your department there. My duties here are of course paramount, but as it will be neither easy nor safe to carry on excavations in this climate throughout the summer, they will not, so far as I can see, interfere with a run to the Barbary coast.

Believe me,

My dear Sir,

Respectfully and faithfully yours,

Geo. Dennis.

He knew he had a sympathetic audience in Layard, who had, during his expeditions to Assyria in the 1840s, always been on bad terms with the Trustees of the British Museum whom he considered to be inordinately mean and niggardly with their funds. In another letter written by Dennis to Layard about the same time (which is unfortunately undated, the first half of the letter having been lost) we see him giving vent to these feelings in even stronger terms. He still hoped that Layard would keep his name before Lord Clarendon with a view to a promotion away from Benghazi.

. . . I am now in a position to carry on excavations anywhere in the Ottoman dominions without neglecting my consular duties, for I have secured the services of an Englishman as superintendent of my workmen, an active, intelligent and trustworthy fellow, whom I am initiating into the mysteries of excavation, and whom I can keep at work with only occasional supervision. He speaks Turkish and Greek fluently. I also am making progress in the latter, and have already dispensed with an interpreter for that language. But to labour for the Museum is to return good for evil. I have been working for the Trustees, as you know, for years past, without any thought of reward. I have saved them expense in many ways. I have made great sacrifice of comfort and of health in their service. And now they punish me for my endeavours to serve them by throwing on me a large portion of the expenses of this expedition, simply because, I conclude, I did not bargain beforehand for justice. I placed myself with entire confidence in their hands, and the result is that I find myself at least £250 out of pocket. In three-fifths of that sum I have made no claim – my demand for the remainder has been rejected. I have therefore small encouragement to continue to labour *under the Trustees*, though I shall always be happy to do my best to enrich the Museum under the auspices of the Foreign Office.

In defence of the Trustees' attitude, however, it must be admitted that Dennis was not, after all, on the staff of the Museum; he was on the staff of the Foreign Office. He could hardly expect them to pay all his expenses, including the travel expenses of himself and his wife wherever he went. They gave him as much money as they could afford, and he did remarkably well with it. Charles Newton on the other hand, who had just arrived in Turkey, was a Museum official; in fact he had been promoted Keeper in the Department of Greek and Roman Antiquities in 1861, having been an Assistant in 1840.[1]   Richard Popplewell Pullan (1825-1888), whom Dennis also mentions in his letters about this time, was an architect and archaeologist who became a good friend to Dennis.[2] Pullan explored on his own account during the winter of 1868-69 at Priene, a maritime town at the foot of Mount Mycale, which had been built by an Athenian colony and had been one of the twelve independent cities of Ionia.

There can be little doubt that the real reason behind Dennis's desire to explore Lydia and excavate Sardis was that he was a staunch supporter of the theory that the Etruscans were of Lydian origin. In the introduction to his *Cities and Cemeteries of Etruria* he stresses that despite the opposition of Dionysius of Halicarnassus, the majority of ancient historians (beginning with Herodotus) believed that the Etruscans were a tribe of Lydians who left their native land on account of a protracted famine and settled in Italy; and, wrote Dennis in 1848, 'I confess I do not perceive that the crowd of authorities who maintain the Lydian origin of the Etruscans have been put *hors de combat* by the dictum of Dionysius. There seems to be life in them yet.' Was he right?

The British Museum had asked him to excavate the great tumulus-tomb of Alyattes, the father of Croesus, which was the most conspicuous feature in the plain of Karabel near Sardis. Herodotus had declared that it was surpassed in size only by the monuments of Egypt and Babylonia. But Dennis had not yet penetrated to the inner chamber when his work had to come to an abrupt termination in the summer of 1869. He felt that he was on the eve of important discoveries when his labours were brought to this sudden halt, partly by reason of his funds running out, and partly because he received the news that at last there was a move and a promotion for him: on July 28th, 1869, he was promoted Consul for the island of Crete, and the appointment was confirmed on August 10th. The

salary was to be five hundred pounds per annum, plus two hundred
per annum for office expenses.[3] This pleased him greatly, and he
returned alone to England, leaving his wife at Malta.[4] He acknowledged his new post in a letter to the Foreign Office written in London on August 26th, and again on September 2nd he wrote asking
to be allowed to take his family from Malta to Crete before going
himself to Constantinople to report to the Ambassador. During
September he sailed again to Malta, and left there on October 2nd,
arriving at Canea in Crete on October 15th. On October 26th he left
Crete for Constantinople, and after presenting himself to the Ambassador he sailed back again, being detained for a week at Smyrna
by tempestuous weather, finally reaching Crete on November 15th.
The six months which Dennis spent in Crete were peaceful and
quiet, although there had before his arrival been several disturbances.

On January 7th, 1870, he told John Murray that he was not
comfortably settled in Crete, and hoped that now Palermo was
vacant he would soon be transferred there. He was, however,
only too accustomed to disappointments and banishments to uncongenial places, and he hastily added, 'But what may be reserved for
me by the Parcae who spin the web of consular destiny in Downing Street I cannot tell'. This time good luck came his way, and
quickly, for on January 17th, 1870, he was officially transferred
to Palermo as Consul for the island of Sicily, the post he most
dearly cherished. He could not go there immediately, however,
but remained in Crete until May. On April 17th he wrote a letter
of sympathy to John Murray who had just lost a schoolboy son:

I have just heard from my brother the melancholy loss you
have sustained, and I hasten to assure you of my heart-felt
sympathy with you and Mrs Murray in this your deep afflic-
tion. My brother only states that you have 'lost a young son
at Eton' but does not give his name. It cannot be John, and
can hardly be Hallam, both of whom I know — I conclude it
is a younger son whom I do not recollect. I hear he was ill
only for a day or two, and died of congestion of the lungs.
It must be a fearful blow to you and to his mother. Truly
when I hear of friends suffering such afflictions, I am almost
content to be childless.

I have not seen the papers for many weeks, or I should
have known the event soon after it happened. But I am in a
transition state, gazetted to Palermo, but as yet without orders
to quit Crete. And my friends at the F.O. ceased to communicate with me for a long time, and now explain their silence by
telling me that a report had reached them from a neighbouring
Council that I was no longer in existence, having dropped dead
suddenly soon after reaching Palermo. The truth is that the
clerk of the Consulate, who was acting as Consul on Goodwin's

death, did die suddenly while signing the marriage settlement
of a young English lady, and my consular brother confounded
me with him. The wish may have been 'father to the thought',
for he applied for the post incontinently.

I am delighted to exchange Crete for Sicily, in spite of the
charms that Hellenic mythology, unexplored antiquities, recent
political events, and scenery unsurpassed in magnificence, throw
over this island. It is a miserable place for a residence. No
comforts, hardly the necessaries of life are to be obtained. I
caught a cold at Xmas, and through want of judicious treatment
and proper medicines, it turned to bronchitis, confined me for
2 months to the house, and still clings to me, changing me from
a vigorous and healthy man to, I fear, a confirmed invalid. I
can't even obtain a plaster to protect my chest in this wretched
labyrinth of filth and discomforts, from which, even with the
snows of Mount Ida in sight, I long to extricate myself.

I rejoice also in my transfer to Palermo to have the opportunity of preparing a 2nd edition of Sicily, as well as of Etruria.
I *hear* that the former has received high praise from a recent
writer on the Mediterranean — I forget his name — who classes
it among the best of your Handbooks. I am not vain enough to
take this *au pied de la lettre*, but he might truly have said that
in accuracy it yields to none. I am fully alive to its defects,
and will take care to remedy them.

The Dennises did not arrive in Palermo until May 22nd, when
George took up his new duties at the British Consulate in the Piazza
Marina, near the harbour, at a reduced salary of £475 per annum.[5]
He was allowed to stay in Sicily for the next nine years; in Sicily
he felt at home, and, while not for a moment forgetting his interrupted archaeological labours at Sardis, he was able to think again
about ancient Italian civilizations and about the desirability and
method of preparing a new and revised edition of his *Cities and
Cemeteries of Etruria.* He had always the support of Charles
Newton of the British Museum, who wished him to continue his
researches at Sardis, but for the opportunity to do so he had to wait
almost another ten years, until 1879 when he was sixty-five years of
age.

CHAPTER 8

CONSUL IN SICILY — AND BACK TO ETRURIA — 1870-1879

SINCE GARIBALDI'S liberation of the whole of Sicily by the end of 1860, it had taken another ten years to achieve the formation of a united kingdom of Italy. 1870 was the momentous year in which this at last came about, and when King Victor Emmanuel II entered Rome in September, 1870, and the brief resistance of the Papal army was overcome, George Dennis and his wife had already been installed in Palermo for three months. Palermo by this time was a city of some two hundred and twenty thousand inhabitants. The British Consulate was a spacious building of twenty-two rooms in which the Dennises soon settled down happily. Gone for ever was all the misery of Demerara and Benghazi. Sicily was going to remain at peace, the climate was delightful, official work was not too taxing, and George was going to revise his great book on Etruria, which very much needed to be brought up to date since its first appearance in 1848. In Palermo he was able to study in the Biblioteca Nazionale and the Biblioteca Comunale, where he was invariably given all possible help by those two industrious local Sicilian scholars, Gioacchino Di Marzo and Filippo Evola.

One of Dennis's first tasks on arriving in Sicily was to write on July 9th 1870, to the Foreign Office, suggesting that the British Vice-Consulate at Syracuse should be re-opened, having remained unoccupied since 1863; and he recommended that Mr N. Bisani should become the Vice-Consul. This appointment was sanctioned by the Foreign Office on July 21st.

Dennis had to send regular reports to the Foreign Office, of course, as a fulfilment of his normal routine duties, but there was nothing very serious to report. In 1871, for example, he reported on an outbreak of scab among the goats in the province of Girgenti; and from time to time there would be the wreck of a ship, which was sometimes a British one, in stormy weather off the west coast of Sicily. On July 8th 1871 he wrote to ask for a month's leave, and on the 16th of the same month he wrote a long letter to Lord Granville, the Secretary of State for Foreign Affairs, complaining of his poor salary and pointing out that he was not a businessman, and must be guaranteed a pension. His salary was only a basic £450, and the cost of living in Palermo had doubled since 1860. He had control over eleven Vice-Consulates throughout the island, and felt that he deserved a much better salary; at the same time he wished to be relieved of the 'mock privilege of trading', which alone, if it had been real, could have brought him in enough money to live on comfortably.[1]

Mr and Mrs Dennis were away from Palermo from July 28th until October 12th 1871, so that he managed to obtain a considerable extension of his leave. During that time they were in London, staying at Hill Side, Streatham, and no doubt George called on John Murray to discuss with him a new edition of the book on Etruria. By the middle of October he had resumed his duties in Palermo. 1872 and 1873 were not momentous years for him; in 1872 we find a tremendous amount of unpleasant correspondence between George Dennis and another English resident, a Mr D.W. Thomas, over the rent of the late Consul Goodwin's house.[2] In November, 1873, George again had to ask for one month's leave in order to visit Malta for treatment for his gout. On June 22nd 1874 he wrote a letter to John Murray on a totally unexpected subject:

Dear Mr Murray,

I write to you on a subject with which perhaps you may not sympathise as much as I do, although as it fills the most prominent and wonderful chapter of the history of modern Italy, it is of world-wide interest — I mean Garibaldi. The old hero, his fighting days over, has taken up his pen to commemorate, like Caesar, his exploits. He has written his own Memoirs, and has intrusted them for publication to a mutual friend, who requests my assistance as regards publication in England. For the General, wishing to make his pen more profitable than his sword ever proved to him, wants to secure the copyright of this work in America, England, France and Germany, as well as in Italy, and to reserve the right of translation for those countries. I therefore write to you on his behalf, and shall feel greatly obliged if you will answer the following questions at your earliest convenience. Is it necessary, in order to secure the copyright or right of translation in foreign countries, that the work should be first published in Italy? Can it not be simultaneously published in various lands and languages, by making arrangements for the exclusive publication in each land? Or could it not be published first in England? Are you willing to undertake the publication of this work, and on what terms?

It is written in Italian. The General has no one to suggest as translator. If you undertake the publication, can you recommend anyone for this service? If so the MS. would be forwarded to you without delay, i.e. if the General accepts your terms.

If you do not care to publish it, to whom would you recommend me to offer the work?

Can you recommend me a publisher in America who would bring it out on advantageous terms for the General?

It appears to me that the work is certain to command an

extensive sale, and beyond the cost of translation it would not
be expensive, for it requires few or no illustrations, and no
annotations. In its original form it occupies 670 pages of MS.,
all alike containing, I am told, 30 lines, and about 300 words.

You may be aware that there is another work by Garibaldi,
'The Thousand', about to be published in England, by some
inferior publisher — Cassell, I believe, but that the General
acknowledges to be a romance, and not strictly true in all its
details; while these Memoirs I now offer you, are his veritable
history, on which he has expended much care and labour.

I do not know Garibaldi personally. I have never seen him;
but I have heard so much of him from those who are, or have
been very intimate with him, that I am greatly interested in
him and am anxious to forward his views as far as lies in my
power. I am commissioned by the friend to whom he has intrusted his MS. to offer the publication of it to you in the first
instance, and I can assure you that no steps have yet been taken
in any other quarter — that friend thinking with me that it
would be better for his interests that the work should be
published first of all in England.

I had hoped to be able to revisit England this summer, but
I find it impossible. Should you ever be induced to extend
your wanderings so far south as Sicily, it would give me great
pleasure to do the honours of this beautiful city and island for
you, so far at least as the brigands, one of its most firmly
established institutions, will allow. With kind remembrances to
Mr Cooke,

    I remain,
        Very sincerely yours,
          Geo. Dennis.

I was grieved to hear of poor Pentland's death. You must miss
him greatly.[3]

Who was this mutual friend of Giuseppe Garibaldi and George
Dennis, and what happened to the General's memoirs? Garibaldi, at
his island home on Caprera, off the northern tip of Sardinia, finished
writing the preface to his memoirs on July 4th 1872, after completing 668 pages of manuscript. The work remained at first in the
hands of Speranza von Schwartz, Garibaldi's erstwhile mistress, who
kept it until the autumn of 1874. On November 17th 1874, Garibaldi
wrote to Madame Schwartz and told her that he had signed an
agreement to sell his memoirs to the Commune of Palermo for
200,000 lire, but this contract was never ratified, and the memoirs
were for a time in the hands of Enrico Albanese, to whom Garibaldi
later wrote (on May 18th 1875) from Rome, asking him to send
them to Menotti Garibaldi, the General's son, in Rome.

Clearly the mutual friend of Dennis and Garibaldi was not Mme von Schwartz; but there is every indication that it was Enrico Albanese. For this man was a native of Palermo, where he was born on March 11th 1834. Having taken his degree in medicine at the university there in 1855, he spent some time in Florence before joining Garibaldi's brigade in 1860, when he was nominated Director of the military hospital at Syracuse. In 1862 he took part in the attempt to liberate Rome and tended Garibaldi after he had been wounded at Aspromonte. He accompanied Garibaldi to the Trentino in 1866, and from 1865 onwards was Director of the civilian hospital at Palermo. It is likely not only that Garibaldi would entrust his memoirs to his faithful personal physician, but also that George Dennis, upon arrival at Palermo in 1870, would soon become personally acquainted with Dr Albanese as Director of the hospital.

Garibaldi's memoirs have, however, a curious history. The first complete Italian edition appears to be that published in Florence in 1888, long after his death. As to the English translations, there was an early version published in 1860, which describes itself as a 'new edition, revised and corrected' although the first edition does not seem to be recorded. This was translated by William Robson and edited by Alexandre Dumas the Elder. After that there was nothing until 1889, when the authorised translation of the full autobiography by Alice Werner appeared, with a supplement by that minor Florence Nightingale and friend of Garibaldi, Jessie White Mario. This work was published by Walter Smith and Innes. George Dennis's appeal to John Murray, therefore, was of no avail, for Murray never published any work by Garibaldi, nor did the General's memoirs see print in England until seven years after his death. Dennis had failed to persuade Murray, just as he had done with his own book on the Sicilian prisons. Murray was determined to avoid publishing any book which dealt with current or even recent political events in Italy.

Soon after the episode of Garibaldi's memoirs, which as far as George's efforts were concerned led nowhere, he began to come into contact with the indefatigable Sir Richard Burton, and it was not of his own choosing. For in 1874 Burton was writing his two-volume work on his visit to Iceland, which was published in 1875 under the title *Ultima Thule; or, a Summer in Iceland*. He wished to add in appendices some accounts of the sulphur industry in other parts of the world, so as to compare them with that of Iceland. He therefore wrote to George Dennis, who obligingly and most conscientiously supplied him with as much information as he could gather. This is printed as an appendix, 'Sulphur in Sicily', and Burton writes: 'The kindness of Mr Consul Dennis of Palermo enables me to offer the following sketch of sulphur in Sicily.

'Sulphur [said Dennis], it is well known, forms the most important branch of Sicilian commerce and exportation . . . In 1864 Sicily

worked about 150 distinct diggings, whose annual yield exceeded
150,000 tons . . .'

To this very fair report Mr Consul Dennis adds: 'I have no notion
that the supply of Sicilian sulphur is nearly exhausted; more deposits
are known than can be worked. There are many spots in the heart
of the island which abound in the mineral, but it must lie useless,
for as yet there are no means of conveying it to the coast for ship-
ment.'

Dennis was just as ready to supply information on any subject
concerning Sicily, whoever wrote to ask him for it. He did not know
that he had not done with Burton yet.

On May 15th 1875, George wrote to the Foreign Office asking
for three months' leave in England to get proper medical treatment,
since he was now suffering from stricture. He left Palermo on May
31st and arrived in London on June 7th. He asked for travelling
expenses from the Foreign Office for himself and his wife. They
stayed at 85 Thistle Grove, South Kensington, until November, for
George asked for, and obtained, further extensions to his leave in
August and October.[4] There are no letters to John Murray for the
year 1875, for the simple reason that there was no need to write
any: George must have visited Murray a number of times between
June and November to discuss the proposed new edition of the
Cities and Cemeteries. They left England once more on November
16th and reached Palermo on December 15th. George spent all of
1876 in Palermo except for one month's leave in May and June when
he revisited Rome and parts of Etruria. The journey back to Sicily
at the end of 1875 had also included visits to Bologna and other
places of Etruscan interest, and there were new painted tombs to be
described at Cerveteri, Orvieto and Corneto (eleven at this site), not
to mention new museums which had been opened since 1848. The
original idea for a new edition of the book on Etruria was to con-
dense the two volumes into one, of manageable size and unforbid-
ding length, but now Dennis realised that this would be impossible,
and the work would again have to be in two quite large volumes.
New maps and more illustrations would have to be added, but
perhaps the historical notes could be abridged. By the beginning of
February, 1876, he was able to tell Murray that he had just finished
revising volume one, which covered South Etruria. A general criticism
of the first edition had been that it contained too few illustrations,
and particularly of the painted tombs. This deficiency must now be
remedied. Dennis also asked Murray to send him a work by a Frenchman, Noel des Vergers, which had appeared in the past ten years,
entitled *Étrurie et les Étrusques*. But when this book came, Dennis
found it much less interesting than he had anticipated: M. des
Vergers, he said, might have written it without visiting the sites. It
was chiefly a history of Etruria, and not a personal account at all.

The new maps or plans which Dennis now prepared for Murray were of Fidenae, Sutri, Falleri, Bieda, Sovana, Pyrgi, Fiesole, Populonia and Rusellae; and to these he hoped soon to add plans of Chiusi, Arezzo, Perugia and Orvieto.

To his relief Murray wrote and expressed complete approval of the scheme to bring the work out again in two volumes, and asked Dennis to try to have the entire manuscript ready by the following November. Dennis asked Murray to try to obtain a photograph of the wonderful Etruscan sacrophagus in the British Museum, or at least of the loving couple on the lid, which he described as 'one of the most singular and quaint monuments of Etruscan art I have ever seen'. He could not have known that this famous object was a clever forgery.

Murray told him that Sir Richard Burton was now writing a book on Etruscan Bologna, and naturally Dennis was surprised and interested: he had no idea that Burton had added Etruscan antiquities to his other multifarious and world-wide studies, and as he himself intended to revisit Bologna as soon as possible during the coming season of 1876, he begged Murray to send him the book when it appeared. More than that, he actually met Burton briefly during the latter's hurried visit to Palermo. When Burton's book reached him the following November, Dennis found it very dull; on opening it he soon found himself described as 'my friend and colleague Mr Dennis'. But as George told Murray: 'I don't feel at all honoured by being booked as his "friend". I only saw him once for 5 minutes when he called on me in Palermo while Lady Denman (not Isabella) was waiting in the carriage, and would not come in. He came to my back-door, looked at my Arab horses, and was off. There is a friendship! But from what I have heard of his antecedents, he must be glad to claim any respectable individual, even tho' as insignificant as myself, as his "friend".' In Dennis's opinion the very first page of Burton's book 'showed the self-sufficiency of the man', and he had not treated Murray's handbooks at all fairly. He could not even quote the title of Dennis's book correctly: he called it 'Cities and Cemeteries of Western Etruria'. Burton was always in too much of a hurry. By the time he wrote the preface to this book in March, 1876, he had gone off to India again; and it was not surprising that *Etruscan Bologna* was badly received by the English reviewers, who called it inaccurate and slapdash.

There were other English-speaking visitors to Palermo whom Dennis found much more congenial than Burton. About Christmas, 1874, he had met an American named Dr Keep who pleased him greatly, as he told his friend Dr Henzen at the German Archaeological Institute in Rome. Then there was a Mr Middlemore, to whom he gave a letter of introduction also to Henzen. But above all there was Colonel Yule, whom George considered to be a fine, cultured gentleman and a true friend. Henry Yule, born in Scotland in 1820, had served for many years in the Indian Army, not only in India, but in Burma and Singapore too. With his delicate wife and their only daughter, Amy Frances, he moved to Italy in 1863, and in October, 1864, they settled in Palermo, the warm climate of which in winter was necessary for Mrs Yule's health. Palermo was their home for nearly eleven years, while Sir Henry worked on his huge translation and edition of Marco Polo's travels, as well as many other learned books and articles dealing mainly with the East. Mrs Yule died in the spring of 1875, and Sir Henry left Sicily for England, where he married again in 1877. His second wife died in 1881, and he himself was for years in poor and even declining health, although he acted as President of the Hakluyt Society from 1877 and President of the Royal Asiatic Society from 1885. He died on December 30th, 1889.

Ever since they first met in Palermo, Dennis and Yule were good friends. George invariably asked after Yule's health when writing to Murray after 1875, for Murray was Yule's publisher too. The daughter, Amy, however, was, according to George Dennis, an eccentric creature, and she did not deign to pay a call on the British Consulate to greet her father's old friend when she was staying by herself in Palermo.

Having for many years been a corresponding member of the German Institute in Rome, George became an ordinary member in 1876, and thus he was described for the rest of his life; the diploma making him a 'Socio Ordinario dell' Instituto Archeologico di Roma e di Berlino' reached him in the new year of 1877.

Meanwhile, after suffering another attack of pleurisy in the early spring of 1876, he was able to tell Murray on March 13th, that he now had six hundred pages of the new edition ready, and was busy incorporating the most important and interesting details of recent discoveries which had been reported in the Bulletin of the Institute during the past twenty-seven years, including, of course, some of his own. Apart from the copies of illustrations of the painted tombs at Corneto, and other scenes which a native Sicilian artist was working up from George's own sketches, he also had the advantage of his friend Edward Cooke's delightful drawings, from which he selected five for reproduction. Cooke lent him the whole of his Italian album of drawings and sketches. 'One was a view of the walls of Fiesole, very picturesque and effective. Another, Leghorn from the sea, a third, Radicofani — and the subjects of the other two I have forgotten, but E. Cooke will know which I selected'.

The maps and drawings reached Murray safely, and next George wished to send him some new landscapes, more pictures of painted tombs, a photograph of the celebrated Gate of Volterra, and another of the diggings-now going on in the necropolis of Orvieto. He knew that his first edition had been greatly wanting in illustrations of 'what are unquestionably the most characteristic and most interesting monuments of that early people — the painted tombs'. The drawings were all too large to send by post, but at the beginning of April he sent fourteen more illustrations, including three photographs. The drawings were later taken to London by the kindness of some willing traveller. Murray wanted the new edition to come out 'in a new page and type, which will make two handsome yet *portable* volumes': George hoped this did not mean that he would reduce the size from octavo to duodecimo. He was at first dissatisfied with the proofs of the plans, for they were not clear enough, and the lettering on them was too big and ugly. These details had to be worked out again.

Having received a telegram from Lord Derby giving him a month's leave, George left for Rome on May 17th 1876, and made a most successful tour, covering Cerveteri, Orvieto, Perugia, Florence and Bologna. He was back in Palermo on June 21st, having been delayed two days at Naples by the steamer.

But although George was so intent on finishing the new edition of his book, and wanted it to be as up to date and as accurate as possible, he was also keeping a close eye on his career, and although in July 1876 he celebrated his sixty-second birthday, he had no thought of retiring. In fact before undertaking the latest tour of Etruria he had written to Lord Derby on April 19th 1876:

My Lord,

I have the honour to state that having only this morning learned that the Consulate of Smyrna has become vacant by the death of Mr Cumberbatch, I took the liberty of sending a telegram to solicit your Lordship's patronage in that instance, should the vacancy be still unfilled.

I have already, through your Lordship's kindness on a former occasion, enjoyed the opportunity of making myself acquainted with that part of Asia Minor and its inhabitants, and without setting an undue value on my own qualifications, I venture to think that I could make myself useful to the Government in more than my official capacity, should I have the honour of receiving this appointment.

My chief object in asking for it, is indeed not so much to obtain an increase of emolument, although I admit that to be an important consideration, as to be placed in a position to carry out my archaeological researches in Asia Minor in the interest of the British Museum, which in 1869 were brought to an abrupt close by the refusal of the Museum authorities to ask H.M. Treasury for a small additional grant to complete my explorations at Sardis; and thus the great problem of the art and language of Lydia, and of their relation to those of

Greece, Etruria and Assyria, which I had fondly hoped to solve, remains still a mystery. In the Consulate of Smyrna I should have leisure to continue such researches, without neglecting my Consular duties; and I feel persuaded that to the principal British residents at that port, with whom I am well acquainted, my appointment to the Consulate would not prove unacceptable.

Humbly submitting this application to your Lordship's favourable consideration,

I have the honour to be, My Lord,

Your Lordship's most obedient humble servant,

Geo. Dennis.[5]

On the same day, April 19th, George also wrote to Mr T. Villiers Lister of the Foreign Office, whom he knew well, saying that he felt sure he would be the right man in the right place at Smyrna; and Lister noted: 'Mr Dennis is a very agreeable and gentleman-like person and really eminent as an archaeologist. He knows the East well but has none of the leaven of the Levantine in him'.

George returned to his duties towards the end of June, and on July 3rd sent Murray the remaining copy for the first volume, including all he had to say about Cerveteri and its painted tombs. As far as possible he had re-arranged the material to follow the course of the railways which had been built since he first explored Etruria. 'The bye-laws of Italy,' he said, 'are not much improved since I first knew them 35 years ago.' He was not satisfied with the reproductions of views of places, only with those of figures. He exclaimed: 'What a mess the man has made of the bridge at Bieda!' By late August he had plans of all the sites of Etruria except Chiusi and Orvieto.

By the end of September the busy season for consular work had arrived, and there was little time for work on Etruria. Sicily was experiencing a very bad wave of violence from brigands, and murder was not an uncommon occurrence. A young Englishman of twenty-two, a member of the Rose family who were among the biggest merchants and exporters in Palermo, was kidnapped and held to a huge ransom. George Dennis sent a letter to *The Times* protesting against the ineffectual behaviour of the Italian Government in dealing with such outrages, and pointing out that English residents were not safe as they walked about even within the walls of Palermo, let alone in the country outside. 'The Government does not seem to comprehend its first duty — to prove that it governs. The brigands evidently laugh at it.'

The printers were very slow at sending from England proofs of *Etruria*, but George was busy enough with official duties. Murray sent him a copy of Mr Gladstone's latest pamphlet which he had just published, and George's never very favourable opinion of the statesman deteriorated much further: 'Many thanks for Gladstone's pamphlet. It is utterly unworthy of him. It is W.E.G. gone mad! He is no longer the statesman, but the wild enthusiast. I cannot wonder, however, that you bring out his ravings, when the pamphlet had already reached the 56th thousand.'

The pamphlet in question was called *Bulgarian Horrors and the Eastern Question,* and it sold in all two hundred thousand copies. Layard too wrote: 'It is grievous to see a man like Gladstone turned into a mere vulgar pamphleteer.' 6

Dennis told Murray on November 13th 1876 that he thought an edition of two thousand copies of *Etruria* might be the most suitable number. 'I know that the first edition,' he wrote, 'was in great request in the U. States, for an English bookseller once offered me 4 guineas for every copy I could sell him for the American market. And that was the sum given for a second-hand copy by Quarritch [*sic*] at a recent book-sale. Therefore I think you may well reckon on selling 500 in the States. So many Americans now travel in Italy, and so many more now feel interest in antiquities than formerly.'

In December he excelled himself in his expression of bitterness against Gladstone and his son. 'I wish I could export Leone [a notorious Sicilian bandit] and his band to carry off Gladstone and Co. from St James's Hall, and keep their mouths shut while the Conference is going on at Stamboul. The vilest instruments may occasionally be turned to good account. "As crows the old cock, so crows the young one." Young Gladstone and Bright are trying to be as mischievous as their fathers.' And on January 13th 1877 he wrote: 'The Conference it seems is likely to come to a lame and impotent conclusion. Russia is proving herself a mere bully, and is unable to put her threats into execution. Turkey not only defies Russia, but her allies, Gladstone, Bright and Co., to drive her out of Europe. What will the next move be?' He would have been surprised to learn how prophetic of many twentieth-century events these words were!

As an intelligent man Dennis could not help being interested in politics, but he never attempted to take part in them. He was pro-Turkish and anti-Russian, and he blamed Gladstone for the way things were going so badly in Eastern Europe.

To take his mind off the Russian threat there came just at this time the exciting news of Schliemann's discoveries at Mycenae, and Dennis wrote to Murray on December 20th 1876:

What a fortunate man is Schliemann! His success may be the result in this case of forethought and skill, for I did not see his account of his first essays at Mycenae. But he is most fortunate in finding so many tombs intact, and so richly furnished. His success at Troy was a mere fluke. He had no right to expect anything where he found 'Priam's treasures' . . . I hardly think

he is to be trusted as an archaeological authority. I hope you
will publish his work on these Greek *scavi*.

I have some intention of visiting Greece next year to see his
excavations and those at Olympia.

1877 was another busy year, but it still did not see the new edition of the *Cities and Cemeteries* published. In March the Duke and
Duchess of Edinburgh visited Sicily for a week, and George had to
show them the sights of Palermo. At the end of April he wrote to
the Earl of Derby to ask for one month's leave in order to accompany
his wife to the baths on the island of Ischia, which her doctor had
advised her to take. Mr Joseph Rap, the Vice-Consul, was left in
charge while the Dennises were absent from Palermo, which they
left early in June for Naples. George had to leave Ischia on June 25th
to attend a trial at Taormina, and returned to Naples on July 3rd.
He resumed his duties at Palermo on July 25th.

Meanwhile that spring Schliemann had been in England again, and
Murray had agreed to publish his *Mycenae*. 'I don't doubt,' wrote
George Dennis to Murray, 'that it will be successful as a speculation.
So far as I can learn from those who have seen his finds, there is
little or nothing of beauty in them, tho' they must be very interesting from the place and circumstances where and under which they
were discovered. I see also that he has forestalled Montenegro, and
made peace with Turkey, and is about to continue his researches in
the Troad. I wish I had the chance of doing the same.'

As far as a return to Asia Minor was concerned, George had to
continue to exercise the utmost patience. Meanwhile he spent part
of his leave re-visiting Bologna, gaining the freshest information on
Etruscan subjects, and preparing more illustrations. In the middle of
the summer workmen came into the Consulate at Palermo to undertake extensive repairs, and like most Sicilians, said George, they
worked very slowly, so that he was constantly interrupted in his
writing. However, by September 16th he had sent all the chapters
of volume two except those on Rome and Bologna to the printers.
He decided to retain the two frontispieces of the first edition after
all. By the end of September he had sent off the chapter on Bologna,
and by October 14th the printer had the entire manuscript but for
the introduction and index. On October 24th he wrote to Murray:
'I am sorry to say that I have been so worried by workmen for the
last 5 or 6 weeks that I doubt if I shall have any of the Introduction
in print or at most a sheet or two. Important despatches also have
occupied much of my time, and tho' I usually rise at 3 A.M. and
don't go to bed till 9 or 10, I find the days far too short for my
wants. As for siesta I have never yet fallen into that bad habit, but
work thro' the day all the year round.'

On October 27th George wrote a long report (of nine large pages)
to the Foreign Office, justifying himself from charges made by the

Italian Government that he had 'raised pretensions contrary to the incontestable principles of the rights of nations' in the case of a visit which the police officers at Palermo proposed to make on board the British steamship 'Castalia', to ascertain whether there were on board any Italian subjects fugitive from justice, and that he had made use of 'unguarded language' in his correspondence with the Italian police on the subject. Such a contravention sounds very much unlike what we know of Dennis's usually placid and gentlemanly character.

On November 2nd he wrote to John Murray expressing his disapproval of the proposed alterations in the wording of the titlepage of his book. Murray had proposed 'New edition revised from recent visits to the Etruscan sites, with a chapter on Bologna'. George did not like this, and wished to keep to his own original suggestion of 'A new edition, recording the most recent discoveries in that land'; and he added: 'It strikes me that my title is not only neater, but more comprehensive than yours'. And so it was.

By Christmas 1877 he had received from Murray copies of Schliemann's *Mycenae* and *Cyprus*. *Mycenae* he felt sure must be selling well, especially as it had a preface by Gladstone, and he feared that *Etruria* coming after these books would strike the public as stale and dull.

On February 18th 1878, he told Murray: 'A few days ago I heard of Pullan's discovery of an ancient city of large size in the Tuscan Maremma, and as I could not omit to notice this I have inserted a 2nd Appendix to the Introduction — very short, which will just complete the sheet. When this is printed my work is finished — nothing now remains but the Index'.

He could not refrain from adding his personal thoughts on the latest political developments in the East: 'What a terrible state of affairs in the East! What a mistake England has made in allowing Russia to crush Turkey in this way! We have to thank Gladstone and Co . . . . I do not see how we can avoid war.'

There were more interesting visitors to Palermo. One of John Murray's sons came with his wife for a two-and-a-half-days stay in April, 1878, and George showed them round as best he could in the time. Murray Junior told him that his father had decided to delay publication of the new edition of *Etruria* until the following November, owing to the threatening political situation, and this he also mentioned in a letter of May 7th to Henzen in Rome: 'My book is finished — in print — but not yet published. The unsettled state of affairs in the East has so affected trade that my publisher says it would be folly to bring it out before the winter.' To Murray he said: 'You are the best judge of such matters. But I should like to know if the storm of war should burst upon us this year, what probability there would then be of publication. My arrangements

are in some measure dependent on your answer to this question.'
On April 19th: 'I had intended revisiting England this year, but if
I can get away at all I think I shall run to Greece, to see Mycenae,
etc., and perhaps to the Troad also. I want to form an opinion as to
Schliemann's four cities, for my faith in him is by no means strong.'

But once again he was denied a trip to Greece, and to England he
went in 1878 after all. Before leaving Palermo, he received two
visits from the famous German historian Dr Theodor Mommsen,
affable but absent-minded like so many great scholars; he was three
years younger than Dennis.

On May 7th George told Murray that he had of late been suffering so severely from an old complaint (it might have been gout, or
pleurisy, or stricture, all of which he had had) which if neglected
might prove serious, that he had determined to sacrifice pleasure for
health, and was returning to London for medical treatment such
as he could not obtain abroad. A week later, on May 14th, he wrote
to the Marquis of Salisbury stating his intention of leaving Palermo
that day for Marseilles on his way to England for urgent medical
attention.

On arrival in London, the Dennises stayed at Durrant's Hotel,
George Street, Portman Square, and on June 14th he asked for
another month's leave on medical grounds. On July 12th he wrote
as follows:

> Right Honourable Marquis of Salisbury, Secretary of State for
> Foreign Affairs.
> My Lord,
>   I have the honour to approach your Lordship with the ex-
> pression of my desire to be transferred from the Consulate of
> Sicily, which I have held for the last 8½ years, to a similar post
> in Asiatic Turkey, where, under the new Convention with the
> Porte, it appears probable that the British Consular staff will be
> considerably increased. An official residence of nearly seven
> years in the Ottoman dominions in Europe, Asia and Africa,
> has enabled me to acquire a varied experience of that land and
> its inhabitants, which I flatter myself might prove, under the
> present circumstances, of service to Her Majesty's Government.
>   My desire for this transfer is strengthened by the belief that
> in the improved condition of Turkey, which cannot fail to
> result from the exercise of British protection and control over
> her Asiatic provinces, it is likely to afford me opportunities of
> resuming my labours in the cause of archaeological science,
> from which the British Museum has already reaped no incon-
> siderable fruits.
>   Should there be no suitable appointment for me under the
> new arrangements about to be effected in the Levant, I have
> the honour to express the hope that I may not be forgotten as

a candidate for Your Lordship's patronage, in case a vacancy
should occur in the Consulate either of Beyrout or of Smyrna.
    I have the honour to be
        My Lord, Your Lordship's most obedient humble servant,
        Geo. Dennis.[7]
This time he was to be lucky. Before leaving England, however, it
occurred to him that the first edition of his *Cities and Cemeteries of
Etruria,* had in 1848, been dedicated to no one; now, thirty years
later, he decided that he wished to dedicate it to the man who had
given him so much help and encouragement, and who had just recently been knighted by Queen Victoria. Accordingly, while still in
London on July 19th 1878, George wrote the following letter to
Layard:

Dear Sir Henry,
    On the strength of an acquaintance of nearly 40 years, I
venture to congratulate your Excellency, which I do most
heartily, on the distinction Her Majesty has recently conferred
upon you — a distinction you have richly merited by your
valuable services to the nation, and which everyone regards as
but the prelude to further honours.
    I write also to ask your permission to dedicate to you the
new edition of my work on Etruria. I am anxious to do this,
because you are the patriarch of British explorers, by whose
example in resolutely overcoming enormous difficulties all
subsequent excavators have greatly profited, while to the
encouragement and assistance I have personally received from
you, I owe what small success I have enjoyed in such under-
takings. The book has been carefully revised, and considerably
enlarged by notices of many painted tombs and other interesting monuments which have come to light during the last 30
years, that is, since the appearance of the first edition, and I
feel entitled to regard it as a great improvement on the original
work, and as almost a complete record of researches in Etruria
down to the present day. If you will allow me to dedicate it to
you, I shall feel highly honoured. It has been in print for many
months, but its publication has been delayed by Murray on
account of the depressed state of trade caused by the impudent
though in great measure abortive Treaty of Santo Stefano.
    The protectorate and control now assumed by England over
Asiatic Turkey seems to open a wide field to antiquarian
research, of which I would gladly avail myself, either to resume
my excavations at Sardis, where I was on the eve of important
discoveries when my labours were abruptly brought to a close,
or to explore some of the many tempting old Greek sites on the
coast of Asia Minor. With this view I asked for the Consulate
of Smyrna, when it fell vacant some two years since, and with

this view I have now made application to Lord Salisbury for
any suitable post in Asiatic Turkey that may be created under
the new Convention, and, if that be not to be had, asking for
the reversion of Beyrout or Smyrna. Charles Newton would
like me to carry out my researches at Sardis, where in an
intact mound I expect to find a treasure like that of Kurium.
There is also much yet to be done in Cyprus, though that
island will of course be under the control of the Colonial Office.
There is some talk, however, of the probability of an antiquarian commission being sent to Cyprus, similar to that despatched to India some time since. Should this project be
realized, I should much like to take part in it: but this would
require a special grant of leave from the Foreign Secretary,
such as I obtained for my excavations at Sardis. This would
not interfere with my claim for a Consulate in Asiatic Turkey
should one fall vacant or be created worthy of my acceptance,
for at my age [he was sixty-four], after a life spent in the
service of the Government, I feel entitled to look for promotion. My official residence also of nearly seven years in the
Ottoman dominions — at Bengazi, in Crete, and in Asia Minor —
which has given me a varied experience of Turkey and its
inhabitants, should strengthen my claim to Lord Salisbury's
favourable consideration. My chief difficulty lies in obtaining
personal access to him. At the present moment, even had I an
introduction, I could hardly venture to intrude upon him, and
I am on the point of returning to Palermo. Although I have
addressed his Lordship officially, and have received a courteous
reply that he will make a note of my request, I feel the want of
a recommendation to his notice from some influential quarter.
If your Excellency will condescend to say a word in my
favour, it will have great weight, and doubtless ensure me
success; and you will thus add to the many obligations I am
already under to you, for the kind and opportune assistance
you have rendered me on former occasions, of which I retain
a grateful remembrance.
   I remain,
     Dear Sir Henry,
       Your most faithful and obliged servant,
        Geo. Dennis.

This letter Dennis sent to Constantinople, where Sir Henry Layard
was now Ambassador. Layard immediately gave permission for the
new edition of *Etruria* to be dedicated to him. Meanwhile the
Dennises left England on August 1st, arriving on the 11th at
Palermo, where in October George wrote the preface to his book
and the dedication to Layard, and sent these to Murray, who
brought out the book before the end of November.

Dennis spent the last fortnight of November, 1878, at Syracuse, working on its antiquities, for he had now conceived the plan of writing a new book on Sicily, of somewhat similar character to his *Etruria*, but not so exclusively antiquarian. He thought of devoting one volume to ancient Sicily and a second to modern Sicily. But no such work ever came to fruition.

On November 30th he wrote to Murray asking him to distribute a dozen copies of the new edition of *Etruria* to friends and eminent people, including one to the Duchess of Edinburgh who had recently visited Palermo, and one to the Marquis of Salisbury, whom he did not know personally, but who was his chief at the Foreign Office.

The new edition of George's book was soon reviewed in the *Athenaeum*, the *Builder* and the *Academy*. He wrote to Murray on January 14th 1879:

> The former [*Athenaeum*] is evidently by Alexander Murray of the British Museum who owes me a grudge for differing from him, and calling in question his opinions on the Etruscans in the *Contemporary* a year or two back. He therefore damns me with faint praise — laughs at me for holding to the oriental (not the Lydian, as he states) origin of the Etruscans, and kindly teaches me that Lydia was not Mongolia.
>
> I have just received another review in the *Academy* by Sayce — which is not ill-natured like Murray's, but finds fault with me for not being a philologist. I have stuck to the archaeological and artistic side of the question — which was quite enough. The philological, if properly treated, would fill two volumes of larger size. "Ne sutor, etc." The book is heavy enough as it is. It does not require to be further weighted with inscriptions which are almost always merely sepulchral, recording merely the names, relationships, ages, etc. of the defunct.

Archibald Henry Sayce was a thirty-three-year-old Oxford scholar, who for many years later held the Chair of Assyriology in the University, and was soon to meet Dennis in person. Sayce had thought the first edition of *Etruria* 'one of the most delightful archaeological books ever written,' but the new edition of 1878, he felt, was 'really a new work, of a much more ambitious character than the earlier book but without its personal charm'. He expressed his regret at the change in the form of the book, and although the review was anonymous, in some way or other its authorship became known to Dennis, who resented the criticism.[8]

On January 30th George wrote to John Murray: 'I conclude you have already sent a copy to Constantinople — Fancy the man on whom the Eastern Question mainly hangs amusing himself with lawn-tennis! Great men have always simple tastes — e.g. Gladstone, with his axe — and if Punch is to be believed D'Israeli grinds a barrel-organ! and Salisbury dances to his music!'

But if Layard played tennis, Winston Churchill painted many pictures and built brick walls. If great men had simple tastes, and George Dennis had no simple tastes, there is only one conclusion to be drawn. A few games of lawn-tennis would have done him good.

On January 28th 1879, Dennis wrote from Palermo, in answer to an enquiry from a certain Mr George H. Pope, who had written to ask him about early urban development in Italy, a letter which came into the hands of Mr John Bradford a few years ago. Referring to the so-called 'Pelasgic' cities, Dennis wrote: 'Years ago I made the tour of all the known cities of that antiquity in Italy and made careful drawings of their walls with the camera lucida, with the intention of writing about them, but I have never been able to put my intentions into execution'. Mr Bradford published a note on this subject, adding that it would be of the greatest value to archaeologists if these drawings could be found and published, but they have evidently not come to light and their whereabouts (if they still exist) are unknown.[9]

The so-called 'Pelasgic cities' of Italy, which Dennis tells us he had drawn, were colonies of the Pelasgi, an ancient Greek people who settled at various places in Epirus, Crete, Italy and Lesbos, apart from the Peloponnese. As Dennis himself explains in the introduction to *Cities and Cemeteries,* the Pelasgi came to Latium and Etruria before even the Etruscans, perhaps about 1800 B.C.

On February 4th he wrote to Lord Salisbury, pointing out that he had now been in government service exactly fifty years, since he swore allegiance to King George IV on February 14th 1829; and he now asked for a promotion so that he might be able to retire on a comfortable pension. If he were not promoted, he would have to retire on a pension of only two hundred pounds a year. On April 9th he asked permission to leave his post for one month. He and his wife, however, did not leave Palermo until May 24th for Naples, and thence for London, where they again stayed at Durrant's Hotel in George Street until July 2nd, when they again left for Sicily, arriving back in Palermo on July 6th.[10]

Above all else, Dennis longed to return to Smyrna to resume the excavations at Sardis which had been interrupted ten years previously, and he had no thought of settling down in England. His dearest wish was that now, at the age when most men retire, he might still obtain the Consulate of Smyrna. This time perfect luck came his way, and the Consulate of Smyrna was his. He felt this was almost too good to be true, but it *was* true. Someone in an influential position must have pulled strings on his behalf, and it was fairly obvious that this someone was Layard. George Dennis's appointment to Smyrna was dated June 23rd 1879.

CHAPTER 9

CONSUL IN SMYRNA – 1879

THE DENNISES arrived in Turkey once more to occupy the Consulate at Smyrna about the beginning of September, 1879, and on the 9th Dennis, in sending his first official despatch to the Ambassador at Constantinople, Sir Henry Layard, enclosed with it a private note thanking Layard most warmly for having used his influence at the Foreign Office to obtain this new post for him. No one had actually told Dennis that he had Layard to thank, but he knew that it could have been none other. Reade, Dennis's predecessor as Consul at Smyrna, told him that the Layards were likely to visit Smyrna that autumn, which indeed they did, in October, and while Mr and Mrs Dennis showed them the sights, Sir Henry and Lady Layard took photographs which they afterwards sent back from Constantinople. Soon after this visit Dennis received a telegram from Sir Henry, asking him to act as guide to two English ladies, the Misses Monk, who paid a short visit to Smyrna. He took them to the Castle Hill, to the Tomb of Tantalus and to Ephesus. They were very pleased with everything they saw, and then they left for Athens.

The British Consulate had seventeen rooms, twelve on the upper floor, including a pantry and three servants' rooms, and the rest, including kitchen and store-room, on the lower floor. In summer it was delightfully cool, but in winter not at all easy to heat, although by no means uncomfortable. Dennis scarcely found his salary to be adequate; it certainly did not permit him any luxuries.

He was as anxious as ever to resume his excavations, but it was now necessary always to obtain first a firman from the Porte in Constantinople or from the local Turkish authorities before anyone could begin to dig.[1] Dennis knew that the Germans were making good progress in their excavations on the acropolis of Pergamon, and were about to start sending back to Germany their most interesting finds. Accordingly he wrote to Layard on November 8th 1879:

Dear Sir Henry,

I have hitherto delayed writing to you on the subject of the firmans I am anxious to obtain for my excavations, thinking you would be too much engaged on your return to Constantinople to pay attention to any matter not of primary importance, but I now venture to trouble you with the request to use your good offices to obtain for me firmans for excavations

on the 3 following sites:— First — Sardis — where I am very
anxious to explore thoroughly the tumulus on the Bin Tépé,
which I was forced in 1869 to abandon for want of funds
before I had completed my labours, and in which I have every
prospect of finding a virgin tomb. Excavations can only be
conveniently undertaken on that site when the Hermus is
fordable; therefore I should wish also to include in the firman
the right of exploring the ruins of the ancient city on the
opposite bank.

Another site on which I have set my affections is Cymae,
now known, I believe, under the name of 'Namurt', on the
coast north of Smyrna, and a little to the S.W. of Ali Agha.
Owing to recent indisposition I have not been able to revisit
it yet, but I saw it 10 years ago, and was greatly struck with
the site as one of great promise. Its proximity to the sea has
brought on it the usual fate of ancient cities in such positions —
to. be stripped of its monuments — hardly one stone remaining
on another — but this, as regards its necropolis, is a most
favourable feature. An article in the *Times* of October 28th,
evidently written by Sayce or his friend Percival, states that
two colossal figures have recently been discovered here, for
which the German Government has paid £1,100. I have also
heard of recent discoveries of a casual character in its
necropolis, which makes me most anxious to explore it systematically. It is so near to Smyrna that I could work there in any
leisure intervals of Consular business.

Another site of great interest is that of Colophon, which I
believe I discovered on my former visit to Asia Minor, together
with its port of Notium. It is among the mountains which form
the northern horn of the Gulf of Ephesus, to the E. of Claros,
and just a few miles inland from its port of Notium, as the
ancients have described it. Its position in fact is so well marked
by ancient geographers that its name is inserted in Kiepert's
map of 1858, though in his later maps it is omitted. The site,
which I was told on the spot was called 'Tornajic', is an isolated hill surrounded by loftier heights, which prevent it from
being seen from a distance. It retains in great parts its ancient
walls, and many remains of early date. But I was too much
pressed for time on my visit to explore it satisfactorily. Its
high antiquity (for it claims to be the mother city of Smyrna)
and its very secluded position, quite off the beaten track of
travellers, and now in a most desolate region, gives it great
interest in my eyes. It is commonly confounded with Claros,
and many people here talk of it, as if they knew the site well,
but I have always found they were speaking of Claros. The
name of Colophon is not even mentioned in Murray's last

Handbook of Asia Minor, 1878.[2]

I fear that if I do not immediately ask for Cymae I shall be forestalled by the Germans. Therefore I will request your Excellency to apply first for that site and Sardis, if it be necessary to obtain a separate firman for each site. If the firman can embrace Colophon also, so much the better. But I am less likely to meet with competition in that quarter. Wood's original firman for Ephesus embraced Colophon also, but his Colophon, as I ascertained at the time, was Claros.

It seems to be putting the cart before the horse to ask for a firman before I have obtained a grant, but as regards Sardis I feel assured of Newton's assistance and I am ready to commence operations at Cymae on my own responsibility, on the understanding that if I am successful I shall be reimbursed. I shall communicate with Newton as soon as I have revisited these sites. He would probably prefer me to work at Cyprus, but that can be done at any time, and there is danger in delay in Asia Minor. I feel certain that he will approve of my selection of the other two sites.

Being well assured by past experience of your Excellency's readiness to forward my views in such matters, to the best of your power,

I remain,

Very faithfully and respectfully yours,

Geo. Dennis.

But exactly a week later Dennis had to write and tell Layard that he was too late for Cymae. The American Consul, Smithers, had obtained a firman for it instead. Dennis was very disappointed, especially as he knew that Smithers had had no experience in such matters; so he asked Layard to help him get a firman for Ephesus as well as Sardis. The Germans had had such success at Pergamon that everyone seemed to be wanting to start new excavations, and Dennis did not intend to lose the chance of Sardis, Ephesus and Colophon. A few days later Dennis met Smithers, who told him that he had in fact obtained firmans not only for Cymae, but for the whole coast of Aeolis, which meant all its twelve cities except Smyrna. So Dennis began to think: if the Germans had the whole of the Troad including Pergamon, and the Americans the whole of Aeolis, why should he not have the whole of Lydia? Thus he asked Layard to ask the Porte to let him have the entire coast from the Hermus to the Meander, including Sardis and Ephesus. 'This will include Clazomenae and Teos, Lebedo, and Colophon, Magnesia, Priene and Miletus,' he wrote to Layard on November 19th 1879.

My object is to explore the necropolis of those ancient cities and if not successful on one I should like to be able to turn my attention to another, without renewing my application to your

Excellency. This region then I shall be able to regard as my peculiar district archaeologically. I shall write to Newton at once and obtain from him some grant, however small, to enable me to complete the explorations at Sardis, which I was compelled to leave unfinished 10 years ago, and from which I hope to draw great treasure of artistic if not pecuniary value. Smithers has no grant yet from his government, but hopes to obtain one. He knows nothing whatever of excavating or of ancient art, but has a brother-in-law, Lawson, in the Ottoman Bank, on whom he relies for assistance. I am anxious to forestall them if possible, by disclosing the contents of an ancient Greek necropolis in Asia Minor — which has never yet, so far as I am aware, been done. I write in haste to save the post, and remain
     Dear Sir Henry,
          Yours most faithfully and respectfully,
               Geo. Dennis.
But then Smithers told Dennis about the new regulations; he would have a formidable obstacle in front of him, for before deciding on the precise spot where he wanted to dig, he would first have to make a trial of the ground, and ascertain to whom it belonged, and then come to an agreement with the owner; then wait three or four months before obtaining permission — thus losing the season. Smithers had applied in July and got his firman in November. Layard sent Dennis a telegram, advising him to write to the Pacha's secretary, asking for permission to make excavations in the interest of the British Government. This Dennis did, explaining to the 'Vali' (the Pacha's secretary) that the sites he particularly wished to explore were Sardis and its necropolis, Bin Tépé, several ancient sites on the coast of Ionia, between the Hermus and the Meander, including Miletus, and also the heights in the neighbourhood of Ephesus.

'I represented to the "Vali", ' he told Layard on December 17th:
     that I was anxious to obtain a firman which would include
     several sites, because in certain localities, owing to the insalub-
     rity and other causes, I could work only for a short time during
     the year, while by obtaining a firman for a district, such as
     that I had specified, I should be able to transfer my opera-
     tions from one site to another, as I might find it convenient,
     without the loss of time which would attend an application
     for an additional firman for each site; and also because until
     I had satisfied myself by tentative explorations, I could not
     be in a position to specify the precise locality where my labours
     would be likely to be attended with the most advantageous
     results.
     I assured the Vali at the same time that my excavations

would not interfere with the public convenience, or prove in any way injurious to the public interests, and also that I should not venture to trespass on private property without coming to an understanding with the owners.

I trust you will approve of my request, and give me your support. I hear that the Germans, when they have finished their labours at Pergamon, will ask for a firman for Sardis and Miletus, and I want to forestall them. I hear that at the latter site there are many reliefs which have been re-covered awaiting further excavations. I have an excellent jackal, who gives me trustworthy archaeological information.

Mrs Dennis unites with me in presenting best compliments to Lady Layard. Believe me, dear Sir Henry,

Most respectfully yours,
Geo. Dennis.

This was how matters stood at the end of 1879. About the middle of December Mrs Dennis had to take to her bed with a bad attack of rheumatic gout, and could not move for a month. Her husband therefore could not go out, but could only attend to the urgent business in the office. However, he must have spent a large part of Boxing Day writing an extremely long letter to Layard on another problem. (He declared that it was written 'amid a thousand interruptions,' but nevertheless he wrote a letter of eleven sides that day.)

Evidently Edwin Freshfield, who was in the habit of paying yearly visits to the property at Smyrna which he had inherited from his father-in-law, had expressed a desire to move Dennis and the Consulate into a smaller house, on the grounds that Dennis's small salary did not permit the upkeep of so large a house as the present one.[3] Freshfield had offered to purchase the Consular property for £8,000, 'or to give in exchange a piece of ground, much smaller than that occupied by the present Consulate, and which has the disadvantage of being cut in two by a street, on which he proposes to erect a new Consular residence and offices, with a church, prisons, and other outbuildings'. Dennis was disgusted with this idea, and had already written to tell the Foreign Office that the sum offered was far below the true value, which he placed at between twelve and fifteen thousand pounds. The Government had received the Consular property from the old Levant Company, and from its situation and the increasing trade of Smyrna, said Dennis, it was becoming every day of more value. He thought that Freshfield was trying to make a nice profit at the expense of the Government, and he told them so, although not officially, as he did not dare to write direct to the Secretary of State for Foreign Affairs on so delicate a topic because he did not know the full details of the negotiation. But the general character of Freshfield's proposal

Dennis had learned from his architect, J. Werry, who had just returned from England, and 'who expects to be employed in the
erection of the new buildings, should the negotiations have a termination favourable to Freshfield and himself'. Dennis called it 'a
gratuitous piece of impudence' on Freshfield's part to claim that
the house was too large for the Consul. The fact was, he said, that
the house was not at all too large; it was smaller than the Consulate
in Palermo had been, and Dennis wanted a few spare rooms to put
up guests who might come to stay, and this, of course, included
Sir Henry and Lady Layard. Dennis was making these spare rooms
as attractive as possible. He was sure that the residence needed
little repair, and he hoped that Layard would tell the Government
so. If the Government insisted on selling the property, they might
at least put it up for auction; but he hoped they would not dispose
of it at all. Thus matters rested as the year 1879 came to an end. But
before the year was over, Dennis had made the personal acquaintance
of the man with whom he at first quarrelled and later became firm
friends; Professor Archibald Henry Sayce came to Smyrna with a
companion, and they were welcomed there by Dennis. Sayce knew
that it had been Layard's influence which had obtained the Smyrna
Consulate for Dennis, and he found Dennis to be a most congenial
host. A few years later, Sayce was to show his good will towards
Dennis in a very practical way.

CHAPTER 10

ADVENTURES IN TURKEY — 1880-1884

IN 1880 Dennis celebrated his sixty-sixth birthday, but his energy for travelling and his zeal for exploration remained undiminished. The next few years were to be most adventurous for him, and were to bring him into contact with new and interesting scholars. Firstly, there was a young Frenchman of twenty-two whom he met for the first time at Smyrna in 1880: Salomon Reinach (1858–1932) who worked for the Louvre and was a brilliant archaeologist. The French were excavating at Myrina in Aeolis, where Dennis visited them and helped them to search for a Hittite relief in the neighbourhood. They failed to find it, although it had been seen and described twenty years earlier by a French land surveyor. George Dennis collected from Myrina at various times a number of statuettes which were described in an auction sale catalogue in 1894.[1] When Reinach fell ill and was admitted to the French hospital in Smyrna, Dennis came to visit him every day, and, said Reinach, he was 'very kind'. For years to come Dennis and Reinach exchanged many letters on archaeological subjects.

By the middle of January 1880 Mrs Dennis was much recovered from her painful illness and her husband was anxious to start moving about the country again, revisiting his old haunts and exploring new sites. He intended first to revisit Sardis, where he wanted to see what damage had been done to the temple. 'Diran Effendi assures me,' he wrote to Layard, 'stringent orders have been given by the Vali to put a stop to these demolitions. Our local papers have just published a decree on the subject, for which we are doubtless indebted to your Excellency'.

As Dennis discovered for himself a month later, 'the beautiful masses of marble, many of them architectural fragments of the Temple, which encumber the site, have not a few been broken up into chips for the lime-kiln, and I hear that the offenders are persons connected with the railway. Similar destruction has been going on among the other early remains of Sardis, especially at the so-called "Palace of Croesus". I have sent word to the Kaimakam of Salikli, the nearest Ottoman authority, to prevent a continuation of this vandalism'.

Meanwhile red tape of one kind or another was making it increasingly difficult for Dennis to advance his plans for further exploration. Turkish regulations forbade any one person to excavate on two sites at the same time; so at the Vali's suggestion Dennis persuaded

Mr Purser, the Director of the Ottoman Railways, with whom he was on good terms, to apply for a firman for Sardis, while Dennis applied for Ephesus.

He continued to be worried about the Germans, who had done so well at Pergamon that the German Government had sent another gun-boat to Smyrna to take away the most recent discoveries. Dennis had heard of some monuments recently unearthed at Miletus, and that the Germans had their eyes on this site too; but he knew that they had applied for an extension of time at Pergamon, and he hoped this would keep them too busy for Miletus.

At the end of January Dennis left Smyrna for a week's tour of Sardis. When he returned, there was a telegram from Layard telling him to go and see the Konak. Further red tape hampered him, as he wrote on February 7th: 'The Pacha tells me I must go to Magnesia and see the Mutasarif about the matter, who will send a person with me to the spot to see if there is any objection, and this person will make his report to the Mutasarif, who will forward it to the Vali. There appears then to be some hope of a firman in this case, in spite of the red tape in which it is wrapped up. But in the other case, where I ask for a firman in my own name, there seems no disposition to grant it. To Diran Effendi I explained exactly what I wanted, and at his suggestion, I asked for permission to dig in the hills around Ephesus. Yesterday, however, I received a letter from the Vali, copy of which I enclose, which appears to me to be a polite but decided refusal.' The objection did not appear to be raised by the Vali, who was on the whole co-operative, but at Constantinople, where the Porte seemed to be jealous of the German discoveries at Pergamon and therefore hesitant to allow any more foreigners to proceed with their desired digs.

Later in February Dennis went back to Sardis, accompanied by one of the officers of the Mutasarif of Magnesia, to whom Dennis pointed out his tumulus of Bin Tépé and the Temple of Cybele as the spots which he most earnestly wished to explore. Bin Tépé, said the officer, belonged to the Government, and Dennis must not touch it, while the Temple of Cybele belonged to a local landowner with whom he could come to a private arrangement. 'At Ephesus,' he wrote to Layard on February 21st:

> It is not so easy as at Sardis to comply with the regulations, for until I have made experiments on the spot, and tested the ground, I cannot state on whose land I wish to dig, and there-fore cannot obtain the written consent of the proprietors. And it is not so easy at the present moment to make such experi-ments, for a friend of mine in that district writes that he has been informed by the Chief of the Police in Smyrna that 49 brigands have just landed on that coast from Greece. Until that district becomes more secure I shall not venture to encounter

such dangers. Therefore, if I cannot obtain a firman for Ephesus without making preliminary researches, I must give it up. Here for the moment matters rested. Dennis had other worries at this time in Smyrna, connected rather with his consular duties than with archaeology. One of them concerned the dispute between the Roman Catholics and the Protestants, and in this he was on the side of the Protestants, calling the Catholics 'aggressors'. The Roman Catholic Archbishop was requesting the cession to him of the old Protestant cemetery. First they had tried to purchase the ground almost by force; but having been thwarted, the Archbishop was now 'content to beg what he was unable to obtain by violence'. Dennis was very sad to think that religious differences were allowed to influence all disputes between one set of the community and another, even when they did not concern religion at all. The other preoccupation of this time concerned the harbour dues at Smyrna. Dennis was determined to protect the rights of the British merchants who landed there against the grasping designs of the Turkish authorities and the French firm of Messrs Dussaud, who were trying to 'force their Tariff down the merchants' throats.' He wrote at great length on this subject to Layard throughout these early months of 1880. 'I have heard fears expressed by not a few,' he wrote on March 3rd,

> that these charges will drive trade from Smyrna. It is already seeking other channels. The coal-trade has already shifted its grand depot to Syra — and Vourla, Chesmeh, and Scala Nuova are indicated as probable rivals of Smyrna, at least in the export trade. The merchants all agree on one point, that the new Tariff is no improvement on the present as regards reduction of dues, and that it offers no adequate compensation for the loss of the 100 pics. When I saw M. Elie Dussaud the other day, I told him plainly that I thought he had acted unwisely in not attempting to come to an understanding with the merchants as to the Tariff. He said he was always ready to meet them, but they were most unreasonable in their demands. I questioned this, and reminded him that whenever they had applied to him for information, he had always repulsed them by telling them he had nothing to do with them, only with the Turkish Government, and I told him that I thought he would not be able to close the 100 pics and put his new Tariff into execution, unless he arranged matters with the British merchants.

So Dennis called a consular meeting to discuss the question, and found that the American and German Consuls were in complete agreement with him, while the rest (Italian and French in particular) were indifferent.

In March 1880 Dennis was still feeling utterly frustrated with

regard to the excavations which he so earnestly desired to resume.
He had a low opinion of the Turkish authorities, who, he said, were
only interested in *backshish*. Moreover the land was overrun with
brigands. At the Vali's suggestion he went to Magnesia and obtained
a favourable report from the Mutasarif of that town. This official
arranged to send with Dennis an escort to Sardis and likewise the
Kaimakam of Salikili sent a man with him; to these two persons
Dennis had to point out exactly where he wished to dig.

> I showed these officers just what I wanted to do, and they, I
> conclude, have made their report, but the result is that I am
> no nearer a firman than ever. He of Magnesia calls on me for a
> plan of Sardis and Bin Tépé, which I am not going to make. My
> journey there and back cost me nearly £10 — and I cannot
> afford to repeat the process with a very uncertain result. News
> reached me yesterday (5th March), that a Railway Station
> beyond Sulikli has been broken into by night by Zebeks, and
> robbed — and the country round Ephesus has for some weeks
> been in the possession of the brigands. So my chances of mak-
> ing myself useful to the B.M. in Asia Minor are small indeed.
> I might do something in Cyprus, if I could be spared from
> Smyrna.

But matters eventually improved, and Dennis did not go to Cyprus.
In the next three years he was able, after all, to carry out his explorations at Sardis, Clazomenae and other sites in Turkey. But not
immediately.

Many of the brigands who were making the interior so dangerous
had fled there to avoid the conscription, but Dennis could not
understand why the Turkish government had to impose conscription when at the same time they were disbanding regiments every
day. The Vali informed Dennis that he had no power to deal with
the brigands: if he ever sent a complaint to the Porte, the answer
always came back that Smyrna was perfectly tranquil, and that he
must diminish the police by one or two hundred men. The Vali, on
the other hand, who had not more than three hundred men, felt
sure that he needed seven hundred. 'The Government,' Dennis told
Layard on March 8th, 'like that of Italy, is far too lenient with these
rascals, who ought to be treated as pirates, and shot down without
mercy whenever they resist the police. They are murderers by
profession, and should be treated like wolves or hyaenas — and not
like prisoners of war, as they are in Italy. I see from the papers that
they have given your Excellency trouble enough of late in Mace-
donia.' And on the 19th March he wrote to Layard that the whole
country round Ephesus was infested. 'A friend just returned from
Priene tells me he was obliged to take an armed escort of 18 men!'

Not until the last day of April was Dennis able to tell Layard that
he had at last obtained the written consent of the owner of the

ground on which the Temple of Cybele at Sardis stood to excavate on that spot, 'on condition that I make good any damage I may do to the ground'. Nothing now seemed to prevent him from obtaining a firman for Sardis and Bin Tépé in the name of Edward Purser, and he sent Layard a copy of the letter which Purser had written on January 19th requesting permission to dig there over a period of two years. 'The two spots where I wish to dig,' wrote Dennis to Layard on April 30th,

> are within sight of each other, but separated by the river Hermus, which is not at all seasons fordable — so that I must regulate my proceedings on this site by the state of the river. In 1868–9 I was sometimes unable to cross the river for 3 or 4 weeks at a time, and was consequently half starved. The Pacha, and his secretary Diran Effendi, not being at this moment at Smyrna, some little delay may occur in forwarding the paper containing the written consent to Constantinople. But I will let you know when it goes hence, and if you will kindly back it up at once, I may have a good chance of success. I have let them know here that if they expect backshish they will get none, and that it is of no use to throw difficulties in my way in the hope of extracting money from my purse.
>
> Mr Smithers, my American colleague, who in November last obtained a firman for Cyme, is about to leave Smyrna, having an appointment in China. I have asked him to transfer his firman to me, but he has not yet decided what to do with it. Hitherto he has done nothing in the way of scavi, not being able to obtain a grant from the New York Museum as he had expected, for that Company is deeply in debt at present and cannot help him. The firman was granted to him personally, not to the American Government, with power to transfer it. If Schliemann heard of this, he would like to take it over, I doubt not. But I hope to make some arrangement with Smithers by which a share of the proceeds of my diggings there should be placed at his disposal. I am now writing to Newton on the subject.
>
> Since writing the above I have seen Diran Effendi, who has returned unexpectedly to Smyrna, and who promises to forward the document containing the proprietor's consent by tomorrow's mail. He assures me there can be no further difficulty, and the firman must be granted at once.

At long last, on May 17th, the firman arrived, and Dennis wrote a letter of profuse thanks to Layard. But ten days previously he had read in the papers with genuine regret that Layard was planning to leave Constantinople for good and return to England. He had feared that the return of Mr Gladstone, whom neither he nor Layard liked, to power might cause Layard to resign as Ambassador to

Turkey, but he hoped that as Lord Granville was again at the Foreign Office Layard would not find it necessary to take such a drastic step. However, Layard did so, and at the beginning of June he and Lady Layard left Constantinople for London. Before going, Layard was asked by Dennis to put in a word for him at Sardis, where he had heard that the Germans too were asking for a firman. The German Government was intending to establish a commission in Asia Minor for the prosecution of excavations, and Dennis was afraid that he might be forestalled at Sardis as he had been at Cyme. But just in time the firman came.

On May 13th, William Ramsay arrived at Smyrna and immediately met George Dennis, whose first thought was that Ramsay could be of immense help to him at Sardis. William Mitchell Ramsay, born at Glasgow on March 15th 1851, was thus twenty-nine when he first came to Turkey, and he brought his young wife with him. He was a brilliant classical scholar at St John's College, Oxford, and afterwards a Fellow of Exeter and then for a short time of Lincoln College, and Professor of Classical Archaeology for one year, 1885 — 86, before moving back to his native Scotland as Professor of Humanity at Aberdeen University until his retirement in 1911. Ramsay early gained the reputation of being the foremost British scholar on the geography, history and theological background of Asia Minor, and in course of time he wrote many weighty books on these subjects, lectured in America, and lived to be eighty-eight. He first came to Turkey under the auspices of the Asia Minor Exploration Fund newly organised by Oxford University. From 1880 to 1884 he spent more time in Turkey than in England, and learnt to, speak Turkish better than Modern Greek. Before long he, Dennis and Edward Purser (the Manager of the Ottoman Railways) were to set out on an exciting journey together.

Nowhere in his voluminous writings on Turkey have I found Ramsay mentioning Dennis by name, but in 1909 he wrote as follows:

> When my wife and I first landed in Smyrna in May, 1880, brigandage was rife, and the streets of the city were unsafe after evening came on. Robberies and murders occurred in the most public parts of the town, and blackmailing was common. Our Consul forbade us to make any excursions, and destroyed my whole reason for existence in Turkey. I had access to information a hundred times better than he could command as to the state of the country. Bands of brigands cannot go about without their movements becoming known to the peasants in the mountains. The Consul, who knew no language of the country, and was far too great a man to have or desire access to the useful sources of information, was quite unfitted to determine what we should do or what was safe, so he freed himself from

possible blame by ordering us to stay at home. We did not obey him, but went about the disturbed country, acting prudently, getting information from a good source, and never letting our plans be known to any one before we actually rode out of the town.

Then I received an official warning that the Consul had written to the Foreign Office, informing the authorities that I persistently disobeyed his orders and warnings, and that he washed his hands of all responsibility for me. My wife, being only a lady, was not included in the denunciation. We set the proper value on this warning, and carried out the work which I had been sent to do. But these facts may show what would be the fate of any Briton who let himself be guided by a Consul ignorant of the country, its people and its language, free from any desire to help his countrymen and only eager to avoid trouble, and above all not to send home any business which might trouble the Foreign Office and endanger his standing with the authorities in London.

From that time on I made it a rule never to go to a Consul on business, but to be on friendly terms with them all in private life. Unluckily, as the years passed, rules in Turkey became more stringent about travelling, and we were compelled to procure some papers through the Consuls. First of all, a passport was required, and in 1884 we got a joint passport at Athens.

The Consuls, however, seem to be personally not to blame in many cases, where they have to refuse perfectly reasonable requests . . . But in private life, apart from official business, it has been my fortune to receive from many Consuls a great deal of kindness and help. As officials they would not move a finger to aid my exploration, but as private persons many of them have been the pleasantest and most useful of associates, from whom one could learn a great deal. The distinction was stated to me by a Consul who unofficially was kindness personified, but who pointed out that officially it was no part of his duty to do anything for me.[2]

The anonymous Consul here referred to can be none other than George Dennis, who had been dead eleven years when Ramsay wrote thus of him. Had Ramsay not been careful to draw a distinction between the Consul's official duties and his personal actions, we could have thought of him as ungracious and ungrateful towards Dennis, who, officially, was only acting in the best interests of the personal safety of Mr and Mrs Ramsay as he would have done with any other British travellers; and unofficially may be supposed to have had every sympathy with Ramsay's wish to carry out his explorations. Indeed, as we shall soon see, the two men were not long after Ramsay's arrival travelling companions on a dangerous excursion into the interior.

In July 1880 there was a severe earthquake which wrecked Dennis's Consulate and compelled him to 'remove bag and baggage to a country-house, where I have been pic-nicking ever since,' as he told Murray in a letter of the following December 31st.

He was violently opposed to the Liberal Government in England. 'How indignant you must be at the present state of things in Ireland! What an inglorious mess the Liberals have made of their government, or rather, negation of government . . . In spite of brigands and the general corruption, life and property are more secure in Asia Minor than in Ireland. I almost wish myself a Turk, when I might at least claim the merit of consistency. If the Porte be sublime, Liberal England is certainly ridiculous!'

As usual, he complained of the lack of funds even though he now had a firman for excavating at Sardis, and he understood that 'it is useless to expect money from the Liberal (?) Government for such absurd and useless purposes'. Anything but liberal! But Dennis never lost hope. He felt that certain friends in England would help him. 'Some very quaint and beautiful jewellery recently found in a Lydian tomb whets my appetite for research. It is of somewhat similar character to the wonderful gold jewellery found at Palestrina a few years since, though more archaic. If I could get only £100 or £200 to begin with, I might do something.'

Later in that year, 1880, it seems probable that Dennis visited Constantinople, but his plans to visit the Troad on his return journey did not materialise.

Early in 1881 Sayce arrived at Smyrna from a tour of Egypt and Palestine. He writes in his autobiography:

> At Smyrna Dr Dennis [Dennis was not a Doctor until 1885] gave me hospitality, and a day or two after my arrival we made an expedition to the Homeric 'Niobe' on the northern side of Mount Sipylos. Dennis had discovered through his glasses what he believed to be a Hittite inscription on the right-hand side of the seated figure, and naturally 'the High Priest of the Hittites', as Gladstone had just called me in the *Times,* was anxious to see and verify it. We carried two long ladders with us; these were tied together, and while their foot was planted in the earth and built up with stones two stout Turks on the summit of the cliff held a rope which was attached to the topmost rung of the ladders. I then climbed up till I stood in the niche in which the figure is carved. Here I copied and took a squeeze of the inscription, which I should translate: 'Adoration to the goddess Mama, the queen of the rocks'. It shows that the figure whose origin had been forgotten when the Greeks of Homer wove their legends round it was that of

the great Mother-goddess of Asia Minor, and that the Hittites
of the East had once come as conquerors to the confines of
the Aegean Sea. Above the head of the goddess I found the
representation of a lotus or ostrich feather which is invisible
from below.

On March 24th 1881, Sayce wrote a very long 'Letter from
Smyrna' which was published in *The Academy* (No. 466, April 9th
1881, pp. 261–3), the relative passages of which are as follows:

A day or two after my arrival at Smyrna, I accompanied Mr
Dennis upon a visit to the figure of Niobe, which I shall leave
him to describe in his own words. I will only say that, by tying
two ladders together, we succeeded in climbing up to the
inscription he has discovered at the side of the figure, and in
examining the details of the figure itself more thoroughly than
had been done before. The inscription consists of four very
legible Hittite characters, the cap, the bent arm, the bull's
head, and the boot — which all occur in the inscriptions of
Carchemish and Hamath — and two, or perhaps three, others,
which are unfortunately much obliterated. Thanks to the ladders, we found that a curious ornament, in form like a lotus
bud or the uraeus serpent, rises from the middle of the back of
the figure's head, and that a single lock of hair is rudely sculptured in an oblique line across each of the shoulders. In fact, I
have been more struck than ever with the Egyptian character
of the figure and its resemblance to the sitting image of Nofre-
tari, the wife of Ramses II, carved in the rock a little to the
north of Abu Simbel. However, when we remember the
Egyptian-ising character of the Hittite sphinxes at Eyuk, or
the close relations that existed between the Hittites and Ramses II, we need not be surprised that Egyptian art should have
had an influence upon the rude art of the Hittite conquerors
of Western Asia Minor. We further found two shelf-tombs
cut in the rock a little above the figure of Niobe on the western side; and, if Mr Dennis's compass is to be trusted, we also
ascertained that the figure faced, not north-west as I had supposed, nor north-by-east as Major Gordon believed, but north-
north-west.

Our next expedition was to Ali Agha, where Mr Baltazzi
offered us kind hospitality and proposed escorting us to the
ruins recently visited by himself, in company with Mr Ramsay
and M.S. Reinach, on a rugged mountain summit called Nimrud
Kalessi, as well as to a figure carved on the rock, and resem-
bling the pseudo-Sesostris which M. Guichon averred he had
seen several years ago in the same neighbourhood. M. Reinach
is at present conducting excavations for the French School of
Athens on the sites of Kyme and Myrina, midway between

which Ali Agha stands. Mr Dennis and myself left Smyrna by
a steamer which called first at Old Phokaea, then at New Phokaea, and finally landed us at Ali Agha. On our way we passed
the sites of Klazomenae and Leuke, where, unlike Mr Pullan,
we saw fragments of ruined wall through the glass, and, as we
sailed past the Arginusae Islands, had a good view of the acropolis of Pergamon rising above Elaea, with the long line of
debris which marks the excavations of Mr Humann glistening
in the sun. After reaching Ali Agha, we walked over to the
scene of M. Reinach's excavations at Kyme, where some interesting archaic stone figures had just been discovered. One of
these, which was unfortunately headless, closely resembled
the sitting figures discovered by Mr Newton at Branchidae,
and still retained traces of the red paint that once adorned it;
the others were sitting figures of Kybele, which seemed to me
archaistic rather than archaic. However, a few days afterwards
a fragment of early Phoeniko-Hellenic pottery was discovered
in the same place. The spot where they were found was a
necropolis of the Graeco-Roman period; and, as M. Reinach
had excavated there down to the rock itself, I can account for
the presence of these archaic remains only by supposing that
the ground subsequently turned into a cemetery had been
originally a suburb of the ancient Greek city, where, perhaps,
a temple of Kybele stood. I fancy that the prae-Hellenic city,
whose foundation was ascribed by legend to the Amazons, lay
on one of the heights farther inland, at a little distance from
the sea, by the side of which the Aeolic settlers built their
'village'. At any rate, I know of no other prehistoric site
immediately on the sea-shore.

Our expedition to Nimrud-Kalessi was prevented, partly by
a snow-storm which overtook us the day after our arrival at
Ali Agha and confined us to the house the whole day, partly
by M. Reinach's report of the ruins, from which we gathered
that they were not older than the Alexandrine period. We
therefore devoted our time and energies to the rediscovery of
the sculptured warrior, who we fancied might turn out to be
of Hittite origin. Our quest, however, was fruitless; but in
searching for the warrior, we made some other discoveries,
which are of possibly greater importance. As soon as the
weather allowed, we rode across the plain to the west of Guzel
Hissar, in a north-easterly direction, passing on our way a
small eminence of cretaceous limestone, containing rifled tombs
and an old raised road of Greek or Roman construction. After
crossing the Koja Chai we rode up a broad and rocky slope,
and found ourselves at the foot of a crag which had a double
summit. This crag was surrounded with the remains of a well-

built Cyclopean wall, and a little examination soon showed that it was the site of a prehistoric fortress. As we climbed the highest or western summit of the crag, we came across other portions of Cyclopean masonry, and at the top found the entrance which faced the east. The two door-posts, each consisting of a single block of stone like those of Mykenae, still remained, though one was fallen and broken in two, but the lintel-stone was wanting. The posts, however, showed traces of the ledges on which it had rested.

According to M. Reinach's measurements, the upright monolith is two metres five centimetres long by one metre twenty-five centimetres broad in the thickest part, while the fallen monolith is two metres fifteen centimetres long by one metre ten centimetres broad. The difference of length is easily accounted for by the fact that a part of the upright monolith is buried in the ground. The path led from the entrance of the acropolis into the valley of Uzan Hassanly, and at a little distance from the gate consisted of a flight of steps. After passing through the entrance, we came to the remains of some building, which may have been a temple. The lower or eastern summit of the crag was fortified like the rest of the acropolis, and one of the corner-stones of its enclosing wall which I measured was eighty-eight inches long by fifty-five broad. The stone had been shaped by cleavage; the drill-holes were still visible in many places, and there was no trace of a metal tool. Nor was there any trace of Hellenic masonry, from which we may conclude that the fortress was deserted either before or shortly after the arrival of the Greeks. This conclusion is confirmed by the existence of Greek tombs cut in the rock of the crag both without and within the Cyclopean walls. One of these is on the very summit of the acropolis, and close to the remains of the building I have spoken of. I noticed traces of Greek letters of large size cut in the rock over it, but could make out only four of them. We found no pottery of the historical age on the site, except fragments of Hellenic ware in the neighbourhood of the rifled tombs. I believe that the site represents the prae-Hellenic city of Myrina, or Smyrna, founded according to tradition by the Amazons, or, as I should prefer to say, by the Hittites. It is about four miles distant from Kalabassary, the site of the historical Myrina, at the mouth of the river (the Kojah Chai) and on the sea-coast.

The day after the discovery of this early site, we first visited the excavations at Kalabassary, and then rode along the northern bank of the Koja Chai, keeping a ruined aqueduct on our right and passing an old raised road that must once have led to Pergamon and have joined the raised road to which I have already alluded. We passed the site we had discovered the preceding day on the opposite side of the river, and noticed two or three rock-tombs below it which we had not observed before, and then came to a point where a narrow channel was cut through a projecting ridge of rock. After this we had to climb a rugged mass of cliff and then descend the opposite side of it in order to regain the bank of the river. Here we unexpectedly came across an artificial cutting through the rock about thirty-two yards in length and twenty-five feet in height at the highest part, the cutting itself being about two feet broad. The channel curved towards the north-east, and at the eastern end led into a sort of natural basin full of deep water. At this end the rock had been left so as to form a double arch. Just midway in the cutting a large basaltic block in the right or southern wall was carved into the likeness of a bull's head, as M. Reinach was the first to notice. The rock through which the channel was cut jutted out into the river; and the remains of a tablet, which probably once contained an inscription, were visible in one part of its external face just over the water. The channel was evidently intended for an aqueduct, the course of which could still be traced by a raised mound of earth as far as the cutting I have previously mentioned, and from thence by means of a ruined mediaeval conduit as far as Kalabassary. I have no hesitation, therefore, in regarding it as an aqueduct made by the Greek inhabitants of the historical Myrina, and used and repaired as late as Byzantine times.

After examining this curious cutting, we forded the river and led our horses up the steep and rugged bank on the opposite side. Here we found ourselves on a lofty plateau, above which towered a crag of broken rock partially covered with snow. Up this Mr Dennis, M. Reinach and myself made our way on foot, and soon discovered that the whole crag was surrounded by a wall of Cyclopean masonry of far ruder construction than that of the site we had visited the day before. We made our way along the line of it with some difficulty, but found nothing that indicated a later date. At the western end a triangular mass of the rock jutted out at a lower level than the rest of the crag, and looked towards the site we had previously discovered, the summit of which lay at a considerable distance below. This triangular mass was carefully fortified with a well-preserved rude Cyclopean wall, and the foundations of a square building lay a little in its rear. From the line of wall we looked down upon Nimrud Kalessi, which rose into the sky somewhat farther up the valley of the Koja Chai. On this side a Juruk village was perched upon the slope of our acropolis; in the valley on the other or southern side was the

village of Uzun Hassanly. As this valley was broad and seemed
to have an easy outlet, while the approaches to both the prehistoric cities we had discovered led into it, I came to the
conclusion that the old road from Magnesia to the plain of
Kyme lay through it. On questioning Mr Baltazzi afterwards,
he told me that this is actually the road to Magnesia still
followed by the cattle-drivers, and considered by them the
shortest route. Mr Dennis suggests that it is part of the road
from the Ephesian territory to Phokaea meant by Herodotus;
at any rate, it is quite possible that Hittite sculptures like those
in the pass of Karabel may be discovered upon it. I must not
forget to mention that we found three Hellenic tombs cut in
the rock within the precincts of the old fortress, one of which
we explored. We found, however, no other traces of late
occupation upon the site, except a fragment of Hellenic pottery
which I picked up near one of the tombs; and the style of
building, as well as the situation, would seem to show that it
was earlier than the site which I venture to call Old Myrina.

The day after our discovery of this ancient acropolis we
rode to Meneman, past the two sites which are supposed to
represent Larissa and Aeon Teikhos. At Meneman I could find
nothing earlier than the Byzantine period, and the hill in which
some explorers have seen the acropolis of Temnos shows no
trace of having been occupied before the Middle Ages. A deserted mosque in the town would probably be of interest to lovers
of Byzantine architecture, as it is a good specimen of a Byzantine basilica, the east end of which has been supported on the
north and south sides by enormous buttresses, as a protection,
I suppose, against earthquakes. I noticed another mosque
which had evidently been once a basilica. According to Mr
Spiegelthal an old site exists on one of the ridges of Sipylos to
the south of Meneman.

Not long afterwards Dennis and I paid a visit to the country
house of Baltazzi (pronounced Baltaji) Pasha at Ali Agha which
stood midway between the ancient sites of Myrina and Kyme
where M. Salomon Reinach was excavating on behalf of the
French Government. As it was the only habitable house in the
locality he was residing there, the Pasha acting as the representative of the Museum at Constantinople which shared the spoil
with the Louvre. We had to land from the steamer in a rowing-
boat and our passage was greatly impeded by masses of dead
locusts which had recently swarmed over the country and
perished in the sea. They formed almost as compact a mass as
floating ice, and our boat had to be pushed through it by
main force instead of being rowed. At Myrina Reinach found
the terra-cotta figurines rivalling those of Tanagra, which are

now in the Louvre. He was still a young man when we met at
Ali Agha, and there began a friendship which has been one of
the valuable assets of my life.

We visited the excavations at Myrina and Kyme on alternate
days; all that was discovered was brought to Ali Agha and then
divided after dinner between Reinach and the Turkish Com-
missioner . . . Before leaving Ali Agha we made two expeditions into the unexplored mountain-heights and forests to
the east. Here we discovered two prehistoric fortresses with
well-preserved 'Cyclopean' walls, and various indications made
it evident that the pre-Hellenic road from Magnesia to Kyme
must have passed near them . . .

On our way back to Smyrna we were half drowned in ford-
ing the Hermos, and a few days later Dennis was called away
from home by consular duties.[3]

A few cases of cholera had occurred in Smyrna, and therefore
there was quarantine in Greece against arrivals from that city. So
Sayce decided to go for a few days to the island of Chios. 'About
ten o'clock one evening,' he writes,

just after Mrs Dennis had retired to her bedroom, I was kneel-
ing at a table in the drawing-room of the Consulate looking
over the illustrations in Dodwell's *Travels* and noting what
antiquities I ought to visit in the island, when the floor suddenly heaved up and down, the doors opened, and the pictures
fell from the walls. Mrs Dennis rushed in exclaiming: 'There's
another bad earthquake.' Fortunately there was no further
shock of any violence, and after breakfast next morning I
started for the office of the Turkish steamer company to
secure my passage to Chios.

But the damage near the harbour and the angry waves and still
threatening sky put him off, so that he stayed another day or two
with the Dennises before sailing instead to Syra and then to
Greece. Had Sayce gone to Chios when he originally intended, he
would almost certainly have perished in the great earthquake which
hit the island on the Sunday when he would have been there.

Dangers in Smyrna were bad enough: a plague of locusts, several
severe earthquakes; and in the country outside the city the ever-
present threat of robbery and violence from brigands. But Dennis
was undeterred in his preparations for further exploration, even
though he was nearing seventy years of age. He again explored the
great necropolis of Sardis and the Temple of Cybele in the spring of
1882.

It was during these excavations at Sardis in 1882 that Dennis dug
a long trench and two pits on the site of the temple. The following
account is taken from the American publication *Sardis*:

Dennis published no account of this work . . . and for information about it we must depend upon a letter written in September 1882 by Mr Francis H. Bacon, of Boston, to Professor Charles Eliot Norton. Mr Bacon was a member of the American excavating party at Assos, and made a trip to Sardis where he was the guest of Dennis in his camp at Bin Tépé . . . The letter reads: 'Mr Dennis has not begun to clear off the temple plan in a systematic manner; that would be an expensive affair. So far he has only dug pits and trenches, and the only thing he has found (which however is well worth all his trouble) is a beautiful colossal head, supposed to have belonged to a statue of Cybele. He measured from the columns at the east to where he supposed the west end to be, and ran a trench from there eastward into the naos. He found a terra cotta Roman pavement and very few architectural fragments (but perhaps these may lie outside his trench). Just beyond the centre of the naos, lying upon about a metre of debris, he found the colossal marble head lying face down. Excepting a mutilated nose, it is almost in a perfect condition. Judging by the position in which it was found, it is possible that the rest of the statue may be brought to light when the trench is extended. I did not see the head . . . I saw only a photograph. It is entirely different from any Greek or Roman head that I have ever seen. The mouth was large, and the cheek bones prominent; it was the head of a matron and not of a young woman; in fact there is hardly any doubt about its being a representation of Cybele. The workmanship is rather noncommittal and it may be of early or late date.'

(At this point the report adds a footnote to the effect that the head, probably representing Faustina the Elder, is now in the British Museum.)

Dennis's trench and two pits were still visible, though partly filled up, when the American expedition began work in 1910.

At Bin Tépé Dennis opened a number of the smaller tumuli, and since then . . . the native population has undertaken the opening of some of these tombs on its own account; but, except for two sculptured slabs, one or two small pots, a few potsherds which Dennis sent to the B.M. and some drawings of others from the tomb of Alyattes, we are in possession of no objects whatever from this great necropolis.[4]

In the following summer (1882) some peasants accidentally found two ancient Greek sarcophagi in the necropolis at Clazomenae, and these became the subject of an article of about twenty pages which Dennis submitted to the *Journal of Hellenic Studies* printed in 1883. He writes:

They are now about to be transferred to the Museum of Antiquities at Stamboul. The site of the ancient necropolis of

Clazomenae is now occupied by vineyards, which produce the choicest raisins for the export market of Smyrna. I have made several attempts to discover the site of the earlier city of Clazomenae, but hitherto without success. I hope in a future search to be more successful. I have passed nearly five years in Asia Minor, and have visited not a few ancient sites, chiefly on the coast, but have never had the fortune to see a single figured vase ascertained to have been disinterred in any Greek necropolis, or even to pick up a fragment of one in my wanderings in such localities.

Dennis was an honorary member of the Society for the Promotion of Hellenic Studies from its inception in 1880 until his death, but this is the only article which he published in its Journal, and, strangely as it may seem for one who travelled so much all his life, there is no evidence that he ever set foot on the mainland of Greece, despite his constant desire to do so.

Dennis hoped to revisit England in the summer of 1883, but put it off because he had not yet seen all his consular district, which extended from the Troad to Adalia in Pamphylia, and included all the Turkish islands. He told John Murray on February 18th 1883: 'I have become a landed proprietor in Turkey, having purchased the celebrated Temple of Cybele at Sardis, and must spare a little time for the cultivation of my estate.'

During that summer of 1883, Dennis received a visit from Heinrich Schliemann himself, who later sent him a copy of his book on Troy, which Dennis read with great pleasure. Sir Charles Wilson, the distinguished authority on Asia Minor, also met Dennis several times, and supported his views of the oriental origins of the Etruscans. Wilson flattered Dennis by saying that his ambition in writing his big book on Turkey was to establish as good a reputation for conscientiousness as George had won with his *Etruria*.

Another acquaintance of those years was James Fergusson, the eminent architectural historian, who offered George fifty pounds to clear the pronaos of the temple at Sardis, which Dennis accepted on condition that he got his firman.

In the month of May (it is not certain which year, but probably 1883 or 1884) Dennis set out with Purser and Ramsay to visit Nysa, an ancient Greek city situated on the north side of the Meander valley and on the lower slopes of the Messogis range. Presumably Mrs Ramsay stayed behind at the Consulate in Smyrna with Mrs Dennis, for this trip would not have been suitable for women. Their object was not so much to explore the remains of Nysa, which they left for a future occasion, but to discover a certain spot in its neighbourhood mentioned by Strabo. 'I shall therefore say no more of Nysa, than that we verified the accuracy of Strabo's description of the peculiar features of its situation, and the position

of the buildings he specifies, and enjoyed the magnificent view of
the Meander valley and its enclosing mountains from the upper
seats of the Greek theatre.' The Meadow, to which the ancient
Nysaeans and all their neighbours used to go in procession to cele-
brate their festivals, lay thirty stadia from Nysa. Chandler, who
visited the spot in 1765, thought he had found this meadow on the
road between Nysa and Nazli, in a 'remarkable gap in the range of
Messogis, opening a view into a green plain at some distance on our
left'. But his green plain could not have been the Nysaean meadow,
for it lies on the Meander side of the range. To reach the meadow you
must cross the Messogis range in a northerly direction, and you will
come to a piece of level ground, commanding a view over the valley
of the Cayster and the southern slopes of the great chain of Tmolus.
Dennis writes:

> We traversed a valley well cultivated with vines, corn, olive and
> fig trees, yet without any signs of habitation. But I was re-
> minded that in Roman times the wines grown on the mountain
> above Nysa were esteemed the best the Messogis produced.
> The valley gradually contracted, being hemmed in by cliffs,
> which in one spot were yellow with sulphur, till it shrunk to a
> narrow, deep ravine with slopes darkened by olive groves.
> These slopes, after a tedious ascent, led us to the village of
> Malagatch, some 2½ hours from Sultan-Hissar. This village,
> which takes its name 'Tree of the Treasure' from having
> been the deposit of the spoils of brigandage, hangs on both
> sides of the ravine, or Dere, through which flowed the torrent
> which we were to trace on the morrow to its source. It was
> very unlike a European village; it had no street, not even a
> mosque. The houses (many were mere sheds of mud and wood
> without windows) were scattered at random on the steep slopes,
> under venerable olive trees. Here in the best house in the
> village, the only one possessing an upper storey, we passed the
> night, meeting with a rude but hearty hospitality, our host
> resigning his own bedroom to his guests and providing them
> with mattresses and coverlids.

Their host, Kara Ali, or Black Ali, had been the chief of a band
of brigands, but had recently made his peace with the Government,
and he and his comrade Baba now both served as guards on the
Ottoman Railway. All the villagers were Zeybecs, and had belonged
to the robber-band. Dennis, Ramsay and Purser were told that they
were the first Europeans to visit the village of Malagatch.

In the morning Ramsay felt so unwell that he decided to return
to Smyrna by the first train. Dennis and Purser then started for the
Meadow with an escort of Zeybecs, all armed, some on foot in front,
seven or eight on horse-back behind, with mounted servants bringing up the rear. His narrative continues:

On our way to the opposite half of the village we crossed the
torrent by a narrow bridge of planks. Here the horse of one of
the Zeybecs, who was leading it, suddenly pulled the bridle out
of his hand and fell backwards upon a shelf of rock, many
feet beneath, but, being saved by his massive saddle, the beast
managed to scramble out of the stream with scarcely a scratch.
We followed the upward course of the ravine by a rugged path
worn by the charcoal burners across the mountain range. The
slopes on either hand were shaded by young oaks, and the
torrent between them fretted its way among rocks of grey
limestone, white marble, or glittering schist. At a spot where
the path was narrowest, we encountered a train of horses,
laden with charcoal, and driven by grimy Bulgarians. In the
attempt to pass, the leading horses of our party lost their
footing, Mr Purser was thrown to the ground, with Baba the
Zeybec upon him, but the accident fortunately resulted in
bruised instead of broken limbs. The path indeed was in many
parts dangerous, especially when it wound round the heads of
the little gullies, which fed the main stream, and kept the
narrow path moist and slippery, just where a false step would
have precipitated beast and rider into a rocky chasm.
   In a few places they observed a clearing, sown with barley or
planted with walnut or cherry trees, but after leaving Malagatch
they saw no other human beings. After riding uphill for two and a
half hours they emerged onto grassy downs thinly studded with
chestnuts. Far away in the distance Dennis could recognise the
Tmolus range of mountains under which lay Sardis, so familiar to
him. An hour and a half later they came in sight of the Meadow,
called Ovajik by the Zeybecs — a green plateau on the northern
verge of the Messogis, just where the mountains sink abruptly to
the wide valley or plain of the Cayster:
   The plateau was apparently about three miles long, by half
   that in width, in parts somewhat marshy, in others, showing a
   gravelly soil, mixed with quartz, and here and there cultivated
   with corn or fruit, inclosed by fences. We crossed it to a clump
   of lofty elms, at the very brow of the height, where a deep
   ravine opens, leading the eye down to the Cayster valley. Here
   stood a low shed now abandoned, but an old Moslem cemetery
   at its side showed that the site had at one time been peopled.
   The view was magnificent; the highest of the distant mountains
were still snow-capped, even though it was nearly the end of May.
The plain beneath was hazy with mist and in parts thrown into deep
shade by heavy clouds, but a ray of sunshine now and then broke
through the clouds and glittered on the bends of the Cayster as it
wound its way through the plain. The deep ravine at their feet
carried the eye down to the town of Boudemia amid its fig groves,

which yielded some of the choicest figs that Smyrna could export. From a higher point on the Messogis, somewhat more to the east, they saw that the Cayster was flowing, not directly westward from the mountains which form the eastern boundary of the plain, as hitherto it had always been represented on the maps, but apparently from the southern foot of the Tmolus, taking at first a south-easterly direction, through a narrow valley separated from the great plain by a low range of hills, which terminated in a sharp promontory at their feet. Doubling this promontory it assumed a north-westerly course as it entered the wide valley or plain to which it had given its name. This discovery Mr Purser was later able to communicate to Mr Kiepert for the emendation of his maps of Asia Minor.

They estimated that the Meadow must be about 5,000 feet above the Meander valley:

> There can be little doubt that the Ovajik is the λειμών mentioned by Strabo. It is a remarkable spot, the only level piece of ground for many miles from Nysa in a northerly direction, and the road to it through the ravine is so marked out by the nature of the ground that the traveller cannot deviate to the right or the left, and is led on his way northwards to this spot. It is true that the valley of the Meander was close to Nysa on the south, but, as has been shown, the Meadow must have been to the north of that city, and there may have been reasons why the secluded plateau among the mountains was preferred by the Nysaeans to the more convenient plain at their feet for the celebrations of their festivals. It was far less exposed; the approaches to it could be more easily guarded, and religious associations appear to have been connected with the locality. The only difficulty in accepting this view appears at first sight to lie in the distance from Nysa, which Strabo gives as 30 stadia, or 3¾ miles; whereas the Ovajik must be between four and five times that distance. But as any site, within four miles from the city, must obviously have been on the southern or Meander slope of the range, it is impossible to place the Meadow, described in connection with the Cayster valley and the Tmolus, on the southern side of the Messogis.
>
> The apparent discrepancy may be explained if we suppose that Strabo wrote '130 stadia' and that the 100 has been omitted by some transcriber of his MS, either by inadvertence, or, it may be, intentionally – the distance of 130 stadia from the city appearing to the transcriber much too remote for the site selected by the Nysaeans for the celebration of their public games and festivals. It would be a very difficult task to measure with precision the distance traversed over such ground as lies between the ancient city and the Meadow; it may be rudely

calculated, however, by the time it takes to reach the latter. Mr Purser, who has had much professional experience in India as well as in Asia Minor, calculated from the time it took us to traverse the ground that it was about 17½ miles or 140 stadia from Sultan Hissar to the Meadow, which, when the distance between the station and the ancient city is deducted, will leave a total closely accordant with the supposition that the distance stated by Strabo was 130 stadia.

Strabo had spoken of the Meadow as the 'Asian meadow' sung of by Homer, who in the *Iliad* writes 'Of storks or cranes or long necked swans in the Asian meadow about the streams of Cayster. Hither and thither they fly rejoicing in their wings'. But this tradition is difficult to accept, for the Meadow is too high to have attracted waterfowl, and too remote also from the Cayster. It is far more probable that Homer referred to the plain of the Cayster, probably nearer to Ephesus, which in winter is a vast marsh, where cranes, wild swans, and geese may be seen in great numbers, as described by Homer and by Virgil. Strabo spent some time in his youth at Nysa, as he tells us, studying philosophy under Aristodemus; we may presume therefore that he visited the Meadow, whither the Nysaeans resorted for their festivals, and that he wrote from personal knowledge of the spot.

This trip to the Meadow of Nysa is the most charming and vivid account of any which Dennis gives us during his whole residence in Asia Minor. On an earlier excursion with Ramsay, he had found clear traces of a Hellenic city on an extensive plateau six hundred feet beneath the hill over Belcaive, on the road from Smyrna to Sardis,[5] and, as Sayce tells us, a figure cut out of the rock at Bujah near Smyrna, discovered by Mr Spiegelthal, was sent to the British Museum by Dennis;[6] but of these episodes, important for archaeologists as they may be, Dennis did not write down his own impressions. He reached the age of seventy in 1884, but he had still before him years of travel, discovery and writing.

CHAPTER 11

A DEGREE AT OXFORD, RETIREMENT, LAST YEARS — 1885-1898

IN 1883 John Murray published what is described on its titlepage as a third edition of *The Cities and Cemeteries of Etruria,* but in reality is a re-issue of the second edition of 1878. The author wrote no new preface for the third edition, but it is clear that the book was still selling well and more copies were in demand.

Professor Sayce in Oxford had a warm personal regard for Dennis, and saw a way of providing him with a practical demonstration of his esteem. George Dennis, like his devoted admirer of a later generation, Edward Hutton, had given a lifetime of service to study and writing inspired by Mediterranean civilizations, yet had never himself been to the university and had no degree. Sayce accordingly persuaded the Oxford authorities to offer Dennis the honorary degree of Doctor of Civil Law. Dennis came to England in the early summer of 1885, and the degree ceremony at Oxford was arranged for Wednesday, June 17th. Those upon whom honorary degrees were to be conferred included His Excellency William Henry Waddington (the French Ambassador), the Right Rev. Harvey Goodwin (Bishop of Carlisle), the Right Hon. Admiral Lord Alcester, the Right Hon. George Otto Trevelyan (Chancellor of the Duchy of Lancaster), the Right Hon. James Anthony Lawson, Mr Whitley Stokes (whom Sayce afterwards described as 'famous alike as a Keltic scholar and codifier of Anglo-Indian law'), Professor Thomas H. Huxley (President of the Royal Society), and Mr George Dennis, Her Majesty's Consul at Smyrna, who was seventy-one. The encoenia was held in the morning, and afterwards they were all entertained to luncheon by the Warden and Fellows of All Souls. The only one unable to be present was the French Ambassador, M. Waddington, whose degree had to be conferred *in absentia.* Professor Bryce, the Vice-Chancellor, speaking naturally in Latin, introduced Mr Dennis as 'an eminent archaeologist', and his book on 'Etruria, and Investigations into the Antiquities of the Early Italian Peoples' was of great value. (This, at least, was how the *Oxford Journal* reported the proceedings, as though the above were the title of Dennis's book, which of course it is not; but how often are newspaper reports correct or exact?)

During this stay in England in 1885, Dennis visited his old friend Colonel Yule, who was ailing sadly. He also saw James Fergusson, whose sudden death during the following winter upset Dennis particularly as Fergusson would have given him a hundred pounds to continue his excavations in the Temple of Cybele at Sardis. As Dennis told John Murray on April 1st 1886: 'I was expecting to continue my excavations there this spring, but the British Museum Trustees have treated me with some want of consideration'.

Just at this time — April, 1886 — Frederic Harrison (who some years later was to write Dennis's obituary for *The Athenaeum*) was publishing his book entitled *The Choice of Books*. In it he referred to Dennis's translations from the Cid which had appeared as long ago as 1845, calling them 'one of my chief delights in early life', and saying that the book ought to be reprinted. But although this gave Dennis the idea to ask Murray for his opinion on where to apply for republication, nothing ever came of it. Nevertheless, Harrison had done Dennis a good turn by giving his early work a word of enthusiastic praise in print: and such praise did not come Dennis's way often enough.

On June 8th 1886, George told John Murray: 'I have just received a telegram informing me of Gladstone's defeat by a majority of 30! What a glorious rebuff to the G.O. Madman! What follows? Dissolution or Resignation? Law in Ireland or Dynamite in England?' So his contempt for Gladstone was stronger than ever.

Dennis was anxious to resume his excavations at Sardis the following September, but failed to obtain the renewal of his firman. As it happened, that season of 1886 was the busiest year for official consular duties since he had taken up public duties so many years before. But he never despaired of resuming the spade, as he told Murray on October 23rd: 'If I can obtain a firman I shall continue to work in my temple, for old as I am [he was 72], I have no intention at present of hanging up my shovel and my hoe'. Instead, however, of being enabled to resume his diggings, he had the opportunity during the spring of 1887 to visit yet another new part of the world, when he travelled to Syria and saw Damascus, Baalbek, the Nahr el Kelb and Sidon. He would have gone on to Jerusalem, but his wife was ill and he dared not prolong his tour any further. He later told Murray:

> I happened to reach Sidon at a fortunate moment, when all but one of the splendid Greek sarcophagi had been disinterred, and I could examine them by the light of day, instead of by candle or torch-light. They are splendid monuments — intact save by the blows of riflers of long past ages, and most interesting. Most of them are of exquisite art, of the Rhodian period of style, and most probably by Rhodian artists, and as they are evidently the sepulchres of kings and princes, they are excellent specimens of the art of the day, the 2nd and 3rd centuries B.C. But their chief interest consists in their being the best specimens yet brought to light of the polychrome art of the Greeks as applied to sculpture. They are in fact, or rather

must have been, for the more delicate tints have faded, pictures in relief, and as such are unique among the works of Greek art that have come down to us. I was not allowed to take a note, nor even measurements on the spot, as the Director of the Museum at Constantinople wishes to give the first description of them, and therefore I have written nothing about them, and have waited in expectation of seeing an account of them from someone more fortunately circumstanced than myself. But I have now arrived at the conclusion that I am the only Englishman who has seen them, and though I could not take notes on the spot, I examined them carefully, and have something to say about them when I can find the time to write it out.

But this he never did. On returning to Smyrna he found that his wife's health was now a permanent cause for concern.

On December 21st, 1887, George wrote at length to John Murray to tell him about Oscar Whittall, a youth of eighteen and a member of the merchant family of that name at Smyrna, who had just died of typhoid fever shortly after being released by brigands who had captured him and two other young Englishmen. This melancholy news particularly interested Murray since young Whittall had an article in the December number of *Murray's Magazine*.

Just about this time too there was a visit at Dennis's Consulate from Murray's friend Guillemant, on his way to Cyprus on an excavating expedition in company with Ernest Gardiner, who had lately been successfully excavating in Egypt. George heartily wished that he could have joined the party, as he had never been to Cyprus. But he had to stay at Smyrna, where he was happy to receive from Murray a copy of Sir Henry Layard's book of early adventures.[1] In writing to thank Murray, George recalled how he had known Layard since 1839 — nearly fifty years — and he sadly reflected: 'In those early days we were on a level, both having to make our way in the world, but he, though after wonderful vicissitudes and adventures, has risen far above me, who remain a hack in official harness to the last, while he has won the Derby. I fully appreciate your kind consideration which prompted you, who were aware of my early acquaintance with Layard, to send me so welcome a present.'

George intended to retire during the summer of 1888, as he approached his seventy-fourth birthday, being probably the oldest fully employed member of the consular service still overseas. He hoped to receive a sufficient pension to enable him to enjoy his leisure for whatever life was left to him. He could not visualise settling down in England, but he wished to revisit Spain, which he had not seen since 1840, and if possible to go for the first time to Greece, the Holy Land and Egypt.

A heavy blow fell upon him when on April 1st, 1888, Mrs Dennis died in Smyrna after a lengthy and painful illness. Despite a recent

search, no trace has been found of her grave in either of the two
European cemeteries in that city. George was left alone, and on May
1st he officially retired. He had no one close to him now except his
faithful brother John, and even he would see very little of George,
who was determined never again to live permanently in England,
because of its intolerable winters.

He had served the Foreign Office for twenty-five years and seven
months, and his annual salary at the time of his retirement was
£1,050. His annual pension allowance was £420, as from May 1st
1888.

A month later, on June 2nd, he was created a Companion of the
Order of St Michael and St George.

In the autumn of 1888 he met Sir Henry Layard at Wimbledon,
when Layard was kind enough to express his willingness to propose
Dennis's name as a candidate for membership of the Athenaeum.
Dennis spent the best part of the following winter in Italy, revisit-
ing the scenes of his youth. In March 1889 he was staying at the
Hotel del Vesuvio in Naples, and on the 8th he wrote to remind
Layard of the promise to propose him for membership of the
Athenaeum, following this up the next day with a letter to Murray
on the same lines. He had made at the hotel the acquaintance of
Layard's nephew, Henry, who was on his way via Suez back to his
post in New Caledonia. Dennis planned to leave Naples for Rome,
and on March 20th to go on to Genoa; but he was delayed, and did
not reach Rome until the end of March, when he received a reply
from Layard (who lived in Venice) saying that he had put Dennis's
name forward for membership of the Athenaeum. John Murray had
written to tell Dennis that the Committee of the Athenaeum had
already made their selection of new members for that year, and
intimated that he stood no chance of admission until the spring of
1890. Dennis adds rather sadly in his letter to Layard on April 5th,
1889: 'If I have to wait 16 years for admission, I had better with-
draw my candidature — for in that time I shall be 90 years old, and
shall have more need of a coffin than of a club', while to Murray he
said 'I shall be fit for no society but that of worms'. Nevertheless, he
was elected a member of the Athenaeum Club in the spring of 1890.

Layard invited him to go and stay at Venice, but Dennis preferred
the south. He had not spent a winter in England for forty years
and more; and he was tempted to take a villa at Naples for the
winters. He was afraid that Venice would be as cold as London.
(Sometimes it is worse.) By the spring of 1890 his archaeologist
friends in Rome had found some more work for him to do, and
would not let him rest. They were anxious to obtain from him a
description of some interesting discoveries recently made in the
Faliscan district of Etruria, that is, in the neighbourhood of Civita
Castellana and Viterbo. Consequently he wrote an article entitled

'The Recently Excavated Objects from Falerii in the new Etruscan Museum at the Villa Papa Giulio at Rome'. It had eighteen pages, and was printed in the *Journal of the British and American Archaeological Society of Rome,* session 1888—89, which actually appeared in 1890. The temple of Juno Quiritis at Falerii (Civita Castellana) had yielded the most important Etruscan treasures. Dennis's article makes the interesting point that an inscription on one cylix ran 'Foied vino pato cra carefo', that is, 'Hodie vinum bibo, cras carebo', or 'Today I drink wine, tomorrow I go without'. The ancient Faliscan language, then, unlike true Etruscan which is still largely unintelligible, was very much like early Latin.

The British and American Archaeological Society of Rome had been founded in 1865, and by the time George Dennis began to take an active part in its proceedings, in 1890, it was holding many meetings, making excursions into the Roman countryside, and publishing a journal which is now so rare that no British Library has a complete holding of it.

Dennis was a Vice-President of the Society from 1891 to 1896.

In London after his retirement he took a flat at No. 21 Queen's Mansions, Victoria Street, S.W.1., which he kept until at least 1893; but he never again wintered in Britain. He spent the summer and autumn of 1889 in London, and at the end of October left for a tour of Spain. He later wrote to John Murray:

> I entered Spain at Barcelona, and after visiting Montserrat — one of the chief natural wonders of the world — visited all the towns on the East Coast, which was new to me, and from Malaga went inland by rail to Granada, which I found much too cold for me at that season, and after a few days' stay — just long enough to refresh my reminiscences of the Alhambra and Generalife — I descended to Seville, where I was laid up for a fortnight with 'el reinante' as the Spanish influenza is termed, but in the Fonda de Madrid, which deserves its reputation as *the hotel facile princeps* of Spain. I had intended to return by way of Madrid and Toledo, and other interesting cities of the North, some of which were new to me, but the 'trancazo', from which I had just escaped, was reported as ravaging the high plateaux of the Castilles with deadly effect, so that I was induced to content myself with short visits to Cadiz, Tangier, and Gibraltar, where I took ship to Genoa, reaching it on 14th February.

At Tangier he met Sir John Drummond-Hay, aged seventy-three, whom he clearly remembered having met there fifty-three years previously. But alas! Drummond-Hay had no recollection at all of Dennis. 'I found him enjoying a vigorous old age, and heard that he still indulged in his favourite pastime of pig-sticking.' So they talked about Layard, and Drummond-Hay at least remembered the first

time he had met Layard at Constantinople, just after Layard had
arrived with despatches which it took him six days' and nights'
hard riding to bring from Belgrade. That was in 1842.[2]

Upon arrival at Genoa on February 14th 1890, Dennis intended
to go straight on to Nice and there spend the last few weeks of cold
weather, but he 'encountered such a furious tempest of folly raging
at Nice on the last Sunday in Carnival' that he was obliged to seek
shelter at Monaco instead. Here he stayed at the Hotel de Nice,
which was most uncomfortable, but there was no choice. He suffered a serious attack of influenza followed by bronchitis, lasting
nearly three weeks, and was attended by some English doctors from
Monte Carlo, who assured him that he would be well enough to
return to England in the late spring. While at the hotel he received
a letter from his brother to say that he had been elected to the
Athenaeum, for which he was indebted to Layard, Dr William Smith
and John Murray. He wrote a letter of profuse thanks to Murray on
March 7th, and a similar letter to Layard on March 13th. He had
known Layard for fifty-one years, he said, and had never received
from his hands anything but the utmost courtesy, consideration
and warm friendship, despite the extremely busy nature of Layard's
public life.

Dennis returned to London for the summers, and was back in
Rome for the winters, during the next few years; and when in Rome
he regularly attended meetings of the British and American Archaeological Society. On March 10th 1891, he was due to read a paper
before the Society on his visit to the Meadow of Nysa in Turkey
some years before, but having been called away to London unexpectedly, he was unable to deliver his lecture, which was read for
him by Captain Richmond Moore, R.N. Dennis was back in Rome,
however, in the autumn of that year, and was chairman of a meeting of the Rome Society on Tuesday, December 29th 1891, when
the Society expressed its regret at the departure from Rome of the
British Ambassador, the Marquess of Dufferin and Ava.

During the same month he received a letter in Rome from his old
friend Edward Falkener, asking him to investigate certain ancient
Roman games. The reply which Dennis wrote on January 2nd 1892,
is printed as an appendix to Falkener's book, *Games Ancient and
Oriental and How to Play Them*:

> Immediately I received your letter I started for the Forum.
> The excavations at Rome of late years have disclosed the ori-
> ginal pavements of many buildings in the Forum, which show
> circles scratched of old on the slabs, evidently from some
> game or other. The diagrams I give are all scratched in the pave-
> ment of the Basilica Julia, or of other buildings which have
> been brought to light of late years; I take it that they must
> have been made in the Lower Empire, when the temples and

basilicas were deserted, and before the capture of Rome by the Goths: because the destruction of the principal buildings at that period would have covered the pavements with debris. I went carefully over all the ruins in the Forum, and could find no other varieties than I here give you. Many of the circles are rudely scratched in the pavement, but a few are geometrically correct: the former are very numerous. There are but few of the squares. I could find no instances of numerous concentric circles. I remember similar diagrams at Pompeii or elsewhere, but I never paid them much attention. I will not fail to report to you any other instances I may note in my wanderings.[3]

George Dennis, now in his seventy-eighth year, was still a wanderer, still an avid investigator of antiquities, still eager to help old friends and supply them with information.

On March 29th 1892, he read the only paper of his life on his experiences of many years previously in South America, when he lectured on 'The Probability of America having been visited in ancient times by the Phoenicians'. This lecture was afterwards published under the title 'The Aborigines of South America and Speculations on their Origin'.

During this spring of 1892 one English visitor to Rome was the thirty-nine years old Flinders Petrie, already distinguished as an archaeologist in Egypt. He wrote many years later in his reminiscences: 'In Rome there was an interesting company just then, Mahaffy, Stillman, Lumbroso, Lanciani and Dennis . . . Dennis was a delightful old fellow with bushy white hair, saying he felt as much a boy as ever.'[4]

Dennis returned to England for the summer, and before leaving once again for the winter of 1892–93, he called at Murray's office in Albemarle Street and left there a present for Layard: a circular table-top and a stand. The table-top was composed of specimens of Sicilian agates and jaspers, selected by Dennis during his official residence in that island. When he reached Italy, he was again severely ill for some time, and it was not until December 6th 1892, that he was able to write to Layard in Venice to say that he had made the gift. This is in fact the last of Dennis's letters to have survived, and it was written from No. 15 Via Ludovisi, Rome. He again took the opportunity of thanking Layard profusely for all his many favours over the years. On July 5th 1894, Layard died in London at the age of seventy-seven, three years younger than George Dennis.

Despite his eighty years, Dennis had not done yet with travelling between Italy and England. On June 29th 1894 he sold at Sotheby's a collection of his terra-cotta figures from Myrina, numbering twenty-three pieces in the catalogue. They were mostly Greek figures, male and female, including a Faun and Eros; and a Roman lamp, a pair of vases of old opalescent Venetian glass, and six old zinc castings, some bronzed, which he had found on Castle Hill, Smyrna, and which were thought to be of mediaeval Venetian make.

On January 29th 1895, Dennis delivered his last lecture to the Society in Rome, on 'Ancient Greek art in the parts of Libia about Cyrene', recalling his explorations of thirty years before.

In 1894 and 1895 his name does not appear in the *Journal* of the Society for the Promotion of Hellenic Studies, but it appears again in 1896–98 with the address 'c/o Lloyds Bank, Ltd., 16 St James's Street, S.W.'.

George Dennis died in his eighty-fifth year on November 15th 1898, at 31 Harrington Road, South Kensington, a house which has since been demolished. The cause of death was registered as 'senile decay; rigors after use of catheter; seven days' exhaustion'. The death was certified by C.E. Baker, F.R.C.S., and present in the house at the time of his decease was Emma de Porter, probably the landlady. He died intestate, leaving £1,888 1s. 5d., the administration of this modest estate being granted on May 10th 1899 to his younger brother John, now aged seventy-four, who continued to live at Crowborough until his own death in February, 1911, at the age of eighty-six. It was a long-lived family on the male side, for John's own son, Sir Alfred Hull Dennis, K.B.E., C.B., Chief Assistant Solicitor to the Treasury and Legal Adviser to the War Office, died on February 3rd 1947 in his eighty-ninth year.

When George Dennis died in 1898, his anonymous obituarist in *The Athenaeum,* Frederic Harrison, wrote on November 19th that he had been 'one of the most unaffected and simple-minded of men, honest, straight-forward and courteous'.

George was buried in a simple grave in the huge Hampstead Cemetery in Fortune Green Road, West Hampstead, where the inscription reads:

> In memory of George Dennis, C.M.G., Hon. D.C.L. Oxon., son of the late John Dennis of Rose Hill, Dorking: who died November 15th 1898 aged 84. 'In thy light shall we see light'.

On August 6th 1902, his sister Maria died unmarried aged eighty-three and was interred in the same grave.

When George and his brother were dead, the only literary member of the family left was one of John's sons, George Ravenscroft Dennis, who wrote a few minor books and died in Bournemouth in March 1940. The nephews and nieces all treasured whatever letters or pieces of Greek or Etruscan antiquities their Uncle George had passed on to them; but the majority of his archaeological finds had found their way into the British Museum, while he himself was best remembered, as he is still remembered, for one of the most astonishing antiquarian books ever written by an Englishman, *The Cities and Cemeteries of Etruria.*

CHAPTER 12

GEORGE DENNIS AND THE TWENTIETH CENTURY

IN 1907, nine years after George Dennis's death, a cloth-bound edition of the *Cities and Cemeteries of Etruria* was published by Dent at four shillings, as part of *Everyman's Library*. It had a new introduction by Professor W. M. Lindsay, who, however, had nothing whatever to say about Dennis, but was writing exclusively about the Etruscans. It seems that already Dennis's own life had fallen into some obscurity, and little was known about him even by those dedicated few of the reading public who were still interested in his writings.

The *Everyman's* edition was reviewed as follows by Thomas Ashby (later Director of the British School at Rome):

> A re-issue of this well-known work in so handy a form would be most acceptable were it not for the fact that it is reprinted from the first edition of 1848, and not from the thoroughly revised second edition, which appeared thirty years later, and which is still, no doubt, protected by the Copyright Acts. It thus does not embody the results of Mr Dennis's latest researches, and omits the descriptions of several tombs at Corneto which were discovered in the intervening thirty years, and one or two chapters which were added to the second edition. Of this fact, however, no hint, so far as I have been able to discover, is given, either by Professor W. M. Lindsay in the editor's preface, which he contributes (at the end of which both editions are cited), or elsewhere in the course of the work. Such a proceeding is hardly fair either to the author himself or to the public, who may (as happened to the present writer) meet with unpleasant surprises when they attempt to use it as a guide on the spot. Professor Lindsay's remark that 'since it was written a good deal has been added to our knowledge of the subject' is true in a sense which he can hardly have intended.[1]

The 1878 edition remained the most up-to-date.

In 1908 Professor Michaelis made the following references to Dennis: 'The naval officers R. Murdoch Smith and E. A. Porcher had with great success, in 1860, explored the district of ancient Cyrene, and found a number of Hellenistic and Roman sculptures, and in the Cyrenaic town of Benghazi, the British Consul George Dennis, to whom we owe one of the most delightful books on Etruria, had been actively collecting for the museum.'[2]

'[At Sardis] the excavations made in the Tomb of Alyattes in

1854 by the Prussian Consul, Spiegelthal, and in 1882 by the English Consul, George Dennis, in other tombs, proved fruitless, as the tumuli had already been robbed.'[3] But Michaelis might have added that not all of Dennis's exertions in 1882 had proved fruitless, as witness the beautiful female head which we have already described.

In 1909 Mary Lovett Cameron published her book *Old Etruria and Modern Tuscany,*[4] in the preface to which she remarks: 'I do not aspire to rival George Dennis's *Cities and Cemeteries of Etruria,* merely to supplement that fascinating, but now in parts out-of-date, work'. She calls Dennis a 'valiant pioneer of research', and she adds:

It is heart-rending to the student to read of the way in which Dennis found excavations being carried on at Veii and Vulci in the years between 1842 and 1847. Such wholesale and wanton destruction as was meted out to these unfortunate cemeteries, would horrify the least instructed peasant of today, who has learnt by observation at least, that all 'roba antica', even that which seems to him most rubbishy, has its worth and must be treated with respect . . . These wreckers were employed by the Princess of Cannino, widow of Lucien Bonaparte, who, one would think, ought to have known better.

She laments that Dennis had to go on his hands and knees when he wished to explore the Regulini-Galassi tomb or the Banditaccia at Caere. She still believed that in 1909 the visitor to Veii, for topographical indications, could not do better than follow George Dennis: 'his minute and exhaustive examination of the site cannot be bettered'.

Thus scarcely more than ten years after his death, there was the feeling that Dennis's work was beginning in some respects to be out of date, but in general his great book was, as it still is, the best available guide to the Etruscan sites.

In the following year, 1910, another substantial book on Etruria was published. Although it is a serious and worthy contribution to the subject, containing about a dozen excellent photographs, it has unfortunately the all too journalistic title *Up Hill and Down Dale in Ancient Etruria.* The author was Frederick Seymour, who had travelled extensively in Italy and Spain. He explains in his preface that he has concentrated on the abandoned sites of Etruria rather than those still occupied: thus he omits Perugia, Corneto-Tarquinia, Cortona, Arezzo and some others; but he has much to say about such sites as Vetulonia, Rusellae, Norchia and the other cities around Viterbo and Orvieto. Seymour frequently refers to George Dennis, whom he had not known personally. His references are all favourable and respectful. Dennis's authority can, he declares, never be disputed, 'but he was here [at Rusellae] many years ago, when the ruins may have been in a less pronounced condition'. For Dennis had spoken of many more than the six gates which Seymour saw. As for Vetulonia, Dennis had been persuaded that the site was in the vicinity of

Magliano, in which he had been subsequently proved wrong, the real discoverer of Vetulonia being Signor Falchi; but for this Dennis could not be blamed. Full praise is given to Dennis's conscientiousness, enthusiasm and accuracy of description.[5]

Frederic Harrison, who, as we have seen, had written Dennis's obituary notice for *The Athenaeum* in 1898, published his autobiography in 1911, in the course of which he writes: 'In 1881 the danger of brigandage was such that the high road from Palermo to Monreale had to be guarded at each quarter of a mile by pelotons of Bersaglieri . . . A few years before this, my father and mother were invited to a picnic party on Monte Pellegrino by Sir George Dennis, the British Consul at Palermo, and they noticed that the whole day the company was surrounded by lines of Carabinieri. Dennis told my father that he could not go outside the walls without an ample guard'.[6] But Harrison's memory was playing certain tricks on him, for George Dennis was never knighted.

In 1928 there seems to have been some thought of preparing a biography of George Dennis, but it came to nothing. Cecil Roth, who for many years was Reader in Jewish Studies at Oxford University, and in his last years a Professor at the University of Jerusalem, and who himself was also a considerable Italian historian in those days, wrote a letter to *The Times Literary Supplement* at the end of 1927 to say that an Italian acquaintance of his wanted information on Dennis's life. On Thursday, January 5th 1928, the following answer to his appeal was published:

> Sir, my valued friend G. Dennis had been Consul in Florence and Tripoli when I knew him as Consul-General in Smyrna (1880). His curriculum must be preserved at the Foreign Office. He was a friend of Professor A. Sayce and of Sir W. Ramsay; he came to visit our French excavations at Myrina (Aeolis) and searched with us for a Hittite relief in the neighbourhood, which he failed to discover, though it had been seen and described twenty years before by a French land surveyor. Later on, when I fell ill at the French hospital in Smyrna, he came to see me daily and was very kind.
>
> I have many letters from him, which I would gladly put at the disposal of a biographer. Dennis had some good antiques, especially terra-cottas; it would be interesting to trace them.
>
> Yours truly,
>
> Boulogne-sur-Seine.   S. Reinach.

But alas! for Reinach's memory (which was even worse than Harrison's) Dennis had never been Consul either in Florence or in Tripoli.[7]

In answer to Reinach's letter came one from George's nephew, George Ravenscroft Dennis, which the *T.L.S.* published on February 2nd. 'Of his collection of terra-cottas, etc., to which Professor Reinach refers,' wrote G. R. Dennis, 'the greater part was presented to the British Museum, the remainder being now in the possession of his nephews and nieces.' At this point the correspondence ceases, and no more was heard of the idea for writing George's biography.

The next writer to have taken any interest in George Dennis seems to have been D. H. Lawrence, whose excellent little book *Etruscan Places* was first published in 1932. On the whole, Lawrence is in favour of Dennis, although he says little about him. According to Lawrence, Dennis does not find much 'art' in Etruscan things: but whatever exactly Lawrence means by this, he finds it necessary to put the word 'art' between inverted commas. Another slightly curious remark of Lawrence's is that 'anything of the archaic east Mediterranean seemed to Dennis Egyptian'. This seems scarcely justified, since it was the Lydian theory of the origin of the Etruscans that Dennis most favoured.

In the years which have elapsed since Lawrence wrote, a number of notable contributions to Etruscan studies have been published by such scholars as Raymond Bloch and Jacques Heurgon in France, and above all Massimo Pallottino in Italy; more and more details have been made known about Etruscan archaeology; but the Etruscan language has not been deciphered, and the basic problems of this gifted and antique race are still a mystery.

George Dennis was one of the great Victorian travellers, and his book is unchallengeable. This is why we ought not to forget his name. His achievements, however, extend beyond his book, for to his hard work the British Museum owes so many pieces of Greek and Etruscan art, not to mention those in museums in Italy, Sicily and North Africa. But perhaps the pleasantest visual memorial of him is to be seen over the central or royal gateway of the old Etrusco-Roman town of Ferento, outside Viterbo, surrounded by its lovely Italian hills and meadows, which are alive in early spring with pink anemones and with darting lizards in high summer. Here we may read:

LA SOPRINTENDENZA ALLE ANTICHITÀ DI ROMA
COMPLETO SCAVI E RESTAURI DEL TEATRO DI FERENTO
CON DANARO OFFERTO DAL CAPITANO A.L. HARDCASTLE
CHE VOLLE IN TAL MODO ONORARE
IL NOBILE SVO CONNAZIONALE G. DENNIS
ILLUSTRATORE SAPIENTE DELLA ANTICA ETRURIA
ANNO MCMXXVII

With these noble words by Paribeni, the Director General of Fine Arts in Rome in 1927, we may fittingly take our leave of old Etruria, and return, in our English homes, to the hauntingly beautiful and charmingly old-fashioned pages of George Dennis, who is surely still our best guide to one of the most perplexing and fascinating civilizations in history.

NOTES

NOTES TO CHAPTER ONE

1 The details concerning John Dennis's career are all taken from the *British Imperial Calendar*. The name of George Dennis is here recorded as one of the clerks to the Receiver General in 1836-1841, and as one of the four Receivers in 1844-45; but as we shall soon see, he had run away in 1836 to Spain, and from then on he was abroad as much as possible, preparing his books and articles on Spain and Etruria.

2 Pen-name of the American writer Washington Irving (1783-1859).

NOTES TO CHAPTER TWO

1 Just at the time when George Dennis arrived in Venice, in late July or early August, 1839, another young man also arrived there from England; he was twenty-two and his name was Henry Layard. He was destined to become perhaps the most famous of all British archaeologists of the nineteenth century. His latest biographer has written of Layard: 'He was interested to meet there [in Venice] Mr George Dennis, who had been making a tour of the ancient sites and cemeteries of Etruria, for he had as a boy been interested in the Etruscan collection in Florence. Mr Dennis was on the way to London to find a publisher for his work on the Etruscans and Layard gave him a letter to John Murray who later published Dennis's classic work *The Cities and Cemeteries of Etruria.*' (Gordon Waterfield, *Layard of Nineveh*, London, John Murray, 1963, p.26.) This is completely mistaken. Dennis did not begin to explore Etruria until 1842, and he had certainly not begun to write anything about Etruria in 1839. Dennis himself tells us in the very first sentence of the preface to *The Cities and Cemeteries of Etruria:* 'This work is the fruit of several tours made in Etruria between the years 1842 and 1847.' When he was on his way home from Venice in August, 1839, he stopped at Berne, and in his letter of August 13th to his parents he remarks: 'I wish I had W. Ord with me. Mountain air, food and scenes would do him a world of good. I have met with many companions of all nations, but none to my taste except one at Venice who is about to make the overland journey to India, and has given me a letter of introduction to Capt. Scott, my rival.' He does not name this man, but it was Henry Layard. 'Capt. Scott, my rival' was Rochfort Scott, who had published a book on Southern

Spain in 1838.

2 A *calesa* is an open, two-wheeled, horse-drawn carriage or gig.

3 *Escopeteros:* musketeers.

4 The correct spelling is Puerto Lapice.

NOTES TO CHAPTER THREE

1 Maria Dennis never married, and died in 1902 at the age of eighty-three. She refers here to her 'darling children'; she must therefore have been in service as a governess to a family at Walthamstow. Octavia was also away from home in service.

2 This visit which George Dennis paid to Horace's farm has been commemorated by the late Rose Macaulay in an unfortunately careless passage in her otherwise excellent book *Pleasure of Ruins* (London, Weidenfeld and Nicolson, 1953, p.209). After showing how Byron, despite his antipathy for Horace, nevertheless made his pilgrimage to the farm, she goes on to describe how young George Dennis 'spent rapturous weeks tracing the Horatian landscape round it', and she is content to give the unintelligible and meaningless footnote 'G.W. Dennis (1842)'. Although she does not say what is her authority for these statements, she clearly took her facts from Milman's Horace, for it is only in the table of contents to that book that we find George Dennis credited with the mythical initial W which he did not possess. In fact he had no second Christian name.

3 Backhouse was a Secretary under Lord Palmerston, who at that time was Foreign Secretary in Lord John Russell's government. Little seems to be recorded about him, except that he died before 1852.

4 Giovanni Battista Vermiglioli was born at Perugia on 25th September 1769. Ainsley drew a sketch of the Grotta de'Volunni near Perugia which he dated from 'Vermiglioli's tomb, Perugia, Wednesday, 10th May, 1843'. This cannot mean, however, the burial-place of G.B. Vermiglioli himself, who did not die until 3rd December 1848, aged seventy-nine, just after the publication of Dennis's book. He must have been about seventy-three when Dennis met him and talked about his Etruscan researches in and around Perugia. 'Vermiglioli's tomb' must mean instead an Etruscan tomb which he had discovered, or which had been discovered on land belonging to him.

5 For Frederick Catherwood see the excellent biography by Victor Von Hagen, *Frederick Catherwood Archt.*, New York, Oxford University Press, 1950. Mr Von Hagen tells us that Catherwood's visit to Tunis took place in 1832, but he does not mention Dennis and was clearly unaware of the friendship between the two men.

6 *Cities and Cemeteries of Etruria,* first edition, 1848, vol.II, p.322.

7 Patrick Brydone's *A Tour through Sicily and Malta*, first edition, two volumes, London, 1773; and many later editions. It is scarcely a pamphlet! Perhaps there was an abbreviated version.

8 Probably William Tooke (1777-1863), President of the Society of Arts (for whom see D.N.B.) Although primarily an engineer and business man, he had wide interests in classical literature.

9 See Nora Nieri, 'Arcangelo Michele Migliarini (1779-1865) etruscologo ed egittologo', in *Atti della Reale Accademia Nazionale dei Lincei*, anno CCCXXVII (1930), ser. 6, *Memorie della classe di scienze morali, storiche e filologiche*, vol.III, 1931, pp.401-543. Migliarini died on 14th September, 1865. Dennis kept in touch with him by letter, even while he was in South America. (see Chapter V.)

10 *Cities and Cemeteries of Etruria*, vol.I, p.208n.

11 Joseph Marryat, *Collections Towards a History of Pottery and Porcelain, in the 15th, 16th, 17th and 18th Centuries.* London, 1850; second edition, 1857.

NOTES TO CHAPTER FOUR

1 Raymond Bloch, *The Etruscans*, Thames & Hudson, 1958, p.40. Dennis did not become a British Consul until 1869.

2 See the long review-article on Dennis's book in *The Edinburgh Review*, July-October, 1849, vol.90, pp.107-132.

3 This is scarcely borne out by the sentiments which Dennis had himself expressed in one of his letters to his parents from Rome.

4 Ludwig Steub (1812-1888), ethnographer and travel writer, had in 1843 published in Munich a book entitled *Ueber die Urbewohner Ratiens und ihren Zusammenhang mit den Etruskern*. It was almost certainly this book which Dennis had read, but he did not agree with the so-called 'Raetian' (Alpine) origins of the Etruscans.

5 See the *Benares Magazine*, vol. 3 (March, 1850), pp.189-212, article entitled 'Ancient Etruria'.

6 Augustus J.C. Hare, *Days near Rome*, London, 1884, vol.1, p.9.

7 M. Pallottino, *The Etruscans*, Pelican Books, 1955, p.126, n.1.

NOTES TO CHAPTER FIVE

1 British Museum, Add. MS. 46,615, fol. 143.

2 At that time Royal Mail steamers from Southampton used to call at Georgetown twice a month, the journey taking three weeks, with a call at St Thomas. There were also steamers from Liverpool which sailed there direct in a fortnight. George Dennis usually, and probably always, sailed from Southampton.

3 It was Richard Ford's second wife, formerly the Hon. Eliza Cranstoun, who had died on 23rd January 1849. He married for the third time in the summer of 1851.

4 See *British Guiana: Demerara after fifteen years of freedom.* By a Landowner, London, T. Bosworth, 1853. The anonymous author of this short book was John Brumell, who gives in an appendix a long extract from Dennis's report. Brumell must have known Dennis personally.

5 See James Rodway, *History of British Guiana,* 3 vols., George-town, 1891-94.

6 The best-known and most important book by Domenico Lo Faso Pietrasanta, Duke of Serradifalco, is *Le Antichità della Sicilia esposte ed illustrate,* 5 vols., Palermo, 1834-42.

7 This Mr Holmes cannot be identified with certainty, but he may possibly be Sir William Henry Holmes, who published in 1862 *Tree Cotton: How and Where to Grow It. With a map of British Guiana.* This little book shows that the author had lived in British Guiana as early as 1838, and he was there also in 1857: but there is no available evidence that he went to the Ionian Islands.

8 Ferdinand II, Bourbon King of Naples and Sicily from 1830 until his death on 22nd May 1859, was known as Bomba. His rule was noted for its oppression and cruelty.

9 Douglas William Jerrold was born in London on 3rd January, 1803 and wrote many plays and other works. He died on 8th June 1857.

10 Denis Mack Smith takes a rather more lenient view when he writes: 'The Bourbon administrators, even in the 1850s, were far from being the black reactionaries painted by patriotic propaganda, especially when compared to these provincial gentry. Bourbon prisons may have been as bad as Gladstone said, but some other foreigners who saw them thought he had exaggerated the facts for political purposes, and we now know that the prisons in enlightened Piedmont were not all that much better.' *(A History of Sicily: Modern Sicily after 1713,* London, Chatto & Windus, 1968, pp. 428-9.)

11 Anthony Trollope, *The West Indies and the Spanish Main,* London, Chapman and Hall, 1859, chapter XII (pp.169-201).

12 See G.M. Trevelyan, *Garibaldi and the Making of Italy,* London, Longmans, Green & Co., 1911, p.5.

13 But he had been well taught by his parents to dislike Roman Catholics, whom he once described as 'always aggressive'.

14 These words were written (or rather, spoken) by Dennis some thirty-five or more years after the events which they describe: when he gave his lecture in Rome on March 29th, 1892, at the age of seventy-eight.

NOTES TO CHAPTER SIX

1 See Sir Robert Murdoch Smith, K.C.M.G., and Edwin Augustus Porcher, *History of the Recent Discoveries at Cyrene, Made during an Expedition to the Cyrenaica in 1860-61, under the Auspices of Her Majesty's Government,* London, 1864. Smith was a Lieutenant in the Royal Engineers and Porcher a Commander in the Royal Navy at the time of their expedition. Their book, which is beautifully illustrated with coloured lithographed plates, does not, of course, mention Dennis, who had not yet appeared on the North African scene.

2 Paolo Orsi, *Gela,* in *Monumenti antichi pubblicati per cura della Reale Accademia dei Lincei* (Milano, 1906) coll. 25, 26. Orsi was reporting from hearsay, and some of his details are wrong. It was not 1860-61 when the Dennises went to Gela; and George was not Consul at Palermo until about seven years later.

3 Foreign Office, 101 (Tripoli), vol.50.
All volumes of F.O. reports which have been consulted are now preserved in the Public Record Office.

4 M. Vattier de Bourville, French Consular Agent at Benghazi, in 1848-9, collected a large number of vases and terra cotta ornaments from the tombs there. His finds are now in the Louvre. See Smith and Porcher, *op. cit.* De Bourville also made a short exploratory visit to Cyrene.

5 Barataria was the island of which Sancho Pança became Governor in *Don Quixote.*

6 Apart from his excavations at Gela in 1863, Dennis also worked for a short time at Centorbi, or Centuripe, a small town inland, facing Mount Etna, which still preserves remains of Hellenistic and Roman tombs. See H.B. Walters, *Catalogue of the Terracottas in the British Museum* (1903) and R.A. Higgins, *Catalogue of the Terracottas in the Department of Greek and Roman Antiquities, British Museum,* vol. 1 (1954).

7 Gordon Waterfield, *Layard of Nineveh,* London, John Murray, 1963, p.305.

8 Lord Clarence Edward Paget (1811-1895) was Admiral commanding the Mediterranean Fleet based on Malta during 1866-77. Although Dennis met him there, he probably made no great impression on the Admiral, who does not mention Dennis in his *Autobiography and Journals,* published posthumously in 1896.

9 Panizzi's successor was John Winter Jones, Principal Librarian from 1866 to 1878, known as a useful subordinate but a rather ineffectual principal. For everything concerning Antonio (later Sir Anthony) Panizzi (1797-1879) see Edward Miller, *Prince of Librarians: the life & times of Antonio Panizzi of the British Museum,* London, Andre Deutsch, 1967.

NOTES TO CHAPTER SEVEN

1 In between being an Assistant at the British Museum in 1840 and being promoted Keeper of Greek and Roman Antiquities there in 1861, Newton served the Foreign Office as a Consul in Mytilene and in Turkey. It was Panizzi who insisted on bringing him back to the Museum.

2 Dennis was evidently never a member of the Society of Dilettanti, which was responsible for so much exploration in Asia Minor. In 1861, Pullan proposed to the Society to explore the ruined cities of Asia Minor. He left London in July 1861 and was paid two hundred pounds for travelling during six months. In March, 1862, Pullan received instructions to begin work at Teos; excavations on the site of the Smintheum in the Troad followed in 1866, and those at Priene in 1869. The results were published in the fourth part of *The Antiquities of Asia Minor,* by the Society of Dilettanti, in 1881. It is noticeable that Dennis's name is entirely missing from these publications. His other friend, Edward Falkener, had visited the site of Priene as far back as 1845. The name of the British Consul at Smyrna on October 20th, 1866, when Pullan was staying with him and wrote a report to the Society, was R.W. Cumberbatch.

3 F.O. 78, vol. 2102.

4 He actually wrote that he had left his *family* at Malta. This may mean that besides his wife there was a maidservant, for as we know he had no children.

5 F.O. 45, vol. 171.

NOTES TO CHAPTER EIGHT

1 P.R.O., F.O, 45, vol. 191.

2 F.O. 45, vol. 207.

3 Joseph Barclay Pentland edited a number of Murray's *Handbooks,* including *Southern Italy* (1868), *Northern Italy* (1869, 1873) and *Rome and its Environs* (1869, 1871, 1872).

4 F.O. 45, vol. 271.

5 F.O. 45, vol. 297.

6 Gordon Waterfield, *Layard of Nineveh,* p.352.

7 F.O. 45, vol. 350.

8 A.H. Sayce, *Reminiscences,* London, 1923, p.124 and p.167. Sayce records that he had published his review in the *Athenaeum,* whereas George Dennis says that it was in the *Academy.* In fact the *Athenaeum* review is anonymous, while the *Academy* review is signed 'A.H. Sayce'. Therefore Sayce's recollection of where he had published his review in January 1879 must have deceived him when he came to write his autobiography some forty-four years later.

See: *The Athenaeum,* No.2671, January 4th, 1879, pp.13-14. This reviewer adheres to the view of a Northern origin for the Etruscans. He accuses Dennis of not paying sufficient attention to recent German and English writers on Etruscology.

See also *The Academy,* January 11th, 1879, pp.23-24, review signed by A.H. Sayce. He complains that Dennis has given too few inscriptions, and has scarcely ever translated those few which he has given. 'Mr Dennis does not profess to solve any problems whatsoever. He is rather the genial and learned guide of the intelligent traveller, the enthusiastic historian of Etruscan greatness and culture, the agreeable companion of the drawing-room and the library.' For a good many years Sayce had, in addition to his concentration on Oriental studies, given much thought to the origin of the Etruscans. Among his many letters to the Rev. Isaac Taylor (author of *Etruscan Researches,* 1874) now preserved in the library of Queen's College, Oxford, is one dated July 23rd, 1875, in which he remarks: 'I was in Tuscany examining some of the Etruscan cities and cemeteries for myself. I have but just returned, fully convinced that the Etruscans were not Aryan, much less Italic. How anyone could hold such a theory after an examination of their *native* art and mythology is to me inconceivable. As you know, I still hold to the belief expressed in my book that Etruscan is *sui generis* — a waif of an otherwise extinct family of speech; tho' your work obliged me to confess that this puzzling race may after all belong to the Turanian stock.'

Thus in postulating an Asiatic origin for the Etruscans, Sayce was in broad agreement with both Isaac Taylor and George Dennis. The exact truth of the problem has still not been discovered a century later.

The wording of this letter shows that Sayce had Dennis's book in mind when he wrote it.

9 See J.S.P. Bradford, 'An unpublished letter from the Etruscologist, George Dennis', *Antiquity,* no. 87, September 1948, pp. 160-1. After declaring Dennis to be one of the best and most accuràte writers on archaeology there have ever been, Mr Bradford adds that 1948, the centenary year of the publication of the *Cities and Cemeteries of Etruria,* would be a singularly appropriate occasion for the discovery of these drawings: but alas, they remain undiscovered.

10 F.O. 45, vol. 393.

NOTES TO CHAPTER NINE

1 The Porte was the Ottoman court, or the government of the Turkish Empire in Constantinople. It was so named because justice

was administered at the High Gate of the palace, and the French translation of the Turkish *Babi Ali* was *Sublime Porte:* hence the government itself became commonly known as Porte. A firman, granted by the Turkish authorities, was a permit issued to a traveller to be used as passport, or guarantee of protection, or, as in the case of archaeologists, permission to carry out excavations. It could be signed by any Minister of the Turkish government, but it was not always easy to obtain.

2 Colophon was one of the seven ancient cities which claimed to be the birthplace of Homer. Its hill, or 'climax', also gave its name to the final or concluding note in a manuscript or printed book which is still known as a colophon, this being regarded as the climax of the book.

3 Edwin Freshfield (born 26th November 1832, died in September 1918) was educated at Winchester and Trinity College, Cambridge. He served for eighteen months on H.M.S. *Firebrand* in the Black Sea during the Crimean War, and became a solicitor in 1858. As senior member of the firm of Freshfield & Co., he was solicitor to the Bank of England. He took his LL.D. in 1884, and was Vice-President and later Treasurer of the Society of Antiquaries in London. While the *Firebrand* was refitting at Smyrna he met the daughter of James Frederick Hanson of the Levant Co., Zoe Charlotte Hanson, and married her in 1861. They had one son, Edwin Hanson Freshfield. Through his wife Edwin Freshfield Senior inherited Hanson's property in Smyrna, and was accustomed to pay yearly visits there for over forty years. He acquired an intimate knowledge of the liturgy of the Greek Church and of Byzantine architecture. He spoke in public and occasionally in letters to *The Times* on the subjects of Turkish politics and rule in Asia Minor. (See *The Times* for September 2, 4 and 5, 1918.) George Dennis regarded him as unscrupulous, dishonest and grasping.

NOTES TO CHAPTER TEN

1 *Catalogue of various objects . . . the property of Mrs Muller, sold by auction 29th June 1894 . . . Statuettes from Myrina, the property of George Dennis.* London, 1894. There is a copy in the Bodleian Library, Oxford, but apparently none in the British Museum.

2 Sir W.M. Ramsay, *The Revolution in Constantinople and Turkey: A Diary,* London, Hodder and Stoughton, 1909, pp.247-250.

3 A.H. Sayce, *Reminiscences,* London, Macmillan & Co., 1923, pp. 200-205.

4 *Sardis.* Publications of the American Society for the Excavation of Sardis, vol. I. *The Excavations,* pt.1, 1910-1914. By Howard Crosby Butler. Late E.J. Brill Ltd., Leyden, 1922, p.7.

5 W.M. Ramsay, 'Newly discovered sites near Smyrna', *Journal of Hellenic Studies*, vol.I (1880), pp.63-74.

6 A.H. Sayce, 'Notes from journeys in the Troad and Lydia', *Journal of Hellenic Studies*, vol.I (1880), pp.75-93. H. Spiegelthal, the Prussian Consul at Smyrna, had made excavations in the Tomb of Alyattes at Sardis as far back as 1854, but without making important finds.

NOTES TO CHAPTER ELEVEN

1 A.H. Layard, *Early Adventures in Persia, Susiana, and Babylonia*, 2 vols., John Murray, 1887.

2 Gordon Waterfield, *Layard of Nineveh*, p.94. In writing a letter to Layard on 13th March 1890, in which he reminded him of this ride, Dennis wrote 'Baghdad' by mistake for 'Belgrade'. It was hardly likely that even Layard could ever have ridden a horse from Baghdad to Constantinople.

3 Edward Falkener, *Games Ancient and Oriental, and How to Play Them*, London, Longmans, Green & Co., 1892, appendix No. III,pp. 364-6, section on 'Lower Empire Games'. Falkener adds: 'All the circular diagrams appear to represent the same game. During my twelve months' residence in Pompeii in 1847, while excavating the house of Marcus Aurelius, I do not recollect seeing any such diagrams; for, as Mr Dennis says, I was not then interested in them: and I do not consider it likely that the Aedile of such a modern watering-place as Pompeii then was, would have allowed the pavement of public buildings to be so disfigured, or idle people to be squatting about and playing at such games, to the great discomfort and annoyance of other people, engaged either in public business or at their devotions'.

4 Sir W.M. Flinders Petrie, *Seventy Years in Archaeology*, London, Sampson Low, Marston & Co., [1931], p.144.

NOTES TO CHAPTER TWELVE

1 T.A. (Thomas Ashby) in *The Classical Review*, vol. XXII (1908), p.133. He adds in a footnote 'The third edition of 1883 is, as far as I am aware, a re-issue of that of 1878'. This is absolutely true, and it explains why the third edition was not in the British Museum, since re-issues do not have to be deposited there under the terms of the Copyright Act. A copy of this edition was, however, bought by the Museum in 1970.

2 Adolf T.F. Michaelis, *A Century of Archaeological Discoveries*, translated by Bettina Kahnweiler, John Murray, 1908, p.102.

3 *ibid,* p.279.

4 M.L. Cameron, *Old Etruria and Modern Tuscany,* London, Methuen & Co., 1909, especially at pp. 74, 88 and 194.

5 Frederick Seymour, *Up Hill and Down Dale in Ancient Etruria,* London & Leipsic, T. Fisher Unwin, 1910, pp.146n., 155, *etc.*

6 Frederic Harrison, *Autobiographic Memoirs,* 2 vols., London, Macmillan, 1911; see vol.II, p.137.

7 I have not attempted to search for these letters in France for the purposes of the present biography. Reinach died in 1932, aged seventy-four, leaving his antique objects, and probably his letters also, to the Louvre. If they still exist, the letters are unlikely to provide any biographical details about Dennis which I have not found elsewhere; they are sure to have consisted entirely of an exchange of archaeological information of mutual interest to the two men.

APPENDIX 1

BIBLIOGRAPHY OF THE WRITINGS OF GEORGE DENNIS

A. ARTICLES

1 Sketches of Andalucia. Three anonymous articles in *Bentley's Miscellany*, vol. V.
(a) A Pilgrimage to Seville Cathedral. No. 25. 1st January 1839 pp.51-61.
(b) Cordoba. No. 26. 1st February 1839 pp.188-200.
(c) Granada. No. 27. 1st March 1839 pp.264-271.
2 *Bentley's Miscellany*, vol. VI, 1839.
The City of the Doge; or, Letters from Venice. By the author of "A Summer in Andalucia". (Dated: Venice, July 1839) pp.615-622.
3 The Cid. A series of twelve anonymous articles in *The Penny Magazine* of the Society for the Diffusion of Useful Knowledge, new series, 1841. Published by Charles Knight & Co., London.

No. 1.	No. 562.	pp. 4-7.
No. 2.	No. 564.	pp. 25-27.
No. 3.	No. 568.	pp. 49-51.
No. 4.	No. 571.	pp. 73-75.
No. 5.	No. 576.	pp. ·113-116.
No. 6.	No. 581.	pp. 153-154.
No. 7.	No. 583.	pp. 173-175.
No. 8.	No. 587.	pp. 201-204.
No. 9.	No. 594.	pp. 257-259.
No. 10.	No. 597.	pp. 284-286.
No. 11.	No. 601.	pp. 313-314.
No. 12.	No. 602.	pp. 327-328.

4 A letter addressed by Dennis to Dr Emil Braun, Secretary of the Archaeological Institute in Rome, and written in Rome on 28th March 1844. Printed in *Annali dell' Instituto di Corrispondenza Archeologica*, anno 1843 (1844), fasc. 2, pp.233-6. It describes his recent visit to the Etruscan necropolis of Sovana, which his friend Ainsley had discovered in May 1843.

5 Art.VI. 1. *Annali dell' Instituto di Corrispondenza Archeologica di Roma* 8vo. Roma, 1829-1842.
2. *Bullettini dell' Instituto*, etc. 8vo. Roma, 1829-1842.
3. *Tour to the Sepulchres of Etruria in 1839.* By Mrs Hamilton Gray. With numerous illustrations. Hatchard & Son.
4. *The History of Etruria.* By Mrs Hamilton Gray. Part 1. Hatchard & Son.
Long Review-article signed: G.D. (i.e. George Dennis). In *The West-*

minster Review, March-June, 1844. vol. XLI - 1844. pp.145-178. (with plates).

p.153: 'We subjoin a description of it (Ponte della Badia, near Vulci) in the shape of an extract from the manuscript journal of a tour very recently made in Etruria, and as yet unpublished.'

He quotes frequently from this journal, which must be either by himself or by Ainsley.

p.171: 'Several instances of Etruscan tombs with temple-facades hewn out of the rock are extant. Some very interesting specimens have recently been discovered at Sovana, in Tuscany, by Mr Ainsley, who will shortly give to the world illustrations from his own pencil of these and all the other most striking architectural remains of Etruria . . .

The most remarkable instance of a temple-tomb in all Etruria is at Norchia.'

The article does not really criticise or review Mrs Gray's work at all.

6 Bullettino dell' Instituto di Corrispondenza Archeologica per l'anno 1845, pp.137-141. A letter by George Dennis written from London in August 1844, describing his Etruscan finds near Volterra a few months previously.

7 'On an Etruscan city, recently discovered, and probably the Vetulonia of antiquity.' *Classical Museum,* London, 1845, vol.II, pp. 229-246. Dennis had discovered what he took to be the site of Vetulonia in 1844.

8 Bullettino dell' Instituto, No. III, di marzo 1847, pp.51-63; 'Viaggi nell' Etruria'. (Signed: George Dennis).

Describes Santa Marinella and Cerveteri.

9 The Works of Quintus Horatius Flaccus, illustrated chiefly from the remains of ancient art. With a life by the Rev. Henry Hart Milman. pp.194, 490, XIV. London, John Murray, 1849.

Contains in pt.1, pp.97-110:

De Villa Horatii. A letter by G. Dennis, Esq. (wrongly described in the table of contents as 'G.W. Dennis'). The letter is headed "Post fanum putre Vacunae", Prid. Non. Sept. (i.e. 4th September), A.D. 1842. A number of the engravings in this book are from sketches by George Dennis. They include Aricia, Anxur (now Terracina), Formiae (now Mola di Gaeta) and Praeneste (now Palestrina).

10 'On recent excavations in the Greek cemeteries of the Cyrenaica'. *Transactions of the Royal Society of Literature,* Second series, IX. (1870), pp.135-182.

Dennis had read this paper on 10th July 1867.

11 'Two archaic Greek sarcophagi recently discovered in the necropolis of Clazomenae'. 22pp. Reprinted from the *Journal of Hellenic Studies,* vol.IV, 1883.

12 'The New Etruscan Museum at the Villa Papa Giulio at Rome'. *Journal of the British and American Archaeological Society of*

Rome, Session 1888-1889, pp.150-168. Also issued as an offprint entitled 'The recently-excavated objects from Falerii in the new Etruscan museum at the Villa Papa Giulio at Rome'. pp.19. Rome, 1890.

13 List of Lectures and Excursions of Session 1890-91 of the British and American Archaeological Society of Rome.
No. 6. George Dennis. The Meadow of Nysa in Asia Minor. This paper was read for him by Captain Richmond Moore, R.N., on March 10th, 1891, and is printed on pp.22-30.

14 'The Aborigines of South America and Speculations on their Origin'. A paper read on 29th March 1892 under the title 'The Probability of America having been visited in ancient times by the Phoenicians'. Printed in the *Journal of the British and American Archaeological Society of Rome*, vol.II (1893), No.3, pp.143-157.

15 'Ancient Greek Art in the parts of Libia about Cyrene'.
A lecture delivered on January 29th, 1895, and printed in the same *Journal*, vol.II, No. 5 (1895), pp.227-242.

B. BOOKS

1 A Summer in Andalucia. (Anonymous.) In two volumes. London, Richard Bentley, 1839, 8vo. In 'Mr Murray's General List of Works' issued in February, 1856, there is an advertisement reading as follows: DENNIS, George, Cities and Cemeteries of Etruria;or, the extant Local Remains of Etruscan Art. Plates. 2 vols. 8vo. 42s. — Summer in Andalucia. *Second Edition*. Revised. Post 8vo. It is certain that this second edition was never published.

2 The Cid: A short chronicle, founded on the early poetry of Spain. pp.220. London, Charles Knight & Co., 1845. 12mo.

3 The Cities and Cemeteries of Etruria.
(a) First edition. In two volumes. (No dedication.) London, John Murray, 1848, 8vo.
(b) Revised edition, recording the most recent discoveries, etc. In two volumes. (Dedicated to Sir Henry Layard.) London, John Murray, 1878, 8vo.
(c) Third edition, revised. In two volumes. London, John Murray, 1883. 8vo. (In fact a re-issue of the 1878 edition.)
(d) Everyman's Library edition. (With introduction by Prof. W.M. Lindsay.) In two volumes. London. J.M. Dent & Co. Ltd.: New York, E.P. Dutton & Co., 1907. 8vo.
(e) German translation:
Die Städte und Begräbnissplätze Etruriens . . . Deutsch von Dr N.N. W. Meissner . . . Mit 106 Abbildungen, 3 Landschaften, 9 Plänen, 18 Inschriften und einer Karte. pp.lxii.743. Leipzig, 1852. 8vo.

4 A Handbook for Travellers in Sicily. Edited (and probably entirely written) by George Dennis. With maps and plans. pp.lvi.524. London, John Murray, 1864. 12mo.

APPENDIX 2

DRAMATIS PERSONAE

AINSLEY, Samuel James. Born probably before 1820, died 1874. Made three tours in Etruria with George Dennis, June 1842 - July 1843. Had exhibitions of paintings in the Royal Academy in 1836 and 1844. Four volumes of his drawings and a sketch-book are in the British Museum (Prints and Drawings Department), 112 items having been bequeathed in July 1874. See Laurence Binyon, *Catalogue of Drawings by British Artists, British Museum*, 1898, 1, 3-14.

ASHPITEL, Arthur. 1807-1869. Architect. Born Hackney. Crippled by an accident. Left England in 1854 for Rome. Died on January 18th, 1869, leaving a valuable collection of vases and books to the Society of Antiquaries and his two drawings of Rome to the nation. See article on him in D.N.B.

CATHERWOOD, Frederick. Born 27th February 1799 in London. In 1832 was in the Regency of Tunis where he made notes and sketches which were unpublished at the time when George Dennis saw them. Drowned in the Atlantic, September 1854. See Victor von Hagen, *Frederick Catherwood Arct.*, New York, O.U.P., 1950.

COOKE, Edward William, R.A., F.R.S. Born Pentonville, 27th March, 1811, son of engraver George Cooke, See *Illustrated London News*, 1864, vol. 45, p.173; L. Binyon, *Catalogue,* 1, 244-5.
Friend of George Dennis in youth; later placed his Italian portfolio at Dennis's disposal, from which Dennis selected four sketches as illustrations for his second edition. There is a small photograph of Cooke in the National Portrait Gallery. He died near Tunbridge Wells, 4th January 1880.

DENNIS, John. Brother of George. Born 1824. Wrote many books on English literature. Lived at Hampstead until about 1896 when he moved to Crowborough, where he died on 8th February 1911. He had five children.

DRUMMOND-HAY, Sir John Hay. Born 1st June 1816 at Valenciennes, was at Charterhouse 1827-32. His father was Political Agent and Consul General in Morocco. He first went to Tangier in 1832, and for forty years he represented Great Britain in Morocco. See

A Memoir of Sir John Drummond Hay, P.C., K.C.B., G.C., M.G., Sometime Minister at the Court of Morocco, based on his journals and correspondence, London, John Murray, 1896.
He died at Wedderburn Castle, Berwickshire, 27th November 1893.

FALKENER, Edward. Born 1814. Travelled abroad 1842-49: Denmark, Norway, Sweden, Russia, Constantinople, Egypt, Nubia, Jerusalem, Greece, Corfu, Turkey, Italy and Sicily. Lived in the ruins of Pompeii all through 1847. Made drawings in Asia Minor. Edited *The Museum of Classical Antiquities* from 1851 to 1853, which was reissued 1855 and 1860. Was a J.P. for Carmarthenshire. Lived to be at least eighty. Had a son named Lyon.

FORD, Richard. Born 1796. Educated Winchester and Trinity College, Oxford. Married three times. Wrote the most famous of handbooks for travellers in Spain. See *The Letters of Richard Ford, 1797 [sic] — 1858.* Edited by Rowland E. Prothero, London, John Murray, 1905. Ford died 31st August 1858, at Heavitree.

FRESHFIELD, Edwin. Born 26th November 1832 at Reigate. Educated Trinity College, Cambridge. LL.D, 1884. Went on cruise to Greece, Jerusalem and Constantinople, 1853-4. Served for 18 months on H.M.S. *Firebrand* in Black Sea during Crimean War. Solicitor 1858. Senior member of Freshfield & Co., Solicitors to Bank of England. Fellow of Winchester College, 1888-95. Through his wife he inherited property at Smyrna and travelled in Asia Minor annually. Became an authority on Byzantine art and architecture. Vice-President, Society of Antiquaries of London and later its Treasurer. George Dennis disliked him intensely. He died 1st September 1918.

HARRISON, Frederic. Born 18th October 1831. Son of a prosperous London merchant. His father and mother were entertained by George Dennis at Palermo some time during the 1870s. Wrote Dennis's obituary notice in the *Athenaeum,* but could not have remembered him very clearly, for he calls him 'Sir' George Dennis in his autobiography of 1911. Died 14th January 1923.

HENZEN, Johannes Heinrich Wilhelm. Born at Bremen 24th January 1816. After travelling to Paris, London, Greece, Asia Minor and Sicily, he settled in Rome for good in November 1842. Friend of Theodor Mommsen. See his obituary notice in *Classical Review,* vol.1 (1887), p.178. He died in Rome, 27th January 1887.

LAYARD, Sir Austen Henry. Born 5th March 1817. Died 5th July 1894. See Gordon Waterfield, *Layard of Nineveh,* London, John Murray, 1963.

MIGLIARINI, Arcangelo Michele. Born Rome, 25th December 1779. Settled in Florence in 1820. Later became Professor of Archaeology at Florence. Dennis knew him in the 1840s, having been introduced to him by Henzen in a letter of 10th June 1846. Died 14th September 1865.

NEWTON, Sir Charles Thomas. Born 1816. Assistant in Department of Antiquities, British Museum, 1840; Keeper, 1861-85. Between 1840 and 1860 he served the Foreign Office as Vice-Consul in Mitylene, 1852, Acting Consul Rhodes, April 1852 — January 1853, Consul at Rome, June 1859 — January 1861. Died 1894.

PAGET, Lord Clarence Edward, G.C.B. Born 17th June 1811. Admiral commanding Mediterranean Fleet based on Malta, 1866-77. Dennis met him at Malta in March 1867. Died in the spring of 1895. See his *Autobiography & Journals,* London, 1896.

PULLAN, Richard Popplewell. Born 1825. Architect and archaeologist, worked much in Asia Minor. See article in D.N.B. Died 1888.

RAMSAY, Sir William Mitchell, D.C.L., LL.D. Born Glasgow 15th March 1851. Professor of Classical Archaeology at Oxford, later of Latin (Humanity) at Aberdeen. Travelled much in Turkey, and his wife wrote a book on everyday life in Turkey. Died 1939, aged 88. Had five children.

REINACH, Salomon. Born 1858. French archaeologist, worked in Asia Minor on behalf of the Louvre. Met Dennis at Smyrna in 1880, and after that exchanged many letters with him. Died 1932.

SAYCE, Archibald Henry. Born 25th September 1845. D. Litt., LL.D, D.D. Fellow of Queen's College, Oxford, and Professor of Assyriology at Oxford. Never married. Knew Dennis and stayed with him at Smyrna in 1880. See his *Reminiscences,* London, 1923, and the portrait of him in Queen's College, Oxford, where there are many of his books and letters, although none from George Dennis. Died 4th February, 1933.

INDEX

Aberdeen, 17
Ager Faliscus, 55
Ainsley, Samuel James, 35-40, 42, 43, 47, 166
Albanese, Enrico, 112-113
Alcester, Admiral Lord, (Frederick Beauchamp Paget Seymour; died 1895), 153
Alyattes, 104, 107, 161, 173
America, South, 57-72, 159; U.S.A., 60, 119
Apollonia, 84, 86, 91, 93, 95
Aquilina, Antonio, 92
Arezzo, 40, 115
Ash Grove (home of Dennis family in Hackney), 15, 32, 41, 42, 43, 57, 60
Ashby, Thomas, 161, 173
Ashpitel, Arthur (architect), 35, 104
Athenaeum Club, London, 156

Backhouse, Mr (Secretary under Lord Palmerston), 22, 39, 61, 166
Bacon, Francis H., 147
Bacquerie, M. (French Vice-Consul at Benghazi), 81
Baltazzi, 141, 145
Barca, 90, 91
Barcelona, 157
Barkly, Sir Henry (Governor of British Guiana), 57, 58, 59
Benghazi, 78-99, 103, 105, 106
Bentley, Richard (publisher), 22, 23, 27, 57
Bergamo, 27
Bieda, 39, 115, 118
Bin Tépé, 102, 103, 104, 128, 130, 134, 147
Birch, Samuel, 70
Blera, see Bieda
Bloch, Raymond, 56, 164
Bologna, 114, 115, 117, 120

Bolsena, 37
Bomarzo, 37, 39
Botta, Paul Émile (1802-70); French Consul at Tripoli, archaeologist), 81, 82
Bournabat, near Smyrna, 100
Bourville, Joseph Vattier de (French archaeologist, worked at Benghazi in 1848), 79, 81, 85, 90, 169
Bracciano, 40
Bradford, John (archaeologist), 126, 171
Braun, Emil, 37, 42, 48
British Guiana, G.D. in, 57-72
British Museum, London, 40, 52, 63, 65, 73, 76, 77, 88, 90-92, 94, 95, 97, 98, 102, 103, 105-107, 115, 117, 122, 147, 154, 160, 164
Brumell, John, 168
Bryce, James (1838-1922; Vice-Chancellor of Oxford University), 153
Brydone, Patrick, 44, 167
Burgos, G.D. at, 29, 31, 32, 34
Burton, Sir Richard (1821-1890; explorer), 113-115
Byron, Lord, 26, 166

Cadiz, 19, 20, 22, 157
Cambolo, Signor, 73
Cameron, Mary Lovett, 162
Cannino, Princess of, 162
Castel d'Asso, near Viterbo, 39
Castellani (collector of ancient vases), 77
Catania, 64
Catherwood, Frederick, 15, 35, 42, 58, 62, 166
Catherwood, John James, 15
Catholicism, G.D.'s attitude towards, 25, 168
Cayster, River, 150-152

Volte

Populonia

Vet

ETRURIA

0   100 miles